Playing By Heart

Playing By Heart

The Vision And Practice
Of Belonging

O. Fred Donaldson, Ph.D.

Health Communications, Inc.
Deerfield Beach, Florida

The author thanks the following for their permission to quote from copyrighted works.

T.P. Kasulis. *Zen Action Zen Person*. Honolulu: University of Hawaii Press, 1981.

Thomas Merton. *The Way Of Chuang Tzu*. Copyright © 1965. The Abbey of Gethsemani. Reprinted by permission of New Directions Publishing Corporation.

Margery Williams. *The Velveteen Rabbit*. New York: Doubleday.

Library of Congress Cataloging-in-Publication Data

Donaldson, O. Fred
    Playing by heart: the vision and practice of belonging / by O. Fred Donaldson.
       p.   cm.
    Includes bibliographical references.
    ISBN 1-55874-253-0
    1. Play (Philosophy). 2. Play — Psychological aspects. 3. Play-Religious aspects. I. Title.
B105.P54D66   1993   92-19975
128—dc20   CIP

©1993 O. Fred Donaldson
ISBN 1-55874-253-0

Publisher: Health Communications, Inc.
             3201 S.W. 15th Street
             Deerfield Beach, Florida 33442-8190

Cover design by Barbara Bergman

Dedication

For Paul, who shared with me a level of imperishable fearlessness and sacred trust, which no cross-examination by intellect and reason could shake.

For Sybil, a wolf, who shared the deep unison of ultimate kindness which is invisible in the heat of contest.

For Holly, a dolphin, who allowed me to see where fear lives.

For Danny, Jenny and Hector, who showed me the transformative energy of love.

For David, who opened my eyes and heart to the original nature of play.

Thank You

This book is the result of a vision and close to twenty years of playing. It is a delightful and properly humbling experience to think back on the many people whose energies in one way or another have gone into making this book a reality. Many people, as I look back over the years of my play, came into my life with just the right encouragement.

I'd like to thank my wife, Jan, whose natural kindness has been an inspiration for my playing and my writing. Her intuition and inspiration have provided the peace and love which brought almost twenty years of playing into this book.

To my many friends, including Des Dornan, Catherine Smedley, Ken Walters, Martha Decker, Jane Westin and Elaine Cormier, who over the years have organized workshops and lectures and made me feel at home away from home. Kristy Clark, Betsy Koenig, Alan Hammond, Chris Foster and so many wonderful friends in Emissary communities throughout the world for their guidance and gracious support. I hope this book in some small way rewards your faith in me and play.

To Dr. Robert Coles, Wendell Berry, Hal Borland and Sir Laurens van der Post. Their writing has influenced me, and their devotion to their work has been a beacon for me to follow. As I've read and reread their work through the years, I would say to myself, "I want to write like him. I want my writing to exhibit the care and respect that he shows in his."

To the masters who shared with me the powerful lessons of play, including: Windsong, Hambone and Sybil, my favorite wolf friends; Holly, a dolphin guide; and Brian, Paul and Robert, human playmates par excellence. And to so many, many children around the world.

To Roselle and my children, Anthony and Etienne, my first teachers, for all those afternoons on the lawn, showing me that playing is more important than the "jobs" of adulthood.

For Craig and Sally McEwen and the students, especially Heather, Mandy, Jon, Zac, David, Justin, Billy, Jamie and Liza, at MOBOC for five years of the most incredible adventures, where I could put play into practice in so many ways.

I also want to thank the following people whose support during the long birth of this book has been invaluable.

Hillary Donaldson, who listened, coached, prodded and paid for so much in our years together.

Mary and Peter Bartlo, for their financial support to travel to Australia and expand my playmate world.

Vicki, Robert, Brian and Ross Williamson, for being family and playmates to me over the years, for putting me in touch with Wolf Haven and for photographing my play with wolves.

Robert Johnson, whose presence, words and trust helped open me to write about play as I know it.

Wade Doak, Jim Nollmam, Bemi Debus and Gia Gawain, for encouraging me to continue exploring play with dolphins.

Jack Laufer and Steve Kuntz, for their continual trust and support in allowing me the freedom to explore play with the wolves, foxes and coyotes of Wolf Haven.

Bill DeFoore, for encouraging me to talk with Health Communications. And my editor, Barbara Nichols, for her support, patience and guidance during the writing process. And the staff at Health Communications, who put so much effort into producing this book.

Other friends exerted an important influence in the development of my ideas. For the many delightful hours spent talking, listening and sharing ideas, I am indebted to: Richard Heinberg, Jim Bull, Sally Richter, Bill Serdahley, Lynda and Michael Sexson, Bill Shaul, Marianne Torbert, John Nance, Jaak Reichman, Pat and Tandy Seery, Chris St. Clair, Tom McDonald, Eleanor Velarde, Ruth Rudner, Michael Frederic, Nikola W. Lisa, Ed Kotin, Cora Austin, Mary Kawar, Karen Williams, Jean Frazier, Will Heikoop, David Gouthro, Marge and Earl Deacon, Alexandra Delis-Abrams, Caroline Harrington and Cedar Brandt.

Dave Ulrey, Shirley Stafford, George Cagni and Donna Johnson, who supported my play with children in the beginning at The Children's School.

Jan Powell, Jan Donaldson and Joann Hameister and the staff of VIP-Tots for their courage and continued support of play as a way of providing love for all children.

George Leonard, Richard Strozzi-Heckler and Ace Atkinson for the loving spirit in which they share aikido.

Jane Carney Schulze, staff and children of the Yellow Submarine Learning Center.

Walkin' Jim Stoltz, who taught me that visions are for living.

I have no doubt that this book is a preamble of preparation for a transfigurative process on its way to consummation. Had it not been for each of you, I would not have been able to add my bit of evidence to all of those who have traveled this same path. I thank you.

Parts of this book have appeared as articles in *Massage, Holistic Education Review, Somatics, Joyful Child Journal, Creation, Lomi School Bulletin,* and various Emissary publications including *The Renaissance Educator, Healing Currents, The Steward's Journal* and *Integrity.*

Contents

Preface

What is the pattern that connects all the living creatures?
Gregory Bateson

For a child to develop normally, somebody has to be
irrationally crazy about that kid.
Urie Bronfenbrenner

On the face of it, these two comments may seem unconnected. But something profound joins them. Developmental psychologist Urie Bronfenbrenner answers Gregory Bateson's question. The irrationally crazy pattern that develops a normal child also connects all living creatures. The love each human being needs in order to develop fully is the pattern that connects all life.

Here is a wonderful, divine mystery. Whatever this crazy pattern is, it is found in DNA, in quarks and galaxies, in Zen masters, in saints and scientists, and in whales, wolves and children. It flows in water and music; it finds voice in poetry and wind. As mythologist Joseph Campbell told us, "The mystery is what's important."

How wondrous this life, beyond description. And yet our understandings must be phrased in words. If we were to make a list of names for the variety of life from the smallest of the small to the largest of the large, our list would include not only human differences, race, nationality, religion, gender, age, education and income, but all types of beings from microbes to blue whales and all known energy forms from waves to supernovas. Intellectually, we know that words put boundaries between ourselves and experience. In naming our differences we empower separation. The trouble is that we live our lives as though our ideas must set us apart and in conflict with the rest of creation. As Jean-Paul Sartre said, "Everything has been figured out except how to live."

Now imagine that there is a way for us to interact with life in which none of these differences we've just catalogued make any difference. Sounds crazy? Good! Then we are on the right path.

Playing By Heart is an invitation to come out and play with our wonderful world, to see beyond our lists and definitions and join the mystery ourselves. To receive this invitation requires a child-like participation of our senses and a way of knowing that is more holistic than analytic, more heartfelt than discriminating. "Coming out to play" is more than an iconoclastic technique, more than a recapitulation of childish frivolity, more than comic relief from stress or a recreational diversion. It involves a genuine transcendence that is grounded in and nourished by life.

I make my living as a play specialist, but this was not always the case. During graduate school in geography at the University of Washington, I lived for two years in graduate student housing. One afternoon my friend Dean and I walked up to his unit. His young son Cort was playing on the grass in front of the door. Dean and I stopped near him, deep into one of our frequent discussions about graduate school life. Suddenly I felt a tug on my pants. "Come down!" Cort requested. Dean and I smiled and sat down with him. In that moment of "coming down" I entered a world of play and playmates that would change my life. It is a world as real or perhaps more real than any I have ever known. It is this experience that I would like to share with you.

Playing By Heart is not a "how to play" book. To translate play's spirit and form into words is like trying to catch my breath: The breath that I am trying to catch is already gone! This book is written for the playmate within each of us who remembers that everything is not said when we create words. As Rene Daumal says, "The door to the invisible must be visible." It is my hope that as the moon shines with light reflected from an invisible sun, my words will reflect a mystery that is beyond the power of language to divulge.

Playing By Heart is not a book about a predetermined line of research or a survey into the nature of children's play. I am not examining moral, social and cognitive development through play. I am not collecting data. This book is a pirate ship sent to kidnap you, as I have been kidnapped by the children, perhaps a kind of ark, which will transport you so that you might come out and play with the world. Our vessel knows no allegiances, no boundaries. Allow it to carry you as it may. Its path of adventure is the delightful journey of the butterfly, not the train rushing headlong toward some goal. It sails out of profane waters into sacred seas. *Playing By Heart* has in its hold a treasure of experience gathered from playmates, my guides and masters around the globe. Their stories are the heart of this book. But there are dangers hidden in the telling of stories. It is too easy to think of them as special experiences for special people and therefore unattainable. It is true I have found blessed moments among hundreds of thousands of playful hours; it is also true that I cannot play in order to experience them. What I do with children was called for years "Fred Play" to differentiate it from other kinds of play. Although my ego liked it, the reality is that when play truly happens, it isn't Fred's play. I'm only playing well when *I* am not playing. There is no such thing as "Fred play," as if it were peculiar to me or something that I invented or own. There is no copyright here. I participate in play, nothing more. The paradox is that when you truly play, your play will be my play. There is only playing.

To retain their life energy, stories must be given up; like playmates, we must not become attached to them. If I remain filled with my playmates or my stories, I will not be empty enough to receive anew. Likewise, if you attach yourself to these stories, there is the danger that you will be playing for a purpose — to learn, to feel loved, to imitate, to belong. Then play will be too boring, too difficult or too unmiraculous.

"This is play" is the universe's message to all of us. It is a message of profound kindness. To play is to be irrationally crazy, to engage in a metapattern of belonging that connects life forms across species and cultural barriers. Original play is a gift of Creation; it is our birthright. When we truly play ourselves, we are authenticated by all things.

Somehow the world has to be set to playing. At times, however, that seems like an impossible dream. The challenge we face is both personal and global: to play with whoever is nearest at hand, refusing no one, however young or old, distasteful or different, accepting all as playmates. Our participation in life's creative energy is necessary to meet it. It will not be enough merely to change the way we do things; we must develop a new kind of consciousness. "Play practice" means keeping in touch with the people and problems encountered in everyday life, while feeling the wonder of it all, experiencing the awe and exploring without losing the mystery. We retain, even under the enormous weight of culture, a choice each moment to be a kind and fearless playmate rather than act out of personal rancor, disappointment or revenge. The choice of reconciliation is ours, and the need to play with each other is urgent.

This new sense of play will fertilize the human spirit and urge us not toward a regressive childishness, but through wonderment and reverence, into new directions of thought, spirit and action. To re-experience this mind-body-spirit unity, it is necessary for us to let go of much of the baggage we carry around with us as adults. We cannot return to play carrying these burdens. Instead of romping with a child or cavorting with a dolphin, we would then be fussing with our luggage. We must learn how to travel light and free, with as empty a mind, as flexible a body and as open a heart as we can manage.

When it comes to play, most adults imitate the caterpillar, who looks up at the butterfly and exclaims, "You're never going to get me up there!" The caterpillar is correct, a metamorphosis is necessary in order to become a butterfly. Likewise for the adult a transformation must occur to become a playmate. *Playing By Heart* is about the unending transformative process of play.

Playing By Heart is divided into three parts. Part One describes the nature of play as an original, creative and universal force. Part Two documents play's "adulteration" into a variety of counterfeit, cultural forms. Part Three presents the invitations sent by life for us to come out and play, sets forth the craft of play and discusses the qualities inherent in a playmate. The Appendix describes the International Playmate Project.

Play as if Life depends on it — it does!

Introduction: A Playmate Apprenticeship

> Kings could not obtain a greater honour
> than to be God's play-fellows.
>
> *Sir Francis Bacon*

My day began early when I was young and knee-deep in summer. I rushed through breakfast, yanked on my oversized cowboy boots, grabbed my cowboy hat and ran through the screen door to play with a world that was slowly awakening.

That old bulging screen door, bowed outward from my daily collisions, was an alchemical opening into a rarefied world. The mist still lingered in the swamp behind the cornfield, as reluctant to dissipate as the sun was to rise. The early morning air hung heavy with a potpourri of smells, including yesterday's alfalfa cutting, the roses next to the house and the clover along the fences. The grass in front of the barn twinkled with its dewy coating. Our four horses huddled and nuzzled each other against the early morning chill in the sunny corner of the barnyard. On such a day the world was a universe of playmates, the robin fledglings in the apple orchard, the kittens in the hayloft, the horses in the barnyard, the caboose in the woods. I had to poke around and visit them all before the afternoon thunderstorms would rumble across the pastures like potato sacks on the barn floor.

I opened the barn door and walked into a quiet, cool shade split by shafts of yellow sunlight slanting in through the cracks and warps of the old barnwood. The air was filled with dust motes of hay, which shone like millions of golden bugs in the splinters of sunlight. I climbed the ladder built into the wall of the barn to get to the loft. From there I untied the large rope attached to the huge ceiling beam, jumped onto the basketball-sized knot and swung myself out over the mounds of hay below. At just the right moment, I let go and tumbled into the hay. I crawled out and made my way to the ladder for another jump.

At six, wonder was my guide and I would follow her anywhere. When I rushed in just ahead of evening, my mother would inquire, "What did you do today?" "Nothin' much," I would answer.

Many years later, on a warm afternoon in San Diego, I was playing with children after school on the grass of The Children's School. All of the children except David had been picked up by their parents. David and I tumbled on the grass, chased around the yard and climbed on the wooden play structures. As the afternoon waned, our play softened and blended with the stillness of the approaching evening. Running slowed to walking, tumbling merged into hugging, climbing relaxed into lying on our backs on the grass and looking up at the changing sky.

Our minds played with the clouds as if they were piles of cotton at our fingertips. We pointed out and shared our discoveries — horses running and prancing, tiger jaws opening and closing, whales breaching then dissolving. We watched our creations come and go. Softly, David said, "You know, Fred, play is when we don't know that we are different from each other."

At Wolf Haven, a two-year-old wolf named Sybil often rested on the ground with her head on her crossed forepaws, watching me intently. Her deep amber eyes encompassed me without the least trace of aggression or confusion. From my seat on a nearby tree stump, I glanced at her every so often. After a time she walked over, put her forepaws on my lap and rested her head on my shoulder. I leaned against her gently. In a few minutes she left as quietly as she had arrived.

Sybil sauntered back to her special spot among the six other wolves, nosed the ground and spiraled slowly downward. I stood up and began to move slowly about the enclosure. Almost immediately, Sybil trotted over. She jumped up and put her paws on my forearm which I held out in an arc in front of me. She mouthed my beard and I jostled her head with my free hand. Our faces were very close. Then we caught each other's eye. Suddenly there was neither wolf nor human, neither Sybil nor Fred, just light. For just a second, something powerful penetrated me and was gone. For just a second, I had been drawn into her deepest life.

Afterward tears ran down my cheek as I realized that Sybil had shared with me an essence beyond all categories. I wondered if she felt what I felt. If she had been human, I would call her or at least write a letter. But how would I let her know that I knew? I smiled at my human thought: Sybil already knew.

Here are three ordinary yet extraordinary meetings, tangible openings into an indivisible ecology in which no element dominates or damages the others. Playmates catch the moment rather than the expectation. There is a give and take as we learn the points of resistance, connection and flow between us.

This book is about the crafting of ourselves as playmates. We are raw material upon which our playmates work through the practice of original play to release the play hidden within.

My playmates, like David and Sybil, opened doors to a vast world of meaning I had abandoned since childhood. With them I sensed that life is in truth simple, subtle, interconnected and one. Part of me — an inner playmate — was emerging like Don Quixote, out of step and asserting a different world, full of wonder and wonderfully full. I realized a principle that unites science and mysticism: Unity lies at the heart of our world and we can discover and experience it.

This was so much more than I ever expected when I first began playing with preschool children. Play not only tore holes in my pants but ripped open many of my preconceived academic notions about the world. A certain humility tempered my joy and excitement with wonder and awe, and generated a whole new set of possibilities. Play with children gave me no alternative but to continually rethink my sense of the universe and my place in it. My vision continues to expand as playmates redefine what I've been taught to accept as real.

"First of all, it should be fun." These words were spoken by Dr. Bill Bunge, a university professor, exhorting me and everyone else in Geography 101 to enjoy and explore the world.

What did he mean? Did he really mean that my education should be fun? Was it some sort of trick? I soon found out that he wanted us to learn and have fun doing it. He replaced memorization of geographic detail and multiple-choice tests with a series of seemingly impossible projects. By the second set of projects, I let go of trying to get a grade and began to play with the ideas he presented. I was both delighted and puzzled. He seemed to be saying the opposite of what I had been hearing for years in school.

I began to follow Bill's advice outside of his class, but the more I tried to play with my education, the more stifled I felt. The university system was not ready for me to play, and like so many others, I had virtually lost the ability to experience the transformative power of play.

After a while, I put away play for serious and productive academic work. My many years of schooling had trained me to see and think about the world in certain ways, and without realizing it, I lost touch with my sense of wonder and a feeling of belonging to the world. I was no more ready to see the ways of play than I was to discover a rabbit burrow to Wonderland.

I finished my academic degrees, but I never did find the university to be a place of scholarship where people engaged in the play of ideas. Frustrated with academic politics I left university teaching in the mid-1970s. I wanted to be with people who were learning. I didn't want to teach, convince, cajole. I simply wanted to share learning. I thought that preschool would be the best place for such learning and found a position at the Children's School in San Diego as a teacher's aide.

On the school playground, children — like Cort years before — tugged on my clothes to join them on the ground. Now my playmate training began in earnest. With the guidance of my new playmates I began to learn that play possesses implications in directions that I had rarely contemplated during my years of college training. No professional jargon was involved here. The children had something else in mind. In fact, they didn't speak to me at all.

I was enthusiastic about my return to play. It was only after the children began to retrain me that I began to realize I had stopped playing many years before. I thought that I had been playing my entire life. After all, I had played Little League baseball and high school football. Now I was beginning to realize that what I thought was play wasn't.

I must have seemed like a very slow learner to my small playmates. It took weeks of rolling, running and resting on the grass before I began to understand that I was being initiated into "playmatehood." I was tutored by masters who were still fluid in mind, body and spirit. I was pirated by their play. Soon, I began to look at the world differently. The rich sense of belonging I experienced in play was too important to be relegated to "leftover" time. I wanted more.

Unbidden, play began to seep quietly into other areas of my life. My teaching, writing and "house-husband" activities took on a new freshness, spontaneity and energy. In the midst of preparing dinner, I would turn off the stove and go out on the lawn when my own children, Anthony and Etienne, would give me a playful nudge. When I worked on my dissertation, if one of them gave me the play "look," I would stop mid-sentence and tussle on the floor. I found out that my adult concerns were unrealistic. I didn't have to play for hours. Dinners were made and eaten just a little later, and my dissertation was finished on time.

I began to sense something beyond the activity that I couldn't explain. I hadn't completely abandoned my academic orientation, and I wanted confirmation of what I was experiencing with children. So I began reading everything I could find about play.

I didn't find what I expected. Instead, I discovered a major discrepancy between what I was feeling and what behavioral scientists wrote about play. I was puzzled. What I read about play was so lifeless and so destitute of feeling; it was impossible to reconcile these dry words with my play experiences. Dutifully obeying the academic rules, researchers wrote about categories, not children. If what academics wrote about was play, I must have stumbled upon an "undiscovered" form of behavior. If what I was experiencing was play, the scientists were describing something else and calling it play. The more I played, the greater the discrepancy grew between experience and books. I became increasingly convinced that I was being initiated into a very different relationship, which scientists variously described as aimless, blowing off steam, acting out, unreal, competitive, childish, pre-learning for adult life and a release of repressed aggression.

I found only a few exceptions to the standard social science treatment of play. One day, rereading Gregory Bateson's *A Theory of Play and Fantasy*, I was struck by his insight: "Play could only occur if the participant organisms were capable of some degree of metacommunication, of exchanging signals which would carry the message 'this is play.' " This was what had been happening between me and my playmates.

As I played I found that this nonverbal message was understood by all children, regardless of culture or disease etiology. I played with children from Mexico who didn't speak English. I didn't speak Spanish but this didn't make any difference. I played with children who had autism and various emotional disorders and found that they played like "normal" children. The labels applied to children were irrelevant in our play. I began to suspect that I was being introduced to a form of intraspecies communication that all young children understand. The Dalai Lama's statement, "Children know in their minds that all children are the same, all human beings are the same," began to take on new meaning for me.

As the number and variety of my young playmates increased, play revealed itself as a more fundamental pattern than I first surmised. I began to suspect that it connects not just humans, but all creatures, and I decided to seek out animal playmates. I felt intuitively that dogs and cats were too domesticated, in a sense too "adulterated" to play as I was beginning to understand it. This meant that I would need to play with wild creatures.

One day on a visit to Seattle, my friend Vicki told me about Wolf Haven, a sanctuary near Tenino, Washington. We went down on a rainy day to speak with Jack, a wolf biologist, and walk around. I told Jack that I wanted to go in and play with the wolves. He suggested that if I wrote it up as a proposal, he would present it to Wolf Haven's Board of Directors. He did and soon, with the provisions that I not hurt the wolves and that whatever happened to me was my own responsibility, I began the long process of introducing myself as a playmate to the wolves. Because I lived and worked in Southern California, I could only arrange to come up and visit for two periods of two to three weeks each in the spring and fall. Nonetheless for nine years I returned each year to play with wolves, coyotes and foxes at Wolf Haven.

In the mid-1980s, we moved to Montana. I began wandering the mountains, searching for playmates. In and around Yellowstone National Park I would find deer, moose, elk, bison and bear. Since then, my wild animal playmates have included a butterfly, a mongoose, lion cubs, young baboons and dolphins.

Along the way I read another of Gregory Bateson's works, *Mind And Nature: A Necessary Unity.* I was struck by a question that he raised very early in the text: "What is the pattern which connects all the living creatures?" I could hardly contain my enthusiasm. Play, of course! My play with children and animals in the intervening years confirmed that playing is a constant in life itself, a principle whose scope is larger than I can imagine. I feel a belonging or kinship to a very large community, around which I can put no boundaries.

The love expressed through play goes beyond the boundaries of culture. This love is what poet Rainer Maria Rilke wrote of as "the beginning of Terror we're not yet able to bear." I've been a part of such love, and I'm simultaneously afraid of it and want it so deeply. It is what living a life on earth is about. Such love is not concerned with questions of ethics or survival. It is a love without categories, beyond our cultural loves. Nothing in my schooling explained it; nothing even postulated its existence. It is a love for a horse, for a child, for a creek, not as a horse, a girl or a creek, for these are only their categories. This "it" is what I call in play "kindness" — beyond everything I know, all life is of only One Kind. Through play with the children and the animals, this love/kindness that lay dormant within me is now being freed.

Our fundamental error in understanding what we have collectively called play is in assuming that it is created by culture, and that it is an activity done by certain people, like children and athletes, and at certain times as in games, vacations and recess. An alternative to this view is that play is by no means a body of childish activities, cultural diversions or personal acting out, but rather a sacred relationship with life that is anything but popular invention. The kindness inherent in play, though aspired to as an ideal by cultures and religions, is in fact devalued in everyday life.

As children we are taught to think of only some of life as our kind. To propose authentic play in a culture is a bold adventure that rips the very fabric of society.

In play our allegiance goes beyond the limits of nations, cultures and religions to life itself. Play touches that which is most profoundly alive within one being to that which is most profoundly alive in another. Compared to authentic play, the cultural counterfeits, however satisfying, are mere decoration or entertainment. Playing is simply the right way of crafting life. In the highest possible sense, playing is kindness made flesh.

Lewis Mumford describes playmates in a letter to Loren Eiseley: "They are those who make no answer to questions, but depart trailing after them a radiance which is not that of the earth we know, or have set down within our books." Lin-chi (Rinzai), a Chinese Zen monk, described what I mean by playmate as "the True Person with no rank or label in this hulk of mammalian flesh."

Becoming a playmate is a demanding process. At times it seems impossible to be a playmate on earth. The journey is predicated on retraining, prolonged practice and commitment in pursuit of a mystery, which is sometimes immensely joyful and sometimes full of doubt. I have arrived at a conception and practice of playing that is very different from the conventional notions of play. When I am with adults, I sometimes feel unsure about what I'm doing and why I'm doing it. It is a radical act to play with children in a culture that discounts both children and play. There is no societal support for play with children. It is often thought of as "nice" or "cute," and my play with animals as "interesting." We have difficulty dealing with a person over the age of five who plays.

A newspaper reporter wrote, "Fred Donaldson never has a hard day at work. All he does is play around." At such times I recall the lessons from the children and animals, and I remember why I am playing. Play is not a job or a career, but my vocation, which I recall being defined as "the work one is called upon to do by the Gods."

I played before I tried to explain what play is. My attempts to conceptualize play followed some time after my participation in it. I understood why the efforts of social scientists to understand play as I knew it were doomed to fail. As outside observers they examined play and took it apart. But in putting it all back together, they had missed something. They had the sum of the parts, but had somehow missed the whole.

I'm thinking of an Indian summer day in Montana. The sky is a bright blue. There are occasional fluffs of cloud. The aspen leaves flutter on the tree and crunch underfoot. The sun is more than warm, the breeze is a little cool; together they make for a day that one should spend outdoors. If I try to analyze it by taking it apart into its meteorological and biological parts, it loses its beauty. But as a participant in the day, it is part of me.

As a playmate I am independent of the codes I otherwise live by, and by this independence I am free to honor a deeper code than we can express in our cultural lives. Playing is not something new. This cosmic play has been present before the beginning of life itself. Every human being's birth — indeed every being's birth — is an expression of this lifeplay.

PART ONE

ORIGINAL PLAY

God sleeps in the stones,
Dreams in the plants,
Stirs in the animals,
Awakens in humanity
And plays with all.

Unknown

In the deeper reality beyond space and time, we may be all members of
the one body.

Sir James Jeans

1

"Come With Me,
I Have A Secret Place:"
A Divine Invitation

The soul is taken by God to a secret place . . . for God alone will play with it in a game of which the body knows nothing.

Mechthild of Magdeburg

Having made a discovery, I shall never see the world again as before. My eyes have become different; I have made myself into a person seeing and thinking differently. I have crossed a gap, the heuristic gap which lies between problem and discovery.

Michael Polanyi

To play is to yield oneself to a kind of magic, to enact to oneself the absolutely other, to preempt the future, to give the lie to the inconvenient world of fact. In play earthly realities become, of a sudden, things of the transient moment, presently left behind, then disposed of and buried in the past; the mind is prepared to accept the unimagined and incredible, to enter a world where different laws apply, to be relieved of all the weights that bear it down, to be free, kingly, unfettered and divine.

Hugo Rahner

A major portion of the world's story appears to be that of fumbling little creatures of seeming no great potential, falling, like the helpless little girl Alice, down a rabbit hole or an unexpected crevice into some new and topsy-turvy realm.

Loren Eiseley

This morning as I sit on my porch reading, Chris, the boy from next door, pedals his bike down the driveway. He stops abruptly and confides to me that he has a secret. Leaning closer, he invites me to visit the tree where the trolls live. "It's not far away," he assures me. Thrilled at the prospect of such an adventure, I put my book aside and we're off. He guides me down a nearby street, to a huge cedar with a long, narrow opening into its dark center. He puts his finger up to his lips, signaling quiet. "They said it's okay to come in, even if no one is home," he whispers, assuring me, "I've done it before." We squeeze inside and wait quietly for a few minutes in the dark, damp and fragrant center, then squeeze out again, transformed.

We're quiet as we walk back home. Although firmly touching earth, I walk as if I'm floating on air. Then I begin to wonder what happened and the very act of wondering is like a pin that pops the experience. Suddenly I am back walking on the road looking at houses and trees. The experience disappears like a dream. And yet it wasn't a dream. I look at the tree once more as we turn the corner into our street. It's different now. I'm back in my usual world, and yet it's not quite the same as before. Most adults who hear this story are bewildered by the possibility that I believe it to be true.

"Of course, you were just humoring a child. You don't really believe in trolls, do you?" Their skepticism classifies such an experience as fantasy. A few adults, however, excitedly ask, "Where is the tree?" There is a profound difference in the assumptions behind the two questions. The child in us eagerly wants to visit the tree. The adult isn't aware of its existence.

Today I went outside to play with Dennis. It was our usual half-hour time together after his lunch and before he goes home on the bus. As I knelt down at his lunch table, he smiled and began gathering up a small pile of leaves, one large leaf and a handful of pieces. He collected them all and we walked toward the door. He put them down on the counter and began playing with them. The large leaf was a mother chicken and the pieces were alternately babies or eggs, depending on whether he put the large leaf on top of the pile of pieces or scattered them around her. Dennis drew me inside his play, talking to me about the chickens he had seen on a field trip before lunch. For a moment my thoughts went back to my own boyhood when I would get home from a horse show and scour the garage and basement for objects to construct jumps for my backyard arena. I would become the various horses I had seen in the morning.

"You be babies." Dennis' words brought me back from horses to chickens.

"Where are you going, Mother?" I asked. Dennis flew the leaf/chicken mother over the chicks, swooped her down and landed her nearby. Suddenly, I saw not a leaf, but a chicken. Just as quickly, I saw again a leaf gracefully bending in the shape of a bird. I smiled to myself. Dennis was a master, and I had been allowed in to share his world. The "fact" that we saw a chicken, the "fact" that our birds were leaves didn't make any difference to either of us. Here were differences that did not make a difference. I smiled and looked around. Did anyone see me? Could they tell that I saw chickens too? Who could I tell about this? Dennis already knew. Everyone else saw leaves.

I found that the more I worked with them, the bigger and bigger [they] got, and when I was really working with them, I wasn't outside, I was down there. I was part of the system. I was right down there with them, and everything got big. I even was able to see the internal parts of the chromosomes. . . . It surprised me because I actually felt as if I were right down there and these were my friends. As you look at these things, they become part of you. And you forget yourself. The main thing is that you forget yourself.

Barbara McClintock

I had the feeling I was perceiving, *and being perceived by*, an immense presence. I was simultaneously speechless and trying to absorb a vast amount of information that I was unable to fit into adequate patterns of past experience. It somehow transcended the human experience, going deeply into unknown mysteries.

This whale's invitation to share her world gave me a glimpse through a cosmic crack between species . . . a oneness of all living things as we know them someday in the future . . . a place we have been before and will return to again . . . a peaceful promise . . . *the* "peaceable kingdom."

Antoinette Lilly

First, you'll need to dream and believe that the invitation to "come out and play" with the world exists. Think of the invitation as a playmate who can be anyone or anything, real or imaginary. The invitation to join the mystery may come in the person of a child like Dennis or a form like the troll-tree or the eye of a whale. To open the invitation is to be seized by a flight of fancy such that you become acutely aware of the epiphanies that surround us. In the last analysis, the material world fades and yields to our yearning to explore its mysterious invitations.

Surprise! Life Comes Without Warning

It's been said that life is what happens to you while you are waiting for something else to happen. Historian Daniel Boorstin tells the story of an obscure Dutch spectacle maker named Hans

Lippershey, who lived about 1600. One day two children happened into his shop and began *playing* with his lenses. "They put two lenses together and when they looked through both at the same time toward a distant weathervane on the town church, it was wonderfully magnified. Lippershey looked for himself and then began making telescopes." To be continually surprised by the world is not mushy sentimentality, but a realization that we are in the midst of a mystery.

Too often our vision has coalesced into categories, frozen into form like ice crystals into sheets. To discover a playmate is to begin to thaw. When we receive an invitation to play, something we've done numerous times before suddenly becomes transforming. Poet Rabindranath Tagore was so transformed: "When all of a sudden, from some innermost depth of my being, a ray of light found its way out; it spread over and illuminated for me the whole universe, which no longer appeared like heaps and things and happenings, but was disclosed to my sight as one whole." The invitations may, and often do, arrive when you least expect them. If you listen attentively with your heart, you may hear the faint, gentle stirring of an invitation/playmate amidst the rush and uproar of daily life. If you make your mind very silent and stop talking to yourself, close your eyes and really see, you may, if neither your eye nor your mind is already focused, come upon such an invitation.

I was standing in the warm shallows; all of my attention was focused on the sea shimmering in the late afternoon sun. I squinted, trying to catch a glimpse of Holly's fin slicing the calm water. Holly, a two-year-old dolphin, became a playmate during my stay at Monkey Mia, Australia in 1988. Silently she would swim up to me and nibble on my fingers or put her rostrum in the sand under my foot and lift up. Today, however, I couldn't see her anywhere. Suddenly, I felt a firm, soft, snuggling hold on my fingers, which were dangling in the water at my side. I smiled and looked down, expecting to see Holly's eye returning my smile. Instead I saw a little girl's smile. She took my hand and led me through an afternoon of play. She climbed up on my knees and dove off. We frolicked in the water and explored the shoreline. Later we walked down the beach, holding hands, not talking. As we skipped under the pier, she saw her mother and ran off to join her. She left as suddenly as she had appeared, and I was grateful for the wonderful luxury of being the acolyte of a young child who could find that puzzling inner place and shine a light there. I was reminded once again that play is receptive to any opening through which it may flare up like a forgotten ember. The universe invites us to join in its play.

Long Long Ago When Wishing Still Could Lead To Something

Play is an auspicious adventure that combines the magic of Alice and the divine of Christ. But even this is not enough because as magic and divine,the passages would seem beyond the capabilities of ordinary people. It would be impossible to say anything about the openings into play were it not for certain extraordinary encounters, experiences and revelations. In their power, significance and feeling and the keen sense of responsibility they bring, they are at once ordinary and utterly different in quality from our usual experiences.

Life has provided as many kinds of invitations as there are people. They are part of the birthright of all humankind. I suspect that many more people have, if only for a moment, come out to play with the world, but for many reasons have chosen to keep the experience to themselves.

One morning Dennis and I were out on the school grounds having our morning play time together. It was October and the big leaves from the sycamore tree were beginning to fall. It had rained the night before. The sun had not yet evaporated the moisture from the grass or from the sand around the play equipment. Dennis lay down on his tummy on the merry-go-round and motioned for me to join him. Together we lay down and turned the merry-go-round very slowly, watching the brown water ripple as we dragged our fingers through it. We didn't talk, but every so often we would look at each other and smile. Dennis picked up a leaf and put it in the water. He twirled it with his finger and said, "Treestar." He saw patterns and made connections where I had seen discrete objects. Dennis accepted the invitation and let the world tickle his heart.

What Sir Arthur Eddington called "the mystic contact with the earth" is available all around us. This blend of inner and outer nature is an integral part of each of us; our own bodies provide openings to play. This is a very powerful idea not only for the healing of ourselves as individuals, but for the earth as well. Deepak Chopra points out, "Research on spontaneous cures of cancer, conducted in both the United States and Japan, has shown that just before the cure appears, almost every patient experiences a dramatic shift in awareness. He knows that he will be healed, and he feels that the force responsible is inside himself but not limited to him — it extends beyond his personal boundaries, throughout all of nature."

Like Alice going through the looking glass, we must take a quantum leap through the opening life provides. As when snow melts and exposes winter's rich collection of the lost and abandoned "stuff" to spring, such openings bring our fossil experiences of original play back to life.

Two Looks Away

Life abounds with playmates. The invitations to lure us away from the normally traveled paths of our culture are ever-present and accessible. Why then doesn't everyone answer life's invitation?

One problem lies in our limited ability to truly see. Perhaps for a moment we receive the invitation — from a leaf or a child or a chromosome. We glimpse more than we think we should, more than we know and fearfully reject the invitation, retreating back within the categories of culture.

During a trip to Montana to track wolves north of Glacier National Park, I visited with some Native American craftspeople. One of the men spoke quietly:

"Most people don't see wolves because they know only how to look with their eyes. Some are trained and can therefore look better than others. Some of these people say that they see wolves. White men use their science to find wolves, but even with these machine eyes they cannot see. It is not good vision alone that allows one to see a wolf in the wild." Then he peered at me and thrust his hand straight out from the middle of his chest. "One must take a second look. And this is done with the heart. The *real* wolf is two looks away."

The "first look" kind of consciousness organizes life into a succession of rigid categories and structures. To survive we perceive the world rationally, order it according to fixed values and attempt to master it systematically. For example, looking through the veils of habit, most adults see children as clay they must shape. Teachers, doctors and psychologists describe children with a bewildering array of labels — gifted, behavior disorder, autistic, attention deficit disorder, learning disabled, Down syndrome, multiple handicapped. Such terms may help professionals communicate among themselves, but they are useless when it comes to playing with a child. The warmth of an awakened heart is more appropriate here than the cold analysis of the rational mind which freezes every aspect of life. Blaise Pascal put it into perspective for us: "The heart has its reasons which the reason does not at all perceive."

Playing requires a second look. This is difficult because our hearts have become overgrown with thickets of ideas, fears and judgments. These cultural perceptions simply do not penetrate deeply enough. Opening the invitation means being able to see beyond the surface, to hear beyond language. With the wisdom of a third eye, play enables us to see the truth beyond appearances. The openings to play are inaccessible to ordinary human approaches, but not to ordinary humans. What Joseph Campbell said of the mythical hero is true for all of us. Answering the call to come out and play, "signifies that destiny has summoned the hero and transferred his spiritual center of gravity from within the pale of his society to a zone unknown." Here lies the persuasive power of play. It is the second look that senses the Greater Life within life.

The real value of play lies in what it indicates about the arrangement of the universe, whose playful nature is of ancient origin. Fortunately for us there are dreamers and explorers who understand the dreamlike nature of origins. George Wald, in his Nobel Prize remarks, noted that, "A scientist lives with all reality. There is nothing better. To know reality is to accept it, and eventually to love it. A scientist is in a sense a learned child. There is something of the scientist in every child." Both the scientist and the child know that, "logically, when one comes to an empty space, one ought to halt. But life is that which leaps," as Michael Adam said. Playmates leap beyond the safety of the old knowledge that secures teachers and parents. The child and the scientist know there is nothing to fear. They beckon us to join them in their adventures.

To accept an invitation to come out and play is to know the plentitude of the cosmos. We are able to poke through the veils of culture and move into new worlds. We are indeed fortunate that the universe provides us with a myriad of enchanted openings — rabbit burrows, and 100-acre woods, black holes and DNA — through which we are drawn to explore its nooks and crannies full of simple gifts and small wonders.

Like a child playing in mud, we can knead the substance of the universe. And in turn we are molded by the universe. Each play experience lives on in us as a bit of memory. When a new playmate interacts with me, he or she is also playing with each and every playmate with whom I've played.

2

Playing God:
Creation's Irrationally
Crazy Gift

Imagine God to be at play with us.
John Donne

God has created the world in play.
Sri Ramakrishna

For the Logos on high plays.
St. Gregory Nazianzen

Life is at root playing.
Alan Watts

All of this spectacle, including me, is the play of DNA.
Deepak Chopra

The creation of the world, all the world over,
is made from the play of the gods.
Lynda Sexson

Man is made to be the plaything of God.
Plato

Original Play

We begin with the vision of original play creating life and life creating original play. I use the word "original" to denote play that is prehuman, precultural before all conceptualizations and learned responses. Play is a gift of Creation, not an artifact of culture. It is the stillpoint and the energy from which all else is evoked. In mathematics according to Michael Adam, "It is the shape of zero, that absence of number that makes possible all numerical play." Likewise it is play's underlying emptiness or absence of cultural categories and boundaries that enables it to encompass the fullness of life. Anything less could not include the vastness of life. Play's patterns, forms and movements are our mother tongue, what Laurens van der Post has called the "forgotten language of God."

As physicist Brian Swimme asserts, "The adventurous play of the life forms burst into the bewildering and sublime diversity of the past five hundred million years. All of this profusion of being and beauty is the outcome of play, of risk, of surprise." Friedrich Schiller suggested almost 200 years earlier that the impulse to play is a unifying force at work between form and matter. In Shakespeare's *The Tempest*, Prospero "discovers through the loss and renewal of self a body of power existing beneath the world's surface of names and things, a body of power he can reach in play."

Beyond the ancestral clay and within the interstellar spaces, the heavens, the earth, the sky and the waters are all playing. Spiral nebulas and quarks play. God plays. We have been in the midst of it all along. Alan Watts understood playfulness as the very essence of the energy of the universe. At age fifteen physicist Freeman Dyson called it "cosmic unity" and realized, "There is only one of us. We are all the same person." Original play is, as theologian Carol Ochs said about God, simultaneously "our creator and our creation, our ancestor and our descendant."

Such play is at the heart of the teachings of sages from many traditions throughout history. An allusion to play as a prehuman, divine force is found in Christian, Taoist, Buddhist and Hindu thought. We find, for example, in the New Jerusalem Bible, before all "was firmly set, from the beginning, before the earth came into being," wisdom speaks of playing: "I was beside the master craftsman, delighting him day after day ever at play in his presence, at play everywhere on his earth." Meister Eckhart describes the Father as watching the play of his own nature and the Son playing before Him, and "the playing of the twain is the Holy Ghost." In the preface to a seventeenth century translation of Jacob Boehme's *Signatura Rerum* we find that "This is that wisdom which dwells in nothing, and yet possesses all things, and the humble resigned soul is its playfellow."

Eastern traditions also allude to play as an original source. In the writings of Chuang-tzu, for example, Tsekung asks Confucius about the lack of manners of two men whom he encountered singing in the presence of a corpse. Confucius replies, "These men play about beyond the material things. They consider themselves as companions of the Creator, and play about within the One Spirit of the universe." In Japanese Zen there is an intensity of feeling in which the self is inseparable from all else. This is *yukezammai*, in which all activity is play. As in the Christian writings, play is with the Source of all life.

In Hinduism the creative activity of the Divine is called *Lila*, the play of God. This is the sacred energy in which *Brahman* transforms himself into the world. *Lila* is the endless cycle of Divine rhythmic play beyond intellectual understanding, through which

the one is tranformed into the many and the many return to the
one. The heart of man is the seat of this *Lila*, which can be
reproduced at all times, in the heart of every true bhakta. A
secondary name for the Hindu gods is *krida*, meaning play. In the
Upanishads the world process is a game the Spirit plays with
itself. In the Hindu scripture on the life and teachings of Sri
Krishna, "The eternal, unchangeable Lord . . . evolves the whole
universe out of himself, plays with it." Swami Ramdas, a twenti-
eth-century Hindu bhakta, agrees that "He Himself is the player
and Witness of the play."

Original play is a sacred force that permeates existence. Original play is our ground of being. We are continuous with it. This
original play is the great sympathy of which the Taoists speak.
According to Chang, "The universal force holds together man,
and man and all things." Rumi, Persia's greatest Sufi poet, writes
about this same play between the Creator and humans, "That all
I's and thou's should become one soul and at last should be sub-
merged in the Beloved." How wonderfully irrationally crazy.

Playing Without The Lines

Four-year-old Michael pointed at the cow in the storybook and
said, "Horsey." Chuang-tzu said, "Everything is a horse." Infancy
and wisdom are not the same, but are they so different? Both
child and elder see "two looks away," beyond the boundaries and
distinctions imposed by their respective cultures. Such "seeing"
carries them from diversity to unity. That Chuang-tzu and Michael see more than most of us is not surprising, for we live in
adulthood, a state too old for wonder and too busy for wisdom.

Do you remember coloring with crayons on blank paper? It
was impossible to color inside or outside the lines because there
were none. Then came ditto sheets and coloring books. Like a
wild horse in a corral, our coloring was tamed when we brought
it inside the lines.

To come out to play again is not to struggle against our cultures,
but to realize as we did when we first colored that the lines are
unneccesary. We can simply play as if there were no lines. In
original play there is no inside or outside. Without the boundaries
play is, as Martin Buber wrote, "the exultation of the possible."

Okay, you say. Such play may be appropriate for gods, mystics and scientists but what about for you and me? In everyday life to play in this way requires either great fearlessness or great foolishness, or perhaps both. A great fool, says Wes Nisker, is one who lives outside blinding routine, remaining open to life's inherent surprises. We must somehow trust that there will be something to hold us if we let go of the sociocultural norms within which we are enmeshed. Constantly confronted as we are with the uncertainty and mystery of life, we may know that total security is illusory. But illusion or not, we think and act as if our culture is a security blanket. To conceive of coming out from under it requires fearlessness. What motivates some people to forego security and explore outside the cultural limits? We must believe that faith, that life is more than we are told, that it goes beyond the ordinary cultural means to give.

The power of play lives in its timeless pattern of sharing. It does not seek to obliterate or transform differences. It allows for interaction because it operates at a deeper level where there are no differences that make a difference.

Let's try a metaphor. Imagine a human being as an artichoke. The artichoke's tough, spiny leaves are the innumerable shields we put up to defend that which is most tender and sought after — the heart. We can tear an artichoke's leaves off to get at its heart, just as we can attack a person; but there is a much easier and more effective way. If we steam the artichoke, it surrenders its leaves, exposing and sharing its heart with us. In the same way, play does not attack a person's defenses. Play creates an environment in which we drop our shields and share our tender human heart, which is what we all want in the first place. But if our shields are ripped off from the outside, we try to build even stronger ones. In play we interact heart to heart, without any of our cultural separations. This requires trust in a supportive web of life that is greater than one's culture.

Playing provides us with an opportunity to participate fully in a primordial eternal moment. Inconceivable as it seems to ordinary reason, when we play with one being, we are indeed playing with all. Meister Eckhart presents us with a brief question-answer exchange that illustrates such unity.

"When is a man in mere understanding?" I answer, "When a man
sees one thing as separated from another."

"And when is a man above mere understanding?" That I can tell
you, "When a man sees All in all, then a man stands beyond mere
understanding."

This is also the message of Jesus in the Gospel according to
Thomas saying to his disciples, "When you make the two one . . .
then shall you enter [the Kingdom]." Then one is truly playing
without the lines of separation.

Playing God

John Donne, St. Gregory, Sri Ramakrishna, Michael and
Chuang-tzu are correct: We all are God's playmates. "Playmate"
ceases to be a cultural term for what we normally regard as
childish friendships. The word playmate assumes awesome proportions when we feel the spiritual implications involved. Playmates, as five-year-old David knew, don't know that they are different from each other. This means that at some level we are not
different from God. In original play it is impossible not to "play
God," because in the very being/doing of original play, one is God
and God is one. In his clear, childlike manner, David expressed
what Meister Eckhart wrote in the thirteenth century: "God and
I are one in knowing. . . . And the manner of our knowing shall
be this, I Him as He me, not more or less: just the same."

When I use God throughout this book, I am referring to the
ineffable presence that goes by many names — The One, Logos,
Tao, Brahman, Buddha, The Goddess, Krishna, Allah, Mana, Wa-
kan Tanka, the Universal Spirit or Principle.

To play God is not to usurp a divine role, as if one were equal
to God, implying a deification of self and a lowering of God until
they are of equal weight on some social/spiritual scale. This would
be pretense on a grand scale. To play God is not to gain a greater
role, but to let go of those we already have. The result is that
there are no roles to play. The connection made in play between

self, other and God is unmediated, unmitigated and immediate. As the wave does not give rise to the sea, play does not originate in us; play is our common ground of Creation.

Original play derives its power from a source immemorial beyond our oldest memories revealing to us the furthest connections of our souls. In most of us such play lies dormant, like fire beneath a pile of ashes. It flares up now and then, sending shivers of delight through those who are sentient enough to be sensitive to them. A sense of grace, a light delirium sparks a sensitive detector in a human spine at the invitation to play. An intimate energy is shared; an appetite for life increases.

Kindness

What we feel in play is a condition of kindness structured beyond our cultural consciousness. This kindness is not an ethical judgment telling us how to act. Play's kindness is like a pinprick of conscience that lies deeper within the unbounded flux of matter and energy. The essence of original play is then a preexisting kindness expressed in the hermetic dictum, "As above, so below."

Play's kindness expresses a relationship to life rather than a sociocultural command, as in Chopra's story about the Indian *sadhu* and the scorpion:

A man is walking down the road when he spots a *sadhu* kneeling beside a ditch. He approaches and sees that the *sadhu* is watching a scorpion. The scorpion wants to cross the ditch, but when he gets into the muddy water, he begins to drown. The *sadhu* carefully reaches down to pull him out of the water, but as soon as he touches it, the scorpion stings him. The scorpion goes into the water again, again it begins to drown, and when the *sadhu* lifts it out, he receives another sting. The man sees this happen three times. Finally he blurts, "Why don't you stop allowing yourself to be stung?" The *sadhu* replies, "There is nothing I can do. It is the scorpion's nature to sting, but it is my nature to save."

Clearly, there is a time-honored tradition of attempting to express the feeling one gets having experienced a sense of kindness

with all life. Astronaut Russell Schweikart was stunned on his trip
to space. "What took no analysis, however, no microscopic exami-
nation, no laborious processing," he said, "was the overwhelming
beauty . . . the unavoidable and awesome personal relationship, suddenly realized, with all life on the amazing planet . . . Earth, our
home." And Soviet cosmonaut Oleg Makarov adds, "For me it was
an embracing of the planet and all life . . . and, like the squirrels
and the pines, it hugged me back."

Aurobindo expressed similar feelings from an equally small
space, although not of his own choosing. When his prison was
no longer a prison, Aurobindo wrote, "The high wall, those iron
bars, the white wall, the green-leaved tree shining in sunlight,
it seemed as if these commonplace objects were not unconscious
at all, but that they were vibrating with a universal consciousness, they loved me and wished to embrace me or so I felt. Men,
cows, ants, birds, are moving, flying, singing, speaking, yet all is
Nature's Play. . . ."

Original play is the unity of photon and light wave at the
infinitesimal level of nature; it is the union experienced by individuals in space at the grandest scale of human perception. Original play is the union experienced in Yoga and in prison. It is also
found at the scale of life as lived by those of us who are neither
quantum physicists nor Indian *rishis*. We are not separate from
the universe in which we are embedded. What is true at the
micro and macro scales is also true at the scale of life as we live
it. A verse in the ancient Ayurveda texts says:

As is the human body, so is the cosmic body.
As is the human mind, so is the cosmic mind.
As is the microcosm, so is the macrocosm.

Play is not just out there somewhere among the stars, nor is it
merely within our DNA. Play is around me, in me, beyond me.
Play is me. Play is you. Play is we.

This is just what happened on that spring day when David and
I were lying on the little hill watching clouds float by. In one clear,

straightforward sentence he told me all there is to know: "You know, Fred, play is when we don't know that we are different from each other." It was so simple. His ability to fathom the uncomprehensible and articulate its essence so clearly stunned me. David not only gave me the best definition of play that I know of, he was pointing out both the fundamental paradox of play and its profound individual, collective and spiritual importance. His spiritual dynamite explodes preexisting ideas of human-Godhead separation. It is not merely he and I who weren't different from each other; more important, he knew that neither of us was different from God.

Original play is simultaneously inside all life and beyond all separations. This is play of an ancient origin, that has never ceased being nourished and whose life has persisted under the cover of culture for thousands of years. This vision is heretical enough, but it isn't sufficient. Original play is transformative because it is more than a vision that can change our view of who we are individually and collectively; it is an accompanying practice that activates this transformation in all of our relationships with each other and all of nature.

To join in this adventurous play is to work as an artisan with the grain of cosmic dynamics and enhance the movement of the universe. The ancient Hebrew wisdom of the Kabbalah teaches that our task in life is to restore to wholeness as many fragments of a split world as we encounter along our individual paths. Then the richness, beauty and playfulness of the Universe become integral parts of us.

Believe what Plato told us long ago, "Life must be lived as play."

3

Conceived Playing

We all begin life as players.

Lynda Sexson

We are told in the language of Jewish myth that in his mother's womb man knows the universe and forgets it at birth.

Martin Buber

From early days,
Beginning not long after that first time
In which, a Babe, by intercourse of touch,

I held mute dialogues with my Mother's heart
I have endeavour'd to display the means
Whereby this infant sensibility,
Great birthright of our Being, was in me
Augmented and sustain'd.

William Wordsworth

When I was a child, God also became a child with me to be my playmate.

Rabindranath Tagore

I tried to teach my child with books,
He gave me only puzzled looks.
I tried to teach my child with words,
They passed him by, often unheard.
Despairingly, I turned aside,
"How shall I teach this child,?" I cried.
"Come," he said, "Play with me."

Anonymous

The child is playing! And not ten minutes have gone by since it was born.

Frederick Leboyer

With each new birth the universe whispers life into a body with the secret, "Aha, this is play!"

We are conceived playing. Play is the Beginning, the Oneness from which we all arise. Divine play precedes human play and is its model writ large. The play that initiates, inspires and flows through the cosmos is in us too. As liberation theologian Matthew Fox suggests, God is our divine playmate and we live in God's playhouse.

Human infants play for the same reason that water flows and birds fly. Play is in the nature of things. Our individual play is grounded in the very nature of the universe. It is an intimate personal rhythm in which every movement is an unbroken flow of controlled abandon and trust, at once available to everyone and our very own. This play of energies back and forth is not only the pattern of intelligence between mother and child, but between each of us and life itself. This play provides our original center-edness, balance and sense of direction. Biologist Lyall Watson asserts, "We are all biologically entrained in the same way to the basic rhythms of Mother Earth — and these are always with us." We would say that we were playing with the universe were it not equally true that the universe is playing with us. Play/touch between child and mother before, during and immediately after birth, is original play brought from the cosmic to the personal.

Conception is a result, not a cause. The cause lies beyond, in the play of the universe. This is a process of consecration in which the ordinary is made sacred. At some level we know; this knowledge inspires our Easters of whatever name. Play is an inherent part of the ancient continuum of not only our species, but life itself. Whether it is the birth of spring or our own child, we are hard put to contain ouselves when we watch with welcome and wonder as life renews itself. For all our learning and sophis-tication, we are humbled by the magnificence of a mystery that touches us when we share in birth. Something deep within re-sponds to the flow of life, to forces beyond self and our accu-mulated knowledge.

Birth Play

Birth is a personal affirmation of play's joyous energy. No mat-ter when or where we are born, each of us begins life in the same way, playing in the dark, as a sphere nestled within another sphere. The womb is our first playground, mother is our first playmate and play is the energy source offering us love, support, trust, energy and possibility. For nine months, we snuggle within our mother's body. We share her body, food, blood and feelings. More "in touch" than we will ever be, we feel the sense of oneness inherent in original play. The womb is a matrix of being that bridges the usual gap between individuals. The result is a power-ful, instantaneous, synergistic and harmonious rhythm.

The womb is our earliest matrix of life. Besides nourishment it provides other truly basic life skills: trust, balance, kindness, touch, blending and love. This is life's play. In play workshops adults often tell me that playing was a profound experience that brought them to tears, but they cannot say why. I believe in such cases we have a fleeting recognition. What we sense is original play, that sense of oneness before we were conscious. In this powerful connection we recognize not just the physical stimulus but that we have been part of such a relationship before.

This is an individual experience of the image of paradise which lies deep in the collective human consciousness. Colin Turnbull alludes to this as he describes the pregnant Mbuti mother and her relationship with her tropical rain forest home in northeast Zaire:

She is . . . readying herself for the creative act about to unfold, giving herself confidence that the forest will be as good and as kind to her child as it has been to her; providing food, shelter, clothing, warmth and affection. That confidence alone would be an auspicious beginning to any life, and until it is proven otherwise, I am not about to believe that nothing of this is transferred to the child in the mother's womb because I have seen that child born, grow through infancy, childhood and youth to adulthood, secure in an otherwise almost incredible trust and confidence in each of the new worlds into which he successively enters as though each were another form of that first and primal sphere, or womb.

This is the sacred stuff of our infancy that in so-called developed countries is later discarded as a childish waste of time.

The fact that we are born about a year premature and helpless makes possible the intimate contact that begins to initiate babies into their culture. But there is another side to this period of neoteny: a union beyond all of our differences, cultural or genetic. The newborn brings with it this direct experience of original play, the very thing we have chosen, against the advice of so many sages, to ignore and adulterate.

Our paths diverge before birth and continue to separate afterward. The fact that we have devalued and debased children's offerings says more about adult wisdom than about child intelligence. We certainly cannot use ignorance as an excuse. Sages from around the world have told us repeatedly to pay attention to our children:

Except ye . . . become as little children, ye shall not enter into the kingdom of heaven.

Matthew 18:3

Wise men hear and see as little children do.

Lao-tzu

You want the first elements?
The infant has them.

Chuang-tzu

The gift of immaturity itself, which has enabled us to retain in our best, most human, moments the capacity for play.

Joseph Campbell

So long as one does not become simple like a child, one does not get divine illumination.

Sri Ramakrishna

Grown men may learn from very little children, for the hearts of little children are pure, and therefore, the Great Spirit may show to them many things which older people miss.

Black Elk

Zen is to have the heart and soul of a little child.

Zen master Takuan

The pupil must regain the child state he hath lost ere the first sound can fall upon his ears.

Tibetan precept

Abandon thought and thinking and be just as a child . . . and the
innate will become manifest.

Buddhist saint and sage Saraha

Life Play

These continue to be difficult messages for us to hear. What is
being suggested is far more subtle than has been assumed. Our
inattention is beyond ignorance; it is based in fear.

Original play as expressed in the life of a human being is the
being/doing relationship prior to conceptualizations and learned
responses. This is what Zen monk Hui-neng called, "Your original
face before your parents were born." Play is a context unlike
other contexts derived from one's culture. This is play before
culture manipulates and controls it. Cultural play is a particular
codification by which a culture helps its children adapt to life as
they see and experience it. All cultures have such play.

Original play is very different; it is a kind of participation that
we may call mimesis or state of consciousness in which cultural
subject/object categories do not exist. It is a fluid balance of spirit,
mind and body. There is no thought of grasping, no energy is
dissipated, no attachment to fear or desire is present. Here play is
not an ethical choice made among cultural alternatives, but rather
as one living, embedded in a world where such a choice simply
does not arise. This is the essential Buddhist idea of nondistinc-
tion: a dynamic balance, not of equality, but of an interplay and
unification of all that is.

The subtle alchemy by which human touch and trust trans-
mutes love and fearlessness from one human being to another
seems often to defy my abilities to explain, but that it happens
and is the essential "stuff" of life is beyond question. Some cultures and individuals do a better job than others at sharing this
mystery with their children. This is reflected in the inclusion of
males in the caregiving process and the increased amount of
nurturing touch given to children for longer periods in some
hunter-gatherer cultures such as the !Kung Bushmen of Botswana
and the Fore and Arapesh of New Guinea, as well as traditional
cultures in Senegal, Malaysia, Fiji, Bali and Venezuela.

In more technologically advanced societies, however, touch de-
clines rapidly after birth to be ignored, discounted and feared by
adolescence. We do not know how to touch. And we are afraid of
what we don't know. The guidelines of a rural elementary school
in Southern California say, "Keep your hands and feet to yourself
at all times." The evidence of abuse and aggression is endemic in
America. But to gather such statistics is not enough, we must
examine our assumptions about human life.

What can we learn from children? Perhaps we can learn what
the unused 95 percent of our brains is for. In *Growing Young*
Ashley Montagu gives us a list of 27 neotenous traits of the
fetus, infant and child which we can encourage and emulate.
These include love, wonder, playfulness, openmindedness, flexibility, enthusiasm, trust, compassionate intelligence. All of these
traits together provide a model for human behavior to which we
pay lip service, but very little attention. We are in such a hurry to
make new adults that we do not provide the time, space and
nurturance for the characteristics that infants bring with them.
Montagu says, "This is a deprivation we, in civilized societies,
visit upon millions of potential human beings, resulting in untold
numbers of human tragedies."

James Prescott believes, "Warm, affectionate touching relationships in childhood or adolescence . . . deter violence in adults."
My play with children continues to demonstrate that the sages
are correct: Children, before they are enculturated, provide a
genuine model of love and fearlessness. With their help we can
provide humans with nurturing support for our explorations without losing our footholds.

The play that I'm describing is not cultural play taught by
adults to "make" children fit better into their cultures. I am not
talking about developing "superbabies" or being "superparents."
Your child is not your toy, neither are you his or her plaything. Neither of you is an object to be used for the pleasure of
the other.

Unlearning

It is impossible for me to teach another person how to play
with a child. There is no formula. I can only help adults unlearn

so that they can be empty enough to absorb what a child is sharing with them. It is surprisingly difficult for us to recapture our childlike genius. In place of all the *doing* associated with teaching, counseling and parenting, I'm suggesting *being*. To be a playmate is beyond technique and skill; it is a total response. Play is a vision translated by hand. We must trust that play is within us, too, though it will require a good deal of unlearning. I'm talking about original play, in which you participate as a playmate. And the only way to accomplish this is by letting go of all your adult roles while you play.

Observing isn't sufficient. You must feel play yourself. Infants are already experts. Get down. Let go. Pay attention. Be in touch. You'll learn more than you can imagine. I'm not just talking about "normal" infants. There is no question of competence in play, as if people with disabilities play less well than those without. I do not play with categories of disease or illness, but individual children.

All playmates have two very special gifts to share with us. *You are lovable* and *There's nothing to be afraid of.* It is touch that provides us with tangible evidence that these gifts are ours to give and receive. These are gifts that everyone needs throughout life. Playing with babies is not only good for them; the joy, love and trust is reciprocal or it is not play.

The very latest research, as reported in Thoman and Browder, clearly shows that playing with your child will help him or her develop not only intellectually but emotionally and socially. Simultaneously, and this is left out of the research, you will likewise be helped through the synchrony of play/touch. Loving play/touch creates trust within both parent and child.

Playing with a child is not parenting, caregiving, teaching or counseling. It is not trying to win a child over, to change the child, to make the child more socially appropriate in school or to make inroads on a neurosis. This is not to argue against these adult-child activities, but they are not play. Nor is every play session an awe-inspiring, life-changing event. Far from it. I have forgotten the particulars of most play sessions. One year I kept track of the number of individual playmates with whom I played; it was over 3,000. I do not play in order to collect wonderful experiences, to be displayed like medals. I play, day after day, with whomever comes out to play. That's being a playmate.

We receive most touch from young children unaware of the gifts that are being presented. We recognize that babies are acutely sensitive receivers of touch, but we haven't learned that they are equally good transmitters of touch. I am still trying to imitate the profound grasping ability of an infant. Anyone who has offered a finger to an infant has felt what I'm talking about.

A master Japanese archer describes this magic moment of touch in Herrigel's *Zen And The Art of Archery:*

"You must hold the drawn bowstring," answered the Master, "like a little child holding the proferred finger. It grips it so firmly that one marvels at the strength of the tiny fist. And when it lets the finger go, there is not the slightest jerk. Do you know why? Because a child doesn't think: I will now let go of the finger in order to grasp this other thing. Completely unself-consciously, without purpose, it turns from one to the other, and we would say that it was playing with the things, were it not equally true that the things are playing with the child."

The archery master puts our task well: We must play equally with the child as the child plays with us.

In play I do not feel secure because of accumulated knowledge, but ready to be present with a child because I have let go of my knowledge. Original play is not a mere vacation from life; it is life. Both you and a child are always growing and changing. Accepting this and playing without answers requires a great deal of openness. Original play is based not on fear, but on a trust relationship with life. As a playmate you join the child in such a way that both of you feel loved, respected and eager to explore. The skills required of you in play — curiosity, trust, resilience, awareness — are those of a healthy child.

Frankie is two years old. He has been diagnosed with spina bifida and doesn't like to crawl during his therapy sessions. He resists and cries. But our walks become marathon crawling sessions. We crawl together all over the school's backyard. One day I put him down, and he began showing me sticks and pebbles. At first I bent over and walked behind him. Suddenly I knew I should be further down with him. So I lay down next to him. He used his elbows and forearms to pull himself along. I watched and crawled. It was hard work; I tired very quickly. He moved faster than I, but he smiled and waited for me. I continued to pull myself along on my tummy as best I could as we explored the backyard. We threw more pebbles, watched ants and planted sticks.

Within play practice is the ever-present possibility of a new "we" being evoked from "you" and "I." One day Christian and Andrea, both of whom have cerebral palsy and are visually impaired, opened my awareness to new possibilities of touch. Normally I lie down between them, interacting with each in turn. But this time I put Andrea next to Christian, and she reached over and touched his chest. He giggled and moved his arm in her direction. Their hands met in mid-air. Their fingers entwined briefly, before releasing. They began to use their hands to search for each other. Sometimes Andrea would touch and sweep gently over Christian's chest or face, eliciting a giggle from him. He'd turn in her direction. When he put his hand up between them, she found it as if she knew where it was ahead of time. Before they touched, their movements were quick and jerky. As they touched they seemed briefly to soften each other's motions. Here were two children who weren't supposed to be able to relate so effectively, yet they interacted as playmates.

Infants are virtuoso playmates. Psychologist Abraham Maslow has called this "love knowledge":

Love for a person permits him to unfold, to open up, to drop his defenses, to let himself be naked not only physically but psychologically and spiritually as well. In a word, he lets himself be seen instead of hiding himself. In ordinary interpersonal relations, we are to some extent inscrutable to each other. In love relationships, we become "scrutable."

The more scrutable I become, the more I am led to new discoveries in the areas of touch, trust and love.

I must keep in mind the words of Ashley Montagu: "We were never intended to grow 'up' into the kind of adults most of us have become." But having grown up to be such an adult, where can I find someone who will not talk to me about becoming a child, but share with me play's gifts?

Find a baby!

PART
TWO

"With All
Good Intentions:"
Play In Service
To Culture

At evening when the lamp is lit,
Around the fire my parents sit;
They sit at home and talk and sing,
And do not play at anything.

Robert Louis Stevenson

All children running loose and unattended will be towed away at owner's expense.

(Sign on store)

4

Adulterated Play

A cage went in search of a bird.

Franz Kafka

We have buried so much of the delicate magic of life.

D.H. Lawrence

The Disenchantment Of Play

T he hallmark of modern play consciousness is that we recognize no elements of the sacred. We fall into the grave delusion that we create play ourselves. In so doing, play undergoes a fundamental shift from a life process to an act in service to culture. This is a profound shift in human consciousness, which has dramatic and tragic consequences at the level of everyday life. How we think about the world is ultimately tied very closely to how we see and experience ourselves as related to others and life itself, which in turn, is reflected in our inability to play with children.

As Morris Berman has shown so well in *The Re-enchantment of the World*, "The modern epoch, at least on the level of mind, is one of progressive disenchantment." It is more than mind; the shift includes spirit and body. From the perspective of the modern adult, to mature away from child's play is to free oneself from the power of the pleasing delusion of childhood's charms and spells in order to carry out the important work of adult life.

Perhaps nothing is more symptomatic of this shift than our inability to provide models of play that sustain the experience of kindness. From a sense of ecstatic belonging, the view and experience of the world grows into one of opposition. The original gifts of fearlessness and love are abandoned in an effort of self-defense; protecting oneself from an increasingly hostile world is seen as life's purpose. While lamenting the lack of intimacy in our lives, we convince ourselves that our physical and emotional safety requires separation and boundaries. To be safe we distance ourselves from the surrounding world, unaware that our very defense mechanisms create the dangers we fear. While teaching horseback riding to children and adults, for example, I found it uncanny that those who were afraid of horses would shy away and walk around horses at the very places that were the most dangerous.

Children grow up with no cultural supports to lean on, no collective myth that makes original play seem real because it is lived and shared by the adults with whom they live. In its place is disenchantment. That is much like the painful process of being extracted, like an impacted wisdom tooth, from the immense world of wonder, magic and mystery to which childhood naturally belongs. Our extraction is so complete that finally we lose all contact with our aboriginal self, discrediting the instincts through which it was maintained. Regarded as childish, original play is outgrown and in the process distorted in spirit, language and form. In its place we put cultural play, which is derived not from children but from adults. We've rejected the notion of belonging-ness inherent in original play. In its place we affirm the impor-tance of the differences between self and other.

Play has been described by Johan Huizinga as "inspired by the feeling of being apart together in an exceptional situation, of sharing something important, of mutually withdrawing from the rest of the world and rejecting the usual norms." I recall feeling "apart together" as a member of my Little League baseball team, my high school football team, my college crew. This feeling requires an "other." Such play conforms to cultural standards. As a means of contest, play is a primary support for culture. Play is adulterated into a world permeated with fear. Dominique La-pierre describes a children's game with kites that is taken over by fathers: "The game had become a battle. The grown-ups . . . had stolen their children's game and were fighting each other like wild beasts."

Disenchantment is a profound split, in which a rational self asserts a commonsense support of cultural play. Another deeply buried part of the self, however, realizes the sleight-of-hand that has occurred and struggles to retain an original sense of integrity with the natural world by reuniting with the authentic source of play. Matthew Fox tells us, "Those who ignore the holiness of creation and the spiritual experience that natural ecstasies can be, end up distorting the faith message and confusing tactical, man-made devices, with spiritual experience." The Upanishads refer to the descent from the experience of *Lila* or divine play to the shallow realm of vain frivolity.

Having chosen to abandon original play, we grow up in a culture stripped of our natural armament, utterly ashamed of childhood's gifts — the life-giving riches that are meant to come to our aid in the terrible moments of rejection. Like an orphan who is not told of his or her biological parents, original feelings and memories are replaced with others in such a way that the person is rendered unable to access the original. Abducted by culture and alienated from the central nucleus of their playful selves, children must abdicate their ecstasy and be exiled from this awareness in order to be educated by those who have been reduced to orphans with faint recall, grieving for the absolute love they once knew. The wide-eyed wonder, the open-ended trust, the sensitive exploring touch and the expansive love of original play are distorted to fit the needs of the culture. The ancient Chinese practice of binding the feet of females is an excellent example of a cultural practice that mutilates a natural human trait, which thus deformed became an object of veneration. Cultural play is venerated in the same way. In both cases what is authentic is first falsified and then revered.

Playing In The Shadows Of Adults

Those learned men . . . are a terror to children.

W.B. Yeats

Do not seek with cold eyes to find blemishes,
Or the roses will turn to thorns as you gaze.

Shabistari

It's hard for children to play in the shadows of adults who've been radically estranged from the experience of original play. Alice reminds us of this when she enters the looking glass room: "So I shall be as warm here as I was in the old room . . . warmer, in fact, because there'll be no one here to scold me away from the fire. Oh, what fun it'll be when they see me through the glass in here, and can't get at me!" Like the dark funnels of summer's approaching tornadoes, adults sweep

through childhood, scattering and destroying play here and ignoring it there, separating children from the fullness of their
worlds. Let me give you three examples:

During summers on my uncle's farm, I played on an old abandoned caboose that was somehow derailed and put in the woods
beyond the pasture. When I was finished in the woods, I herded
the farm horses down the lane from the pasture to the barn. I
was out in my own world all day, beyond the control of adults. At
the dinner table, my mom, dad, aunt and uncle usually asked me
what I had been doing all day. The dialogue proceeded something
like this:

Mom: "What did you do today?"
Me: "I played outside."
Mom: "Did you do anything special?"
Me: "Nothin', just played."
Dad: "You didn't play with the horses, did you?"

I wasn't supposed to play with the horses. But what else would
I do with them? They were in my world. Play included everyone
I met out there.

Here's another example from my childhood. It was a bright
Saturday morning. The sun streamed through the double
windows of my room, creating sun windows on the oak floor-
boards. I was lying on the floor, soaking up the sun's warmth,
totally engrossed in the plans and movements of the metal and
rubber cowboys and Indians who were battling each other over
the wooden plains and blanket mountains. My mother opened my
bedroom door. Her presence came from somewhere outside my
world. She walked to the windows to let in the morning air, as if
a larger-than-life mythical goddess had moved over and through
the miniature battlefield. "Fred, why don't you go outside and
play? It's such a nice day." Then she left. A moment later she
reminded me as she walked down the stairs, "Come on, now."

The war ended. I reluctantly scooped everyone up, dropped
them in their box and gathered up the mountain range and threw
it on my bed. I would go outside and sit on the porch steps. My
mother had stopped me from playing so that I could go play.

Lynda Sexson describes a similar experience from her childhood:

"When I was three years old, we moved into a little house and my mother set about cleaning. I watched. Her broom disrupted seemingly animated toys that scuttled out from under the bed.

I wanted to keep them.

"No," said my mother. "They're just dirt. Lint balls."

"I could play with them. They look like animals."

"No."

Something is not quite right in our play encounters with children. Something is out of order with us. We just don't seem to be able to let go of our adulterated ideas about play so that we can join children in their play. Most of our assumptions about play are so obvious, universal and self-evident that we are not conscious of them. Virtually everyone assumes that they know what play is and what it means: fun! Yet what is play for a child is quite often perceived by an adult as frivolous, unsafe or destructive.

On a flight from Montana to California, I experienced the following uses of the word, "play." Having settled into my seat, I leafed through the May 1991 issue of *Esquire* magazine, which had been left in the seat pocket in front of me. I read an article entitled, "Caution: Hookers, Flyboys and Stud Monkeys at Play," about a young woman and American soldiers enjoying "R&R" (rest and relaxation) off the Saudi coast during the Gulf War. In their magazine, Delta Airlines asked: "Take us to play. Delta is your perfect playmate." In the same magazine, American Express added, "The pressure is off, the weekend is on. I'm going to play tourist all weekend." In another ad, Las Vegas was described as "The American Way To Play." And "If you're a serious player, the Tropicana's got what you're looking for." Later in the flight, a mother in the seat in front of me seemed to be frustrated with her young son's approach to his milk. She angrily said to him, "Drink it. Don't play with it." Walking through the Salt Lake City airport, I noticed a small sign asking parents to hold on to their children so that they would not play on the escalators.

The term "play" has been used historically in the fields of social and behavioral science, as well as in common English language, to include behavior ranging from infants exploring their toes to children bullying on school playgrounds, from the contests of professional sports teams, to the killing of animals to the killing of enemies, from recess to vacation. In common usage play includes a wide and contradictory range of behaviors and attitudes, from the intrigue and scheming of "playing politics" to the cooperation of "playing ball" with someone; from pretense, as in "playing possum," to taking a subordinate position in "playing second fiddle"; from fomenting disagreement to serve one's own needs, as in "playing both ends against the middle," to acting according to the rules, as in "playing the game." Its connotations can be negative as in "play with oneself," "playboy" and "play up to," or positive as in "play by ear."

The adulteration of play is captured very well in our aphorism, "Play is a child's work." Play has been given a purpose, without which it and children are burdens. For young children play is preparation for the assumption of the responsibilities of the next phase of development. Early on, play becomes training in work. Like work, play should be useful, productive and fair. This is play that adults can live with. What a wonderful way to learn — teachers are in control, play helps teach children how to become better adults and program goals are met. This "whoever does not work, does not play" problem was pointed out by Erik Erikson years ago: "To be tolerant of the child's play the adult must invent theories which show either that childhood play is really work — or that it doesn't count." The most popular theory and the easiest on the observer is that the child is *nobody* yet, and the nonsense of his play reflects it. It is not difficult to understand why, for many educators, researchers and health professionals, play by anyone other than young children is considered regressive behavior.

Psychoanalytic theories tend to see play as reductive, reducing play to some other process, and as regressive, an expression of unfulfilled childish desires. The infant's world of play is described by Norman O. Brown as, "Built out of wishes uninhibited by the reality principle and satisfied by unreal, hallucinatory fulfillment." In this case play becomes something that is separate from reality, an imaginary world. Michael Fordham says, "All play is based on anxiety and is the means whereby a child seeks to master it." Norman O. Brown adds, "The psychoanalytic notion of the repressed unconscious seems necessary in order to define the play element in culture." Many adults believe that play involves rejection of realistic constraints and consequences. When so viewed, it is easy to understand why play is thought to be nothing more than childish.

Stifled by theories and petrified pedagogies, and above all imprisoned in our own fears, adults remain at an emotional and physical distance from children's play. Unwilling to expose ourselves to the love of which we are so afraid, we abandon the position of playmate. In its place we substitute any number of adult roles behind which we can hide.

This process begins early in life and takes on a momentum of its own. Like a Chinese bowl whose layers of glossy lacquer hide the true patina of the underlying wood, fear adds layer upon layer, covering up our original play face with cultural veneers from early childhood through adolescence and on through adulthood. These innumerable protective masks anesthetize and disguise our splintered hearts, torn apart through continual separation from and conflict with life. By adulthood our play mask is a multilayered mosaic pieced together over the years of growing up, as one might rifle a human junkyard of old heroes and disheartened losers. Nothing forces us to try to break through our masks; inertia, fear and the pull of old habits encourage us to maintain the masquerade. We escape within the mask's protective layers and live the illusion that the mask is the real self. All experience is then translated back into the thoughts which built the interior walls in the first place.

Instead of learning how to be playmates, adults learn how to observe and participate as support personnel who teach and guide children's play. Over and over again teachers and parents are told by professionals to watch and facilitate their children's play. In their preparation, teachers are not taught how to play with children. Play is something that kids do. Participation is limited to strategies of teaching and coaching. With all good intentions adults are taught how to help, encourage, challenge, supply, manage, guide, facilitate and plan.

When adults do participate, we do so not as playmates but as supervisors. In a rejection notice I received from a major parent-child magazine, the editor wrote, "Basically . . . [our publisher] said parents [adults] need to be playful within themselves, rather than playing with their kids. Play is for children. Parents need to 'let' children play and do their own play and not necessarily be their playmates." Where is the feeling of true participation or reciprocity in which the adult is actually feeling the joys of play with the children? The teacher remains a teacher, the parent is still a parent. Our choice to remain apart from our children is a tragedy of staggering proportions. Not only do adults not know how to play, they aren't aware that they don't know. Having been orphaned from original play for years, we no longer have access to a way of being that has been banished.

For too many adults, working with children is a job and caring for children is a duty. Far too often, when the job is done, the duty is relieved, but the children are left essentially alone for much of the time. A child can be left alone even in someone's lap as the adult stares off into space or discusses any number of things with a co-worker. In a world that stresses practicality and efficiency, children are barely noticed once they are absorbed into a routine.

In January 1991 I walked around a maze of grey highrise apartment buildings in Budapest, Hungary. Jan, Tunde (our Hungarian guide) and I were lost, searching for a school we were to visit. I felt the overbearing presence of the tall concrete structures, their oppressive greyness, the lack of green from the small, worn-out trees and the overtrodden patches of dirt, strewn with human litter and dog droppings. It was chilly, though sunny. People walked briskly, hurrying on to get where they were going. On the ground floors of some of the buildings were preschools with fenced-in playgrounds. Like kites darting around in a cloudy sky, children's color, sound and spirit added sparkle to an otherwise drab environment. Like hawks perched on treetops, keenly watching for an errant mouse, a few adults stood around huddled in their dingy coats watching the children swirl below them.

I see this in schools and playgrounds around the world. Play is commonly not a time for children and adults to *be* together. Even though adults walk around in the same space, there are essentially two different worlds on the playground. Children play, adults have playground "duty," which is to police and manage children. Every so often they intersect, usually when an adult intervenes in a disturbance. Adults stand around as if nothing below eye level interests them and wander aimlessly through children at play, as if all that is called for is judging and warning. Otherwise it is taken for granted that our commitment or participation is never called for. From their vantage points, adults can't see play, for if they did, they might connect with a common joy. When differences dissolve, authority and separation are extinguished. This is frightening.

Play is leftover time in our already overburdened schedules. We'll play later, only later often never comes.

I recently received a letter from a grandmother who wrote, "My granddaughter and I played until she started school. She still asks me to play, but for fairly poor adult reasons, I haven't. What really hurts is that the last time we visited, she had two friends to play with, but she came to me and asked if I would go out and swing with her. I told her I would later, but I didn't." This is more common than we'd like to imagine and has more far-reaching consequences than we realize.

In *For Your Own Good*, psychoanalyst Alice Miller shares the story of Jurgen Bartsch, an imprisoned murderer of four boys, who at one point was finally able to reproach his parents, crying, "Why didn't you play with me one single time in twenty years?"

I recently had the opportunity to play with a man who knows what it means to be told "Later, son," and never have it happen. During a national play conference, I asked Doug, who has had cerebral palsy since birth, if he would like to get out of his wheelchair and play with me. His "Yes!" carried so much enthusiasm that I thought he might leap out of the chair himself. With his help I got him out of the chair. We rolled around, tumbled over and under each other on the hotel ballroom floor like two little boys on a lawn. We rested on the carpet, breathing heavily, and hugged each other. Later at dinner Doug cried as he told me about his parents' fear of touching him. He had always wanted his father, who had died recently, to play with him. He never did.

Do we ever allow children to give us what they truly have to give? And if children were allowed to give, could we receive them without trivializing their gifts on our deliberate, material scale of adult value? We need each other, adults and children.

When Dennis first came to school, he was filled with curiosity, joy, humor, and sensitivity even after a very harsh early childhood. Yet these admirable qualities are not negotiable currency in school or, for that matter, in the larger world into which school is supposed to provide an opening. Dennis' resistance to being in school was not that he was unwilling to learn, he has done that very well, but he was reluctant to be adulterated. Children ask for playmates and we give them adults.

The de-meaning of play's spirit fundamentally alters the context of children's lives. Our adulteration of play transforms how we view ourselves, how we act with children, not merely in the abstract, but in the particular circumstances in which real people live everyday lives. Truly, the world is at our fingertips. Yet for many the playmate within each of us has not been allowed out to play with the world. Children are told the who, what, when and how's of acceptable play:

"Don't play on the grass!"
"Don't play in the house!"
"Don't play with your food!"
"Don't play with yourself!"
"I don't have time to play now."
"I'm too busy/old/tired/big to play."
"Go outside and play!"
"Don't play in those clothes!"
"Play quietly."
"Don't play so roughly."
"Don't play on your bed."
"Don't play in the rain."
"Don't play around."
"You shouldn't play with them."

In place of the all embracing love of original play, cultural play narrows the world down to safe and unsafe, "us" and "them."

We have built protective inner walls to keep our hearts from extending out toward what we perceive to be a hostile world, making it difficult not only for us to play with children, but to allow them to explore their worlds. On school playgrounds children are directed, for example, to use the equipment "right," which means as it was designed by adults to be used. (Never mind that adults make play equipment for children out of materials that are unforgiving and unsafe in the first place.) On the slide

this means to sit down and face the bottom. The possibilities of
the slide are restricted by adult fears. To "play" on the slide and
explore all the different ways of going up and down the slippery
surface is considered unsafe by adults.

Sometimes words have the weight of a grizzly bear pouncing
on a delicate glacier lily, utterly crushing the life out of it. Our
babel of words is a mirror in which we see not the joy and
wonder of child's play, but an arid reflection of our adulterations.
Play is demeaned in language as well as spirit and form.

Children sense the difference between what they feel in their
hearts as play and what they are being taught is play; but they
have no language to speak about what is essentially ineffable. Put
another way, the child is aware of the absence of a presence,
while the adult is unaware of the presence of an absence. Having
lost touch with original play, on the other hand, adults have language but can only talk about cultural play. Original play is a
child's way of making another child. Cultural play is an adult's
way of making another adult.

A Profound Forgetting

Adults are unhealthy for children and other living things.

Anonymous

You're not here to play.

Adult's admonition to child

Heaven lies about us in our infancy!
Shades of the prison-house begin to close
Upon the growing Boy . . .
At length the Man perceives it die away,
And fade into the light of common day.

William Wordsworth

He already had his suspicion that what people called growing up was, in
a measure, one of being educated out of reality, above all the great
invisible realities which matter so much more to a young person than the
physical ones by which men set by far a greater store as they grow older.

Laurens van der Post

I wanted only to live in accord with the promptings which came from my
true self. Why was that so difficult?

Hermann Hesse

It was my first visit to V.I.P.-Tots. I was kneeling on a blue and
white gym mat when Sandra entered. She turned, tilted her head
and peeked at me, as if to say "Are you in there? Are you afraid
to come out and play?" At two Sandra was like a candle in the
dark, and I was like a moth attracted to her light and warmth.

Sandra's intense and mischievous eyes completely absorbed
me. She inched a little closer and stood directly in front of me.
Her eyes twinkled above her impish smile; our eyes were at
about the same level. She didn't change her gaze, which was
alive, sharp and calm like a sword master's blade. It was as if she
knew exactly who she was looking for. I began to realize why
most adults just pat kids on the head and go about their busyness. It is easier — a whole lot easier. This was no casual encounter. If I was to play with Sandra, I would have to let go of
my adultness. Play required this of me. There was no other
way; it had to be done. It was scary, yet it was also exciting. I did
not know what would happen.

From the first moments of our fingertip greeting to the roly-
poly rambunctiousness at the end of the half-hour, we moved as
if in a large, invisible web. She was careful with me; I didn't
trespass on her. We touched and rolled and teeter-tottered and
hugged.

It was a while before I touched down from my play with Sandra.
I was, as I often am, mentally and physically exhausted after our
play. Her intensity and subtlety amplified every touch. We shared
no words; they would have been redundant and out of place.

I know now that Sandra was looking for me inside out, not
outside in. Sandra was not interested in my outside — the adult
play specialist. It was me, the playmate, she was inviting out to play.

How long has it been since your own inner child has been
invited out to play? Like the imaginary friends we had when we
were young, we don't know what happens to our original play.
What is spontaneous and full of wonder at ten minutes of age
becomes, at age five, selectively appropriate, at age ten a contest,

and thereafter a pastime. Having long ago put aside such possibilities, adults remain physically and emotionally separate from
child's play. We watch, like the elder in Robert Louis Stevenson's
poem, unaware that in doing so we've abandoned an essential
part of ourselves as well as children:

> Now in the elder's seat
> We rest with quiet feet,
> And from the window-bay
> We watch the children, our successors, play.

Why doesn't everyone play all the time? For years now I've
wondered why adults don't accept the invitations to play with
children and the world about them. Go out with children and
catch snowflakes on our tongues, watch raindrops on window-
panes, jump in piles of leaves, roll down hills, wander off and
discover secret places. We have known the heartbeat of play as a
prompting that comes from deep within. But we continue to say
no to the invitation.

What makes it so difficult for us to join children in their play?
As poet e.e. cummings put it, "as up I grew, down I forgot."
Psychoanalyst R.D. Laing agrees, "We have forgotten most of our
childhood, not only its contents but its flavor . . ." Ours is a profound forgetting.

I have seen adults whose eyes gleam with envy as they watch
children play. They feel undernourished by adulthood, but they're
embarrassed about not knowing how to play. For example, at a
day-long play session, 12 adults and I spent the morning talking
and going through a number of "training" activities. After lunch
my plan was to merge the adults with their children and play
together. But it was not that simple. One young woman pointed
to a little boy in a sandbox and asked, "What do I do? What do I
say? I don't know how to start. I want to see you play with him."
This woman spoke for many of the adults who were uncomfortable with the idea of actually joining a group of children as playmates. They were lost without their normal roles of teachers and
parents. Such openness was frightening, as if they had nothing to
hold on to.

Some were forced to grow too fast and missed childhood altogether. One of the mothers in this group had five children between the ages of three and twelve and said that she didn't play with them. After some discussion she said quietly, "I don't remember playing myself as a child."

George Eison records the words of a woman who survived the Holocaust: "I couldn't play because I don't think I ever played, and I really believe play is a learned thing. I mean you have to play to know how to play." She is not alone in her feelings. Adults who grew up in the Depression have told me that they had no time to play. When they did, it was with imaginary playmates who accompanied them on their chores.

On the second afternoon of a two-day play workshop in Tallahassee, Florida, I gathered approximately 20 adults into a circle sitting around me. One by one I pointed to them to come in and play "puppies-and-kittens" with me. "Puppies-and-kittens" is an activity I use to teach adults the roly-polyness of play. I glanced up, smiled and invited an older woman to play. Her smile said she wanted to play, but she hesitated. I crawled forward and touched her hand and returned to the center of the circle. She followed on her hands and knees. We tumbled and laughed and held each other. She flipped me over her back to the delight of the other playmates. Afterward, she told me the reason for her hesitancy to come right out when I had invited her. She was 76 years old and afraid that she didn't know how to play. She had been raised as a "proper lady" in the South and had never been allowed to get dirty. She wept as we hugged. Later she wrote to me, "I always vaguely felt there was more inner and outer life than I was open to. Now I just feel expanded."

Play may look and feel funny. Adults often laugh nervously about how they must appear to passersby. It looks funny to see an adult playing with children but only because so few actually do. Without our roles, our bodies may be as lost as our minds. "Do I stand up? Do I sit down?" "I'm afraid of my breasts getting touched or hurt. How do I protect myself?" "What if my hair gets pulled?" "How do I touch children?" The questions from adults seem endless.

When I began playing, I felt like a cube trying to become a sphere. I kept bumping my elbows, knees, shoulders and head. My corners were in need of rounding off. I couldn't roll or fall; I clunked and banged. I got up slowly and went home sore each day.

One day I was introduced to Billy, a five-year-old with autism. We met on the grass of a learning center in San Diego. We watched each other for a little while. Billy began running around the yard. He combined skipping, running, jumping, hopping and falling into one continuous motion. I ran, skipped, hopped and fell with him. But I could only do one thing at a time. Billy came to the center once a week, and I began to pay close attention to how he fell. He didn't "go boom" and bump to the ground like me. He didn't fall at all. He would glide to the ground as if he were a cobra relaxing its defensive posture. One day in the midst of our play he went down; I imitated him. He smiled, as if to say, "Maybe someday you'll get it, Fred." Then he stood up and walked over to me. He held out his hand. We ran holding hands. He fell with me, guiding me into one of his descents. I began to learn roundness.

The Unbearable Fear Of Playing

The beginning of terror we're not yet able to bear.
                                    Rainer Maria Rilke

The person who does not make a choice makes a choice.
                                    Jewish proverb

I've heard many adult excuses to avoid play with children: too busy, too old, too tired, too big, too dangerous. All of our reasons are based on fear. We're afraid of losing control, looking foolish, getting hurt, hurting children, being sued. Like plaque that blocks the flow of blood in our veins and arteries, fear attaches to our spirits and bodies hindering the free flow of love.

In the late 1980s, a friend and I gave a three-day course/workshop on play for preschool and kindergarten teachers at a Chicago teacher's college. During the three days not one of the teachers would get down on the ground to learn how to play with children. It was very difficult for them to do something so different from their previous teacher training. They explained that they would get dirty, were expected to dress professionally, didn't like children with runny noses hugging them, were afraid of getting sued and would be in conflict with their district's rules against touching children. The same thing happened when I taught an extension course on play at the University of California, San Diego. In this group, only one of the 30 teachers and childcare professionals would get on the ground.

Adults are being driven out of work with young children by the fear of being accused of abuse. Over and over, male teachers tell me that they simply can't afford to touch children. The consequences of a misjudgment or a retaliation by student or parent is just too great. According to Ned Bennet, one report says that annual turnover in elementary education in the United States in 1988 was 42%. Teachers see their role as being a facilitator or manager of children's play, not a participant. Sadly, this reluctance is the norm.

Perhaps adults believe that getting down to play with children lowers their status in the eyes of other adults. In a society that discounts both play and children, it is considered degrading to participate voluntarily and with delight in something so "childish" as play. A kindergarten teacher in Southern California shared with a colleague that she did not play with the children in her class because, "If they [other teachers] think I'm playing too much with the children, I get in trouble."

By the time we reach five or so, what was once universally appreciated as our way of being and doing is now reserved for recess at school and leftover time at home. Very early in life children learn two things: first, to separate play and work, and second, that work comes before play. In the minds of adults, it is appropriate to tell a child, "Play is all you ever think about. It's time to work. You can play later, after you finish your homework, chores, dinner." No one questions why something that was so crucial to a child's life becomes so quickly an afterthought. Dorothy Einon comments, "Adults play when they have nothing better to do; in fact, a philosopher once described play as 'useless in the eyes of the beholder.' "

Because they have such a difficult time seeing any purpose for play in their own lives, adults also discount play as unimportant in children's lives. Play is often subverted to meet teacher-parent needs for productivity. In supporting their use of play in elementary classrooms, teachers often tell parents that children may not

choose to be unproductive. Teachers often say that the distinctions between play and work disappear in the young child's activity. It is true that play vanishes in early childhood, not because
adults support the child's unconscious blend of play and work, but
rather because adults switch one (work) for the other (play).

Many times when I play with preschool and kindergarten children, teachers will come out and say to us, "It's time to come in
and work now. Fun time is over." If the children resist, the teacher
adds, "They would play all day if we let them. They would rather
stay out and have fun with you than come in and work." Knowing
this, teachers often try to make play a reward for acting appro-
priately or doing good work. Play has lost its importance in the
adult's mind.

During my play with Irwin, a boy of 16 months who is blind,
an occupational therapist said to me, "When Irwin comes to me,
he'll have to attend." I wondered what she thought he was doing.
It is very difficult for adults to see benefits to "just playing."
Clearly she thought that doing therapy was more important and
more purposeful than playing. The fact that the child is attending
and learning and teaching simply by playing in his way did not
occur to this childcare worker.

In my position as play specialist, I often take "problem" children
out of their classrooms to play with them alone. Dennis, whom
we met earlier, was a severely abused four-year-old. He had a
very difficult time adjusting to the classroom structure when he
arrived at school. In place of the classroom activities, I would
spend time with him outside. One day he found a bug in the
grass. He flopped down on his tummy and excitedly followed the
bug across the sidewalk and into the grass. He invited me to join
him. So I lay down on my tummy next to him, and we followed
that bug through the grass. His teacher came out to see if he was
ready to join the group. I waved her off. He was animated, excited
and focused. I recall thinking to myself, "Dennis is learning out
here; his exploring and sharing is the essence of science." We
continued following that bug for at least half an hour.

From the viewpoint of the teacher, I was to play with Dennis
to make him more suitable for classroom activities. That is, I was
to increase the child's ability in those areas that are the negotiable

skills of school life, like being better able to take directions and develop a longer attention span. But I don't do these things. I play.

Often adults are afraid of losing dignity. I know from my own experience, however, that such "dignity" is really an infirmity of the mind. During my first years playing, I tried to maneuver my body while I was down on the ground with children so that adults would not see my baldness. Since I am over six feet tall, I thought that most adults didn't know because they couldn't see it. The charade lasted, at least in my own mind, until one day when I sat on the ground in the midst of a group of children I had been playing with in the morning. We were all waiting quietly for a group of Native American dancers to enter our circle for a special presentation.

One of the girls had been playing with my hair. "Look, Fred doesn't have any hair on top!" Her voice split the silence. The audience's attention turned from the dancers' entrance to my bald spot. My sheepish glances were returned by adult smiles. They knew. The children laughed. Children near enough to me ran over to see for themselves and touch my head. Teachers scrambled and gathered children, refocusing their attention on the dancers. Every so often I felt a small finger touch my head, followed by soft joyful giggles. A child's touch can cure any infirmities of the mind.

My bald spot continues to be a focus of children's attention. In South Africa I played with young girls at an orphanage in Soweto. At one point I heard some giggling behind me and felt a slight push on the top of my head. Then there was more giggling and more fingertip pressure. The girls were gathering to take a look at something they had never seen before: the top of a white man's head turn from red to white as they pressed on my sunburned bald spot.

Reading *The Velveteen Rabbit* finally helped dissolve any false dignity I had left. I smiled full of joy as I read the Skin Horse's discussion with the Velveteen Rabbit about being Real. He said, "Generally, by the time you are Real, most of your hair has been loved off, and your eyes drop out and you get loose in the joints and very shabby." I laughed. I am becoming Real!

Unseen Gifts

Still, it doesn't add up. The gifts of play are so valuable. Yet most of us are unable to see what is right in front of us. We grow up and away from life's mysteries, afraid of them as though they were darkness, within and without.

In *A Walk With A White Bushman*, Laurens van der Post tells an African story that illustrates our inability to contact our innermost selves. It is a story of a man who lived alone with a truly wonderful herd of black and white cattle.

One morning he walked out to milk his cattle, but they had no milk to give. He thought that this was very strange since he had given them everything he could. So he moved them to a better grazing area and thought that tomorrow he would have milk. But the next morning there still was no milk. He did this repeatedly; still no milk. He thought that there must be something more to it. So he watched the cattle one night. In the dark of the night he saw a cord come down from the stars. A number of beautiful young women came down the cord and began milking his cows.

Well, he ran into the *kraal*. The star women ran away up the cord, but he caught one. She told him that she was happy to live and work with him on one condition: that he would never look in her container without her permission. He promised.

They lived together happily for months. Then one day she had gone into the fields. He was very hot. He saw her container and became very irritated. Thinking it was ridiculous that he should not look in it, he took the lid off, looked inside, laughed and put the lid back on.

That evening when his wife returned she saw that the lid had been removed and replaced. "You looked in my container!" she exclaimed. "Yes, and it was empty all the time. Why did you make such a fuss?"

"Empty?" she cried.

"Yes, empty."

She became very sad, turned away and left his house never to be seen again.

Laurens van der Post points out that, "It did not matter him breaking his word so much. What really mattered was that he could not see anything in the container, the other things which she had brought from the stars for both of them."

This is a story of the terror we feel when we can neither see nor experience our gifts of love and fearlessness. Many stories of childhood remind us that as adults we do not or cannot perceive the entrances to play's magic.

Our reasons, some more trivial than others, aren't reasonable. They're excuses. We hide from play behind the masks we feel will keep us safe. Teenage gang members demonstrate the same embarrassment as teachers and childcare professionals. The former hide behind their macho, tough masks, while the latter conceal themselves behind their academic facades.

Baldness, age, time, exhaustion, runny noses and all the rest simply cannot account for the lack of adult play with children. What could we be afraid of? After all, we do parent, teach, coach, manage, analyze, organize and direct children. How are we to understand the mindset of adults who lack the imagination, courage and compassion to play with children? There is more to it, deeper fears of which adults are largely unconscious.

To knowingly approach and embrace the world as it really is, with love and fearlessness, certainly is liberating and exhilarating but also it is devastating and terrifying. Even though we mask it with our logical reasons, we are often afraid of our own possibilities, unable to face the wonder and awe of creation's mystery.

We are profoundly ambivalent about and estranged from the love and fearlessness of original play. Such powerful gifts carry with them terrific freedom. We are deeply afraid of the responsibility asked of us in return. Playing is an awesome burden of individual openness that demands a total reversal of priorities of values, discipline and trust.

We know that play's love is something superior, beyond what we know as romance, desire, preference, favor, wish and endless self-deception. Play's love, which "bears all things" and "endures all things" is the most heroic of all experiences. The creative work required is the hardest thing of all to ask of a fearful person who feels unlovable. Ordinary fears are felt more intensely: the failure of efforts, the loneliness of social isolation, the awareness that the process is necessary, the shock of rejection, the endurance of beginning again and again, the pain of letting go.

We are born with a sense of belonging that we reject, shying away like frightened horses from some hidden movement in the bushes. We know what we are to do, but the task seems beyond us, almost godlike in scope. What would happen if we were to love so deeply? Fearlessness and love place a trembling animal at the mercy of the entire cosmos.

Lewis Carroll's Alice spoke about our fears:

"What a curious feeling!" said Alice. "I must be shutting up like a telescope!"

And so it was indeed: she was now only ten inches high, . . . she felt a little nervous about this. "For it might end, you know," said Alice to herself, "in my going out altogether, like a candle. I wonder what I should be like then?"

Like Alice, we're mortally afraid. If we participate in such fear-lessness and love, not only will we dissolve as adults, but we fear we'll go out altogether, disappearing as individuals, extinguished like a candle flame deprived of oxygen. Our terror comes from not knowing and not feeling known. To take such a leap into the unknown means we'd fall away from everything we depend on. Such an experience may be bliss for an infant, a *rishi* or a saint; but for a normal adult who doesn't feel the certainty of such love, it is disorienting and bewildering, to say the least. Unlike Gandhi we have not experienced the exhilaration of the ego becoming zero, when instead of shriveling to nothing, it expands to include everything. But to us, both seem equally self-destructive.

humility

A number of years ago I found Monkey Mia, Australia, a place I could be with animals without the constant bother and presence of tourists or scientists. Once there, Holly found me.

Holly is a dolphin, and we spent part of each day together for a few weeks. One hot day I hurried across the burning beach sand to the warm water and splashed around for a while. Suddenly, I felt my foot being pried up from below. Through the water I could see Holly. She put her rostrum under my foot and lifted up. We began our ritual of swimming up and down the coast with my hand on her side. I stopped swimming and ran alongside her in the shallow water. She always moved at my speed. Once in a while she would dart directly in front of me when I was running. I would tumble over her. When I got up she seemed to be smiling and chattering to me. Then we'd play our seaweed game. I put a piece of seaweed in my teeth and she would come up, touch my lips, take the seaweed and swim away. I'd follow and take the seaweed from her. Every so often she would swim off to find Holey Fin, her mother.

The following afternoon we returned to our swimming game. It changed. She began swimming slowly out toward deeper water. I kept my hand on her side. Suddenly I felt afraid of the sharks in the bay. I turned around to begin swimming back. She was right with me. I looked over to her. She told me, "Don't worry, Fred, when it's time, you'll come." She swam me back to the shore. I realize how strange this seems to many people, and I don't often speak of this exchange. When I describe this experience to some, they try to add words to explain it in their own minds. "You mean, Fred, that you thought she spoke to you?" Or, "You mean that she communicated to you, sort of telepathically?" I smile and let it go. I mean, Holly spoke to me in English. Like the troll tree, it is a wonderful mystery, not to be solved but to be savored and lived with.

As I walked back across the sand, however, I felt deeply disappointed in myself. I was ashamed that I had allowed my fear of sharks to overpower me. Afraid, I didn't follow Holly.

Before coming to Monkey Mia, I had what I call a "dolphin dream"; these are dreams that have a special sort of reality about them. I dreamed I was taken by a dolphin out into the ocean to someplace like a city and then brought back to the shore. As I rested in my bed that afternoon I recalled that dream and wondered if I had dreamed of Holly's invitation only to reject it. This made me even sadder.

Play may be relief, therapy and even enlightment, but it is all these things solely because it is a return to a sense of belonging that we know intimately but tend to forget and fear. Play is a haven devoted to the experiences of childhood and the birth of dreams. In this sense to play is to return home, to overcome for a time the alienation and fear of being an adult.

Play is a great container where we, like the woman from the stars, store life's spirit. Like the man who lost his woman because he lifted the lid and declared the basket empty, we observe play, make excuses and rules and see nothing. We don't believe. We have abandoned the capacity to look inward and see what nature has put there.

Many years of contesting makes playing especially difficult as the patterns of contest thinking and behavior impose themselves on new learning. Play-faith requires that we expand ourselves into the unknown, but this is what the contesting mind cannot do because it has no collective supports for such a leap of trust. In the fearful and contest mind, trust, hope and wonder are banished. It is this isolation which Bertrand Russell felt as he saw the intense suffering of the wife of his friend, Alfred North White-head. He wrote, "The loneliness of the human soul is unendurable; nothing can penetrate it except the highest intensity of the sort of love that religious teachers have preached." Our separation from original play is profound, a deeply felt loneliness that cannot be satisfied by cultural alternatives. Play penetrates to the core of loneliness in each person and speaks to them.

We become so far removed from the play in ourselves that we can hardly honor it in others. Like the child Moses hidden among the bulrushes of the Nile, each new child is both a way out of bondage and a reminder of our own previous abandonment. To play with children would be, as R.D. Laing put it, "to remember to remember, or at least remember you have forgotten." We would access the great emptiness within and hear the inner child's voice which is crying out for recognition. But more than that, we would play with children.

We've come up with a myriad of reasons why we cannot play with children. We need to recognize these for the excuses they are. I am persuaded that it is only by the experience of the gifts of play that this art can be realized. Intellect and hearsay do not uncover play's secrets. Adults will discover play not in definitions or philosophical statements about play, but in the reality of playing to which their words give, however true, only a limited expression. We are obliged to play.

Much of our struggle in life is to reconcile ourselves with the evidence of love that is placed before us, but which we cannot and will not acknowledge. Chogyam Trungpa, a Tibetan meditation master, pointed out, "If we look into our fear, if we look beneath its veneer, the first thing we find is sadness, beneath the nervousness." This sadness is a sense of loss for the love we know is possible. By not loving fully, we break our compact with life.

Playing For Keeps: Trying To Win The Game That Can't Be Won

The Golden Ball which, driven to the Goal, Wins the World's Game but loses your own soul

Attar

Disenchantment infects the spirit with a deep metaphysical doubt. Fear replaces love as the prime motivating emotion. As a self alone in a world of contests, we are constantly in search of teammates who can serve as buffers. We are in a constant state of contest, of fibrillation, as if we were individual muscle fibers twitching out of coordination. In the normal course of experience, we learn to adjust to contest relationships by suppressing our inner need to trust life. The result is a schism in the individual consciousness.

The self is split. Having lost part of ourselves out of fear, we assume that we can "win" it back, as though life were a contest. Michael Balint believes "The yearning for this feeling of 'harmony' (original play) is the most important cause of alcoholism or, for that matter, any form of addiction." We can't see that our efforts can never lead to a unified self, because every contest further splinters the self. The more we try to regain who is lost, the more we are trapped and the more the self is lost. So we continue to contest. Contesting becomes our primary addiction, which we try to satisfy with secondary addictions like alcohol, drugs, sex, sports, but when the momentary thrill is worn off, we are left with the need to contest again. It's very difficult to compete just once.

The "game's" need for losers is insatiable. The foundation of contest relationships is that in order to experience oneself as a winner, one has to suppress one's awareness of our contingency, our state of radical need for losers. Once success is achieved, it must again be achieved at a higher level; at every level the rate of losers to winners increases. Finally, we are left with a world champion, symbolizing an absolutely horrendous rate of losers to winners, roughly, 4.5 billion to one!

We cannot become contestants without becoming divided against ourselves. We cannot be enticed into a contest unless our attention is first drawn to our inadequacies. We will remain oblivious to any invitation until we are afraid of our own inadequacies. As contestants we are trying to win love from others — parents, teachers, peers, audiences — hopefully validating ourselves enough to heal the schism within that led us into the "game" in the first place. As contestants we press our efforts on others because we need to show them and ourselves that we do not live as the failure whom we think others think we are. But contests are not truly self-validating processes because such self-esteem as may be attained comes at the expense of others, and we know it. We rely on the fabrications of the "game" to meet our innermost needs for belonging, something it cannot do.

The contestant mind/heart divides and evaluates. Every contest is a further splintering of the mind/heart into an increasing number of categories and divisions. The fearful contest mind/heart, out of feelings of self-defense, must stop and focus on differences. Such a mind/heart is distracted, jumpy and rigid; and the more categories it fixes, the stiffer it becomes. Such a mind becomes tangled in its own categories, inhibited and unable to move freely. Such a mind/heart must defend its boundaries, which are constantly increasing. Each time it tries to defend itself, it creates another contest, which further splinters the self.

Our addiction to contest is the result of our substitution of culture for Creation as the source of our play with the world and believing that the former is the latter. The effects of a pervasive contest addiction can so disintegrate the personality that out of fear one firmly believes what one would know to be false if their fear permitted them to know it. The longer we live under fear, the more energy it takes to manage our anxiety, the less inner energy remains for the courage to act, and the more we are thrown back on our estimate of externals to provide our protection in times of stress. But this puts us at the mercy of these external symbols of status and security and with very little remaining inner strength. Addicted to contests we can no longer interact with the world in a nonthreatening way. We present a distorted contest self to the world and perceive the world as presenting contests to us.

Although the problem may seem to be a bit philosophical and remote from our daily experience of play with children, it is intimately related to the giving and receiving of love and kindness. Many things cause our minds to evaluate and reject.

I recall a meeting with a 37-year-old man following a play workshop in Wisconsin. He was very excited and wanted to talk with me. "I can now do something I haven't ever been able to do," he said and then paused. I remember thinking to myself, "What could this be?" I didn't know what to expect. "I can now ask a woman out," he beamed. I hesitated to respond. He went on to describe how because of cerebral palsy he had always been afraid of asking because he was fearful of the rejection that he took for granted would follow. In the day's play, however, he experienced acceptance. Cerebral palsy was not a difference that made a difference.

Children with emotional or physical disabilities who are loud, unresponsive or aggressive may be neglected and allowed to lie or sit alone constrained to their chairs. Adults stand or sit nearby, afraid to be too close.

One day I wanted to increase the variety of my play with Andrea, but I was hesitant, unsure about whether I could accurately read her signals. I often heard the therapists and teachers talk about her unresponsiveness and her dislike of touch. I was going slowly. Christian, who also has cerebral palsy, helped me play with Andrea. Sometimes those who do not recognize differences may provide the nudge to those of us who hold back. One day I was holding him in my lap, forming a protective kind of basket around him as we did aikido back rolls together. He squealed with delight each time we rolled back. When we were upright, I asked, "Again?" He flexed and pressed his back against mine, his signal to do another roll. After a few rolls, we were resting next to Andrea's chair. I noticed that she had the faintest smile. I brought Christian closer, holding him so that he could touch her. She seemed to like his touch as well as his laughter. I knew then that she wasn't as nonresponsive as we thought. Christian helped me to open up and play with Andrea.

As children, we asked adults if we could go out and play. Now we're grown up and we're still asking if we can go out and play. We arrived "trailing clouds of glory," our gifts from the farthest, innermost reaches of the universe. Adults turned their backs on us and our gifts. Having abandoned the same gifts, we don't want them from our children. It is as if we enter our own individual "Dark Ages" from adolescence through adulthood, abandoning the very gifts that enlighten in favor of cultural trappings and rewards. Stop the heart and the body dies very quickly; stop playing by heart and the spirit dies slowly, but with no less certainty.

5

The Duchess' Game: Pathogenic Play

Whatever its form competition is always play.

Johan Huizinga

Tweedledum and Tweedledee
Agreed to have a battle;
For Tweedledum said Tweedledee
Had spoiled his nice new rattle.

Lewis Carroll

I am in blood
Stepped in so far, that, should I wade no more,
Returning were as tedious as go o'er.

William Shakespeare

Has there been another age that, knowing so clearly the
right things to do, has so consistently done the wrong ones?

Laurens van der Post

Recently I went to a yearly staff review of Dennis, the five-
year-old abused, neglected child with whom I had been
playing daily for about nine months. Sitting around a table were
15 adults who care for this boy in school and in the residential
center where he lives. As the meeting progressed, I began to
understand more about why I don't normally go to such meetings.
I grew increasingly uncomfortable. The child I knew was not the
person they were describing. In their review process, they had
separated themselves so far from Dennis that I couldn't recognize
him. The woman leading the discussion seemed to recognize my
discomfort. She stopped the discussion momentarily and spoke to
me, saying that they didn't mean to be harsh or distant, but being
so close to the children requires that they sometimes use humor
to protect themselves emotionally.

Later in the discussion, one of the childcare workers described
a race she had set up for the kids in the unit. She was concerned
about Dennis' "refusal to play" with the others. With a mocking
laugh, she said, "He didn't even know how to race." She related
how he ran along laughing, going every which way but straight.
Dennis' response was recorded as "refuses to play" on his indi-
vidualized treatment plan.

Dennis didn't know what to do in a competitive situation; he
was still a playmate. But, like all of us, Dennis' training in the

lessons that cripple the human spirit began early in life. He was laughed at by an unknowing adult for not participating in a contest, which she called play. As Dennis was discovering, it is difficult to remain a playmate around adults. It is also extremely difficult to speak against what everyone knows to be true: that play is a childish activity to be put away so that we can learn to compete effectively in what I call the Duchess' Game. We look too soon for the adult in the child and once having created an adult, it is very difficult to retrieve a child.

Playing The Duchess' Game

The more there is of mine, the less there is of yours.
The Duchess' moral, Lewis Carroll

The Duchess' Game is a way of being and acting based on the Duchess' Law from *Alice in Wonderland* which states, "The more there is of mine, the less there is of yours." The Duchess' Game is an antagonistic encounter in which we succeed by defeating an opponent. This "game" can be cynically expressed in a slightly different manner as The Three Laws of Thermodynamics quoted by Dennis Overbye:

1. You can't win.
2. You can't break even.
3. You can't get out of the game.

In this zero-sum game, everything including life itself can be won, lost, possessed and awarded. It can be played anywhere and anytime with balls, guns and words and on sports fields, corporate boardrooms, political arenas, international battlefields, family living rooms, freeways, schoolrooms and playgrounds.

The Duchess' Game is a shared value system between people who need a symbolically and externally constituted sense of self-worth-contest and a society, which by granting it to them, reduces them to playthings. The game is sustained by a socio-economic, educational and political philosophy, with organized groups and a code of contest ethics. This adversary system is accepted, in part, because it has been an integral part of society for a very long time. So long, in fact, that people both as individuals and as groups cannot conceive of any other way of interacting. Throughout our history we have used one form of contest such as the courts to try to remedy the failures of another contest system, such as elections. We fundamentally believe in the efficacy of contests to cure social, economic and educational problems. But one form of cancer does not cure another; instead the patient now has two forms of cancer.

Just as grammar gives order to our words, so culture's consensual forms organize and give meaning to everyday life. Filtered through cultural traditions, the Duchess' Game isn't merely a metaphor; it is realized emotionally and physically, millions of times over, as a process in the nervous system of individual people. Having already had our connection to life's source thwarted, most of us feel threatened by life on earth. The Duchess' Game is our self-defense mechanism. We seek to find our sense of significance through its contests by rooting our self in its delusions so that we do not have to worry about our own lack of self-esteem.

The game requires a great deal from its participants: that we give our allegiance to a contest devoted to the creation and maintainence of a false self cut off from being and condemned to ceaseless contesting. We have so little self left that any sense of internal steadiness must come from outside sources. As Ernest Becker says, we must suck in other human beings to keep from losing or disappearing altogether.

Having been depersonalized ourselves, we go about depersonalizing others. People become epithets, abstractions, euphemisms and enemies. In their war games, nuclear theorists dehumanize human death with the term "collateral damage." In sports the opponent is often conceived of as the enemy and as former Canadian professional football player John McMurtry writes, "The truly professional attitude is not to think of the opponent as a human being at all—he is a 'position.' "

R.D. Laing wrote, "If our experience is destroyed, our behavior will be destructive." To be prepared to win at any cost, everyone is a potential adversary. Infected with such a state of disease, a contestant does not survive without huge expenditures of personal energy and social resources. Out of fear we still choose to pay the price of endemic violence to maintain our allegiance to the Duchess' Game in its myriad forms, rather than choosing love and thereby dissolving the game itself.

Contestants are fictional selves, parts of people invented to play in cultural games. We identify this fictional self with roles such as breadwinner, awards like bowling champ and titles such as CEO. This self is blamed and praised, charmed and threatened. Our efforts to win over others lead to their control over us. We are trapped by our own devices. This is the false heart of the Duchess' Game which Chuang-tzu described centuries ago:

When he tries to extend his power over objects,
Those objects gain control over him.
He who is controlled by objects
Loses possession of his inner self:
If he no longer values himself,
How can he value others?
If he no longer values others,
He is abandoned.
He has nothing left.

The price we pay for this contest-created self is the necessity to defend it endlessly from all assaults, real and imagined, in order to keep from being undervalued personally and professionally. This is an extremely dangerous position: We are pinning our well-being to the arbitrariness of the contest order, in whose every action we have something to gain and something to lose. Our equilibrium is out of our control.

The Only Game In Town

Why do we play the game? Because the rewards are great. First, we get membership in the group which annuls the fear of being alone in a dangerous world. Second, we get an enemy on whom to redirect our anger and aggression. Finally, we get a false, comforting sense of justification for our actions.

The Duchess' Game is the only game in town. We know no other way of interacting, of valuing our lives and those of others, or the life of our environment. Much of what passes for culture tends to be a form of the game. This is a very effective reward, as everyone we see is participating in the game with us. The Duchess' Game has been, as Morris Berman emphatically points out, the "normal" consciousness in the West since 1600 A.D. Alexis de Tocqueville noticed in the 1830s that a habitual cloud hung upon the brows of Americans. Our restlessness and sadness was intensified by "the competition of all." Dr. Rodrigo Carazo, President of the Council of the University for Peace in Costa Rica, puts it clearly, "The culture of today's world has been based on competition."

The sustaining myth of the Duchess' Game is this: The world is a contest, and we must learn to play the game if we are to survive. This is actually two myths in one. First, competition is innate; it is the way life works. Therefore, the logic goes, it must be natural for us, too. Second, we must learn to play the game well if we are not to become its victims.

So in the normal course of experience, we learn to become contestants. This is accomplished in such a way that it does not appear to be imposed but freely chosen.

The professional literature presents play as a means for children, with adult help, to learn about life. But this is life as culture sees it. Play becomes a strategy that adults must help a child learn in order to develop the competitive skills necessary for later life.

Children are conscripted into the Duchess' Game early in life. It is played in classrooms and on the streets, with grades and guns. If, like Dennis, children wish to be playmates, they find out that there are no clear models of how to proceed. The result is that we feel isolated whenever we fail to behave in accordance with contest values.

A mother recently shared with me that her ten-year-old daughter in a Southern California public school received an unsatisfactory grade on her report card, with a note that she was "not competitive enough." Following a number of play sessions with a fifth-grade class in another Southern California school, one of the boys told his teacher that he no longer wanted to participate in the P.E. class because it was competitive. He wanted to play instead. She came to me and confided that she didn't know what to do because the school had no way of dealing with such a request.

It's not just noncompetitive children who are seen as unfit; adults are not immune. Bruce Newman reported in *Sports Illustrated* that New York Jet running back Freeman McNeil "committed a flagrant act of compassion" in a game against Indianapolis when he was distraught after accidentally injuring Colt linebacker O'Brien Alston. Flabbergasted, his coach commented, "That's the way the game goes. Obviously it [allowing his remorse to affect his play] was not a good thing." Bullied by his coach and by himself, McNeil said after the game, "I let the team down." And Myriam Miedzian tells us, "When former Los Angeles Kings hockey player Paul Mulvey refused to participate in a fight between his team and the Vancouver Canucks, he was ordered off the team and immediately shipped to the minor leagues." As John Bowlby explains, "How to compete, how to take hard knocks, how to win gracefully; when to assert oneself and when to forget self-interest are all learned through play." According to Richard D. Lavoie, a recent study of teachers indicates that "competitive activities comprise the majority of classroom on-task time." This is adult-directed competition. Teachers' comments include, "The kids love it," and, "What else can I do?"

Some professionals even question children's innate ability to play. Children are born limited in creativity, according to Jerome Singer and "do not automatically learn how to play." Deborah Rosenblatt agrees that "the young infant does not know intuitively how to play with objects, and it is only by experience that he builds up a repertoire of play actions."

In his discussion of the biological criteria for being human, Frederick Franck writes, "A capacity for play evolves together with parental care." Other's such as David Carlson and Bernie Ginglend believe that "retarded children have to be taught to play." In still another study Paul Wehman writes that "In the severely handicapped, however, social play does not readily evolve and must be programmed" and "the higher the functioning level, the greater the amount of play behavior." Still another researcher Schlein, finds that children with autism "do not usually exhibit appropriate play skills." Susan Golant writes that gifted children, "Don't necessarily play the same way that average intelligence kids do." These authors describe play as an activity in which children learn to master the Duchess' Game.

What is it that "ungifted" children know less of and children don't know about play that adults can teach them? Culture! There is an extensive educational, therapeutic and scientific literature in which play is described as an activity that: (1) provides opportunities for the child to develop a strong ego; (2) provides a safe outlet for aggression; (3) develops competency; (4) uses up surplus energy; (5) reduces psychic tension; (6) provides practice for the young in developing social contest skills.

Competition instills discipline, produces loyalty, builds character, teaches teamwork, emphasizes mastery — the traits that we reward, especially in boys. As Janet Lever points out:

> Experience with complicated rules and strategies of team sports gives boys a more direct rehearsal for the competitive dynamic in a work situation, and for survival in bureaucratic organizations. . . . Girl's play prepares them for interpersonal relationships and develops their empathetic skills.

So it is the cultural rules of the game that adults teach. Our society provides the child who desires to be competitive with a great variety of examples to emulate.

We learn the game so early and so well that it becomes our unconscious, natural and moral belief about the way the world works. For example, an underlying assumption of the game is that creativity, truth and moral rightness are derived from conflict. What is not so openly expressed is the corollary that our obligation is not to creativity, truth and moral rightness, but to winning. This assumption appears so obvious that we are unaware of what we are assuming, because no other way of expressing our reality occurs to us. The language used to describe the competitive process is such that to not accept it would make us seem weak, unsuccessful and even unpatriotic.

Americans, for example, are given to believe that if our children don't learn to compete, we will be unable to maintain our superior position in the world. Our survival depends on it. Football coach Vince Lombardi put it this way:

It is and always has been an American zeal to be first in anything we do, and to win and to win and to win.

In the recession of the nineties, Americans, like fifth-graders in a spelling bee and college football players, are exhorted to achieve so that America can meet the stiff competition virtually every major industry is facing from abroad. We are told that education and training can help the country compete globally.

To participate effectively in the game, we need an enemy. For so long it was the Soviet Union. Now with the reformulation of Eastern Europe and the Soviet Union, Americans have lost an enemy. In place of the Soviet military we seem to be substituting the Japanese economy. It seems as though our national self-esteem depends upon having an enemy. At the individual or national levels, the loss of an enemy leaves us empty and bereft; we find peace unnerving and boring.

Contests are a centrifugal force, scattering and atomizing people as groups and individuals whose self-awareness depends on identifying others as outsiders. Our very identity is confirmed within the groups playing the game. Families, clans, tribes, gangs, teams, countries — the list of groups to which we can belong is endless. In order not to be thrown back upon our own meager resources, we cling desperately to those with whom we identify. In a society of contests, people must somehow counteract the experience of their day-to-day existence as losers. The contestant comes to be defined as the sane, well-adjusted person. As Thomas Merton points out in *Raids On The Unspeakable*, this person is like Adolf Eichmann, well adapted to the needs and dictates of the social system which he or she carries out in an orderly cool fashion. Deprived of our own sense of self-esteem, we can inflate ourselves with the honor, glory and revenge of the group.

But membership comes at a high price. Being a normal and dutiful member requires us to acquiesce to the group's definition of membership. In contests we cannot affirm the "others" as a spontaneous source of life because they do not belong as we belong. As co-contestants we agree to treat each other as playthings.

We are all splinter individuals, who can and will be replaced. Manipulated and coerced by the games, we in turn manipulate and coerce others. Allegiance to the group requires that we give up our rights to play with everyone. Membership teaches us how and when we are to play and with whom. Groups define players as well as enemies.

Not long ago two adults from different parts of the world brought this to my attention. In Arizona a Native American man watched me play with children of his tribe. Afterward he told me that he too would like to get down on the floor with the children, but he had a problem. He pointed to some of the children and said, "How can I play with them? They are of another clan. What do I do?"

The same issue came up in a play session in South Africa. A Zulu man asked me how he was to play with a child from another tribe. He was afraid of what might happen, not in the play, but to both of them from tribal members outside of the play. In both cases I replied, knowing that for each man to follow through with what I was going to suggest would require a great deal of courage, "You must learn to be a playmate for all children. During play, you give up your allegiance to your clan or tribe." The key word here is *during*. You can have your allegiances back after playing. Of course, the more we play, the more we let go of those allegiances based on fear. This is exactly what makes play an act of insurrection in a dehumanized world.

This may seem like a nearly impossible request at a time when so many people throughout the world are trying desperately to acquire and hold on to a group identification as personal ballast so as not to get swallowed up by a majority culture. But original play is neither determined nor confined by culture and its divisions. Play is not a plea for cultural homogenization or social equality; neither does it support the fractionalization of people into groups. Both of these are positions in another contest. Play has nothing to do with sides.

In the normal course of experience, we learn to adjust to contest relationships by suppressing our inner need to trust life. In place of life we install cultural mirrors, those reflections we see of ourselves in others. Virginia Woolf wrote, "Whatever may be their use in civilized societies, mirrors are essential to all violent and heroic action." It is only in their defeat that people can serve as mirrors to magnify the winner to twice their size. Like the magic mirror on the wall of the Wicked Queen in Snow White, our mirrors must tell us not the truth, but what we want to see. For as Virginia Woolf has pointed out, with the telling of the truth, "The figure in the looking glass shrinks; his fitness for life is diminished."

Competition becomes the ruling principle in our understanding of reality and our explanation of economic, political, social and personal aspects of life. The living person, animal and plant become competitors. What counts is not one's ability to be kind or to spare one from suffering; what counts is whether one has triumphed.

Suffering, destruction and aggression are not scandals, but rather graffiti on a wall, body counts and academic ciphers in a journal — ways to measure the scope of the contest. It is possible, for example, to read Dennis Overbye's story of the scientific quest for the secrets of the universe as one huge contest in which academics publish papers "against" each other, choose sides, and make and break careers. It doesn't take much to discover that beneath their claims of objectivity and technical expertise there exists in these scientists the need to belong to an elite and the same thrilling power in the shattering of worlds. People are hurt with as little regard in academia as they are on the streets or battlefields. As astronomer John Huchra put it, "There are only a handful of people in this game, and they all hate each other." Scientists compete like urban street gangs, or American and Japanese automakers, or two children for their toys.

It is hard to imagine our world without contests. In a world that is believed to be essentially hostile, the "only game in town" is conceived of as a form of psychological salvation, a kind of self-defense. The game is about winning — position, prestige, title, turf or any number of material objects. We compete and destroy for a position, a classroom, a gang, a prize, money, and a country — the bribes are endless. These are decoys cleverly marketed to keep the categories of play and contest confused. The bonding power of the bribes maintains the delusion that trinkets are the stuff that satisfies the soul. Just like indigenous peoples the world

over, when faced with shiny trinkets, we have sold our birthright
for the proverbial mess of pottage.

Playing For Keeps: Playing As Preying

The gift of immaturity itself, which has enabled us to retain in our best,
most human moments the capacity for play . . . It is, in fact, only those
who have failed, one way or another [to preserve this gift] in their
manhood or womanhood, who become our penny-dreadfuls, our gorillas
and baboons.

Joseph Campbell

Play clearly has been thought of as a survival technique; it
becomes one of our self-defense mechanisms against personal
annihilation. This is a cultural adaptation of the "survival" theory
of play developed in the early 1900s by Karl Groos: "Play emerges
out of natural selection as a form of necessary practice on the
part of the child or immature organism for behaviors that are
essential to later survival."

Writing about play therapy, Dr. Haim Ginott says, "One of the
important objectives of psychotherapy is to help children to develop sublimations that are compatible with society's demands
and mores."

In developing *Sports Illustrated for Kids* in 1988, John Papanek
remarked, "We'll never stop paying attention to our games." And
Joseph Chilton Pearce points out in *The Magical Child*, "Beneath all
the studies and comments about animal and child play runs a
central, if unrecognized, thread: Play serves survival."

Each generation willingly propagates the game systems that
hold them in bondage; and since everyone plays, no one is able to
see through the farce. On a sports field, in a corporation, on the
streets or in first grade, you have to play by the rules of the game
if you are going to survive. The real scars of the traumatic mind
shocks and body breaks are painful and debilitating. Beyond these,
however, are the daily contests of ordinary life that result in a
grinding sense of futility and meaninglessness. We learn that we
must defend ourselves against the normal, repetitive, almost invisible contests of life. This is where the sustaining power of
contest consciousness is found.

While playing with some children, I watched another group of five-year-olds play around us on a school playground. They, four boys and a girl, played for about 15 minutes before disbanding. Three boys and a girl would all run to the boy who was on a "bus," a piece of metal and wood play equipment. As they got close, the boys threw punches and "ninja kicks" as they scurried around the bus. The boy inside would look up and growl like a bear. They retreated to talk, encourage each other, saying, "Let's kick him." Overhearing this, I gathered them around me and told them that they were to stop the punching and kicking. While the four were with me their prey was invited in by his teacher. When the four returned, he was gone. They looked around briefly but couldn't find him. Then they disbanded, running off in different directions to engage in other play.

What appeared to be a playful encounter of five children was, in fact, a contest of four against one. The language the four used among themselves was "us" against "him." In fact, victimizing was the glue that held the four together. As soon as there was no one to "attack," there was no need for them to be together. Such contestant training disguised as play is very often unseen or excused by adults as "boys will be boys." "What's the big deal?" adults ask with a shrug of their shoulders, the kids are only learning how to compete.

People split in their core may actually know no other way to feel good about themselves other than outward aggression and power over others. Elliot Currie quotes Blaster, about having fun: "We used to jump a lot, pull guns on people, you know, throw rocks at the police cars. We used to do anything to have a good time. One time we used to kick in people's door like we were a task force! Having a good time." And Eric Brady tells us that, "crunching a quarterback gives professional football player Bruce Smith such inner joy. Paul Verhoeven, director of Robocop, said, "I've always liked violence." Dan Wieden, head of a Portland, Oregon, ad agency, adds that he enjoys a good fight. Anne Strick writes, "Enemies is what our legal system is all about."

One way to differentiate contest from true play is the presence or absence of "get-backs," or the escalating ladder of retaliation, increasing the level of aggression until one player is out of the game. Get-backs are inherent in contests but absent in play. I remember a number of games that were built on this principle. One was punching each other's shoulder, another was wetting our fingers and slapping each other's forearms, another was grabbing each other's forearms with both hands and quickly twisting them in opposite directions.

Often the level of aggression is raised well beyond sore arms to include death. In 1989 a four-year-old boy was shot in a driveby shooting in an Orange County barrio. This came as a shock. "Gang members deserve everything they get," said the wife of a former gang member. "But when it comes to innocent little kids who get shot for no reason, that's different." The shooting raised the stakes in the war between the two gangs. What would the retaliation be? "What if the 17th Streeters kill another child when they take their revenge?" The dead boy's 19-year-old aunt stared back defiantly. "I hope it's one of theirs," she said. The cycle continues.

In a Chicago housing project, a 12-year-old boy's stepfather is beaten by ten teenagers with fists and sticks. He decides to stay in. "If they can't get to him [the stepfather], they'll try to get to me," he says. "It has to get better. We can't keep living like this." He gets back first. The next week he and six others beat up a young girl.

Get-backs are as much a part of adult contests as they are of childhood games. In baseball, for example, a pitcher can protect his own hitters by "dusting" or throwing the ball too close to opposing hitters, since retaliation is the best defense.

Freeway driving is a good place to experience get-backs. On the way to do a play workshop in Pasadena, I was listening to a car talk show on public radio. A male caller phoned in to complain about truck drivers. He was in the slow lane on L.A.'s 405 freeway. He was tired after ten hours of driving. Suddenly, a semi pulled up behind him and flashed its lights. At first he looked around in his rearview mirror, then lightly pressed his brake pedal. The truck tailgated him and continued to flash its lights. So he slowed to about ten miles per hour and stepped on and off his brake. Finally, the truck passed. As it drew up parallel to the car, the passenger in the truck spit on the car's windshield. This is the escalating nature of get-backs in the Duchess Game. These men were like little boys in a sandbox; first one grabs a truck away from the other, then a little sand is thrown, then a hit. They were lucky that the game stopped when it did. There have been incidents on Los Angeles freeways and others that have escalated to shootings and other forms of violence.

This get-back mechanism operates as a ladder of escalation in which each player retaliates at an increasing level of intensity or aggression. In the initial stages of tickling, "play" or sexual interaction, the touch may be soft or gentle enough to make its contest nature invisible. But interaction and contest continue escalating by small increments until one person has had too much. The victim may lash out by crying, screaming, punching or trying to escape. But escape from this spiral of escalating mutual response is often very difficult.

Our contest world is full of such escalating interactions; most do not end in observable violence. But even when an interaction stops before getting overtly violent, each person leaves the encounter already high up on their personal ladder of aggression. They're ready to fight and attack the next person they meet.

In a society where so many interaction patterns are defined and condoned as contests, it becomes "normal" for violence to be an integral part of life in family relations, teenage peer relations, business interactions and sporting events.

The cover story in a 1988 issue of *Newsweek* magazine, for example, covered the Steinberg/Nussbaum child-abuse case. The lead article was accompanied by two related items on family violence. The same issue included three other major articles on contest behavior. Two described ethnic conflict between black and Hispanic "have-nots" in the United States and between blacks and white vandals. Two were major business stories: One was the R.J.R. takeover fight, and the other was on the use of toys by fast-food chains to draw child customers. These articles referred to the issues as "fights" and "wars." In the fast-food war, companies lure customers by whatever means available. For kids and some parents alike, the toys can become as addictive as "a bag of salted fries." The men in the R.J.R. takeover "fight" are described as "enemies" in "the Wall Street equivalent of gang warfare . . . Nothing seemed to propel it except greed. . . ."

Americans do not see the connection. We decry violence on the one hand and promote the contests that perpetuate it on the

other. Contests are insidious threads that run through the fabric
of society. Whether it is a father and mother who become entangled in family violence, ethnic groups in a neighborhod, or
men and women fighting it out in boardrooms and law offices,
we see human beings who lose the ability to think and act outside
of the contest framework. We continue to teach abuse in human
relations throughout the culture.

Whether from father to son or country to country, a violent
response to aggression does not diminish it, but increases it. This
simple lesson is very difficult to learn. I was watching a news
broadcast on Kuwait after the recent Gulf War. While the news-
caster described how Palestinians were being attacked by Kuwaiti
police, army personnel and vigilante squads, the screen showed a
number of reputed victims of this aggression. Then the picture
shifted to the acting Kuwaiti Prime Minister who regretted "these
isolated incidents" and explained that they were only reflections
of human nature — the people getting back at someone after
seeing their country destroyed. I wondered if he would call the
Iraqi incidents of cruelty against Kuwaitis merely "human nature." We have assumed for so long that such get-backs, whether
on the playground or street, playing field or battlefield, are human
nature. This is an unending cycle of violence and we have chosen
to live under its shadow.

"If you strike without compassion against the darkness," says
Gary Zukav, "you yourself enter the darkness."

Predators, terrorists and rapists are described as "playing with
their victims." There is a great deal of literature and common
knowledge that describes violent acts as play and fun from the
point of view of the aggressor without any acknowledgment of
the victim's position. Violence is portrayed as fun in sporting
events, music, toys, TV and film.

This was brought out clearly in a *Newsweek* article entitled "Vampire Agents At Play," about literary agents who stalk "tragedy for
fun and profit." We have come to believe that the ecstasy of play
is the ecstasy of violence. In Missouri, students killed a fellow
student just for fun. In Montana I heard men excuse the shooting
of highway signs and coyotes as "just funnin.' "

"The producers of slasher films assure us that their films are
not really violent. They are all tongue-in-cheek, humorous, lots

of fun." We say that when a cat stalks and leaps upon a mouse it is a playful act in which the mouse becomes a toy. Hunting is described by Spanish poet Jose Ortega y Gasset as occupying "the highest rank in the repertory of man's happinesses."

It is as if we believe that we can't be fully male without the thrill of contest and its violence. The American press hailed President Bush's invasion of Panama as a successful initiation rite in which he demonstrated his willingness to shed blood. Likewise, Atsumori, a young and inexperienced son of a Japanese general was filled with excitement on the eve of the Battle of Ichinotani in 1184. "He felt as though this was the moment he had lived for, that at last he was a man, playing the exciting game that the older men had talked about so often." Atsumori is killed the next day by the veteran warrior Kumagai, who succumbing to peer pressure, kills the 15-year-old. Stung by his cowardly act and the "useless" death of Atsumori, Kumagai returns the boy's body to his parents with honor, cuts his hair and becomes a Buddhist priest.

Following a recent play session with a 12-year-old boy, he shared with me his fears about not joining the neighborhood gang. The pressure from his peers, neighbors and relatives who are members is relentless. He feels he has no choice.

The proof is in the winning. There is nothing else that produces such excitement. "There's nothing like winning," is not only a proclamation among athletes. The hunt, matching oneself against another, and the conquest all feel good. Anything less feels boring. Eddie, a 14-year-old gang member wants "a job with action," he says. "I'll probably be a cop. If I don't get to be a cop, I'll be a fireman. If I can't be none of these, I'll make my own action — buy a gun and start killing people."

There is a game played among young Israeli boys with a number of variations, but the object of all is to place oneself in front of an onrushing car and see how close one can get to the car without getting hit. As one boy put it, "It's a game of life and death." When high school students hear that I am there to play with them, they often prejudge it as boring and "sissy."

The child who kills a mouse, the hunter who shoots a deer, the rapist who attacks a woman may so obviously enjoy the control of life and death and the power of taking another life that the birth of meaning for the victor is the death of the victim. Killing is the ultimate victory in the drive to possess. The victims become trophies. It is as if males learn that the most powerful feeling of life is achieved in killing, while women learn that the most powerful link with life is achieved in giving birth to new life.

The thrill of engaging in a contest is that, unlike any other way, we can participate directly in nature by pitting our cunning, skill or strength against another. Killing is often an integral part of the satisfaction because until there is a death we cannot fully feel that we have won the contest. In a genuine contest, if there is a winner there must be a loser, and the only way another can "acknowledge" its loss is to be dead.

Miedzian points out how important their first deer kill is to some American males. "Your first deer is a big deal. It signifies you have done something significant approaching manhood." The same initiation rite occurs when a gang member shoots his first rival.

This same importance of killing is found in Achilles' speech to Hector near the end of Homer's *Iliad*. When they are finally face-to-face, Hector appeals to Achilles' reason. Achilles responds:

"Hector, argue me no arguments. I cannot forgive you.
As there are no trustworthy oaths between men and lions,
Nor wolves and lambs have spirit that can be brought into agreement,
But forever these hold feelings of hate for each other,
So there can be no love between you and me, nor shall there be oaths between us, but one or the other must fall. . . ."

Achilles sees Hector not as human as himself but as prey. This contest is lived out continually in cultures of contest. In a recent issue of *Sierra* magazine, readers were asked to respond to the question: "Should environmental groups accept contributions from polluters and developers?" One answer was: "The moral issue of accepting or rejecting aid from an adversary in the notion that it might attenuate your position presupposes a fair fight. This is war. Take everything they give and use it to crush them."

Fighting, even killing, has been described as play. For example James S. Hans writes, "The ecstasy of play and the ecstasy of violence are the same." Play may be thought of as "good" aggression, and S.L. Washburn and C.S. Lancaster said, "The skills for killing and the pleasures of killing were normally developed in play." Psychologist William Betcher writes, "It's completely compatible with a close friendship to want to figuratively whip the ass of your squash partner, and sports have a been a highly ritualized way, particularly for males, to sublimate aggression and feel 'safe' to make physical contact." Play is often couched in survival language. "In true play there is always a tension between mastery and submission," Betcher reports, and Ortega y Gasset says, "Hunting is the free play of an inferior species in the face of a superior species." Both Betcher and Ortega y Gasset place play squarely in the midst of contest.

It is important in a conquest that the aggressor not come face-to-face with a recognition of the living spirit of the prey. Then the recognition of kindness may obliterate the urge to finish the game. We may then be called to the awareness that our "play" destroys the world around us, which may startle us out of the game altogether. Then we become spoilsports. This is exactly what happened to Aldo Leopold on the day he and some friends shot a wolf family for fun. As he approached the dying wolf he saw "the green fire die" in her eyes. He saw in her death a deeper meaning, the kindness of life.

As a young boy I lived in an apartment in Harper Woods, north of Detroit, Michigan. Our complex was surrounded by empty fields with trees and ponds and little hills. I spent a lot of time roaming there. It was just right for me to play my adventure games. One day I saw a long garter snake moving along the side of a little mound. I stood atop the next mound and threw my spear, a long piece of pipe I had found, at the snake. I missed and the snake continued to crawl away. I ran to pick up my spear and bring the snake back. I repeated this until finally I hit the snake. Instantly I was thrilled. I had won. Watching it writhe in spasms and jerks of death, however, I was drained of all elation. I walked home immediately after pulling the spear out of the snake. I was sad for the rest of the day. I didn't tell my parents about it; I knew they wouldn't be pleased. I felt ashamed. After school the following day, I returned, apologized and buried the snake. The incident has stayed with me ever since.

I didn't seem to have a reason for killing the snake. I knew it wasn't dangerous. It just felt good, up to the point of killing. Seeing the snake die triggered something that altered my view of life.

Every time we win or lose, the self is splintered. Perhaps the basic, unacknowledged purpose of the Duchess' Game is to distort our children's conceptions to believe that living things can and should be defeated and considered separate from and lesser than the winners. The children are thus prepared for what civilization, through a complex series of manipulations, is going to do to them. Thus destroyed in spirit, children are ready to join adults in life played as the Duchess' Game.

Much of our world has been destroyed by fun-lovin' people who are just playin' around!

Play: A Touchy Subject

"Travis, don't hit!" "Jamie, don't bite!" "Jason, stop kicking!" "Mark, use nice hands!" Adults are constantly telling children how to touch. But telling isn't enough. We must model the kind of touch that we want children to use.

Extensive research with both animals and humans shows clearly not only the benefits of touch but the absolute necessity of touch for the healthy development of a young being. As Ashley Montagu points out in *Touching*, "Tactile stimulation appears to be a fundamentally necessary experience for the healthy behavioral development of the individual." In a study on the origins of violence, neuropsychologist James W. Prescott found "that the deprivation of body touch and movement . . . is the cause of a number of emotional disturbances, which include depressive and autistic behaviors, hyperactivity, sexual aberration, drug abuse, violence and aggression."

Yet we don't know how to touch. Like play and contests, we confuse love and violence. We say, "I'm doing this because I love you" as we hit children. A teenage girl confided to me, "I know my father loves me when he hits me." For some, adult violence against children is also given the sanctity of Solomon's so-called wisdom: "He that spareth his rod hateth his son; but he that loveth him chasteneth him betimes." And: "Foolishness is bound in the heart of a child; but the rod of correction shall drive it far from him."

In recent talks in small communities in Southern California and South Africa, I was surprised to find so much adult support for hitting children not only with their hands, but with objects like spoons and rods. Individuals, like countries, hide behind any number of religious, psychological and familial traditions to lash out at those who are weakest. Out of fear we pass on violence instead of love.

Most people are not aware that they don't know how to touch. As children grow older, what began as sensitive, nurturing full-body touch becomes more restrained, and by adolescence is demeaned to ritual handshakes and perfunctory hugs, if not completely terminated. We stumble through as those before us, passing on our confusion and conflict about touch to those we love. The same parents who cuddle their son or daughter at 10 months are likely to feel hesitant when the child reaches 10 years, and inhibited when the child is 14. The child who shared a kiss at one year thinks kisses are dumb at ten, surreptitiously wants one at 14, but won't say so, and then at 17 can hardly live without one. We know that skin hunger has not decreased with age. Yet in our inability to treat it honestly, touch becomes inappropriate, abusive and destructive. After long periods away from nurturing touch, we become cold, stiff and awkward.

We virtually stop touching after infancy. Imagine if we dealt with our other senses in a similar manner and told children to close their eyes or ears while at school. This would seem absurd. Yet, we do exactly that with our primary sense, the body's largest sensory organ, our skin. As a consequence we suffer from skin hunger.

Like giant crustaceans we literally become uptight in our character armor. Ashley Montagu points out, "The unloved person, taken at any age, is likely to be a very different biochemical entity from those who have been adequately loved." Deprived of touch we become standoffish and aggressive. We are still interacting with children as if we believed what Dr. Broadus Watson wrote in 1928: "There is a sensible way of treating children . . . never hug and kiss them, never let them sit in your lap. If you must, kiss them once on the forehead when they say good night. Shake hands with them in the morning. Give them a pat on the head if they have made an extraordinarily good job of a difficult task."

People who are thought to be less than human receive even less touch. The human history in the treatment of leprosy, and more recently AIDS, are prime examples. The shunning of lepers for hundreds, if not thousands of years seems to be repeating itself anew in our treatment of AIDS victims.

However, the classification of being "untouchable" is much more common than these two diseases. Sandra K. Larson and Tiffany M. Field report that child and adolescent psychiatric patients are rarely touched. Indeed, "most child and adult psychiatric units have a no-touch policy." Increasingly schools impose the "Keep your hands to yourself" standard. Educators use touch as a form of reward and punishment — a comforting tap on the shoulder in passing as a reward for a good test score or for sitting quietly and not causing trouble. Most teacher-touch forms manage, restrain, direct, and organize children, and are used when necessary to carry out the job.

Like a leg that "falls asleep," without our sense of touch, we experience a sensory cutoff which results in difficulty in initiating touch because the impulses are not adequately given or received. Just like adults with their cars, children from kindergarten to high school bump into one another and immediately blame and attack. Playgrounds and neighborhoods are turfs, defended and fought over. Bullying, as described in 1989 by the National School Safety Center, is "perhaps the most under-rated problem in our schools today." The root problem in such bullying may be that children cannot imagine an alternative form of touch.

Skin hunger is not satisfied by sex, food, drugs, busy-work, frenetic entertainment or other varieties of escape we so often associate with cultural play. Nothing but truly meaningful and caring touch meets this need; and this need does not diminish with age. After talking to a Seattle area high school class for unwed mothers about touch and play, one teen-age mother stopped me and quietly asked to speak to me alone. Sobbing, she raised her eyes to mine. Filled with confusion and hope, some anger and desperation she confessed that she didn't know how to touch her infant son. She said that she didn't want her son to grow up like the men she knew. She wanted him to be different, to know how to be both gentle and strong.

Contest Touch

Touch can easily become a contest. We see this commonly in such areas of human touch as discipline, tickling and playfighting in which our misunderstanding of play leads to abuse and aggression. Adults often comment about the tricky nature of touch in tickling and rough-and-tumble play, and how suddenly and easily it turns to crying, retaliation, humiliation and pain. Unaware of the differences between play and contest, we assume that play "gets out of hand" and "turns" into aggression. But play doesn't turn into contest, love doesn't turn into rape and tickling doesn't turn into torture. Contest, rape and torture begin as such. It is our lack of awareness that hides this fact from us.

We have not yet realized that touch is the healing power for those who have been abused by touch. Alice Miller writes:

Since the injured child in us can express himself only by means of *physical sensations and feelings related to his traumas,* it is essential that therapy secure access to these sensations and feelings and enable the person to articulate them. However this access remains completely blocked whenever we are satisfied with intellectual speculations, as in the case of psychoanalysis. (Italics mine.)

Verbal articulation does not release an attack delivered through touch, nor does it teach new ways and understandings of touch.

Tickling

When I first began giving play workshops, I didn't mention tickling. As I noticed adults try to tickle and others leave the playspace, I began to talk about it. Then I began to say that

during our play together, tickling was not appropriate. Increasingly women would come up following the session and thank me
for eliminating tickling in play. Some would go on to tell me
stories behind their fear of tickling. Women, and more recently
men, have helped me realize that tickling is a very powerful and
potentially dangerous form of touch.

Tickling is a touchy subject. It seems to bring such delight. But
all too often hidden beneath the laughter is pain and abuse. Suddenly tickling can become disabling, as laughter and movements
become uncontrollable. Pain becomes rage. The victim's laughter
entices the aggressor to continue. This is "tickle torture." Such
tickling is a form of abuse and can have devastating consequences.

Tickling may begin in a way that seems nonaggressive and
pleasurable for both people. But, like rape, tickling is often used
to control another person, to take control of another's body and
use it for pleasure. It is common for men to hold down women
and for parents and older siblings to hold down younger children
and tickle them relentlessly. This becomes agonizing. The person
doing the tickling is a predator, trying to stalk and corner the
other, who is the victim. The laughing of the victim encourages
the tickler, who responds to the laugh and not to the verbal and
physiological messages to stop. The game for one is fun and for
the other is pain. At some point the pain may turn to rage. Then
if he or she is able, the victim lashes out. This is perceived by the
tickler as unprovoked, and the aggressor retaliates at a still higher
level of aggression. If the tickler stops, he or she will likely feel
embarrassed and hurt by the victim's accusations. After all, the
victim was laughing. How does one tell another that you were
laughing and feeling pain and rage?

For many children such attacks are so threatening that as adults
they still react violently even at the hint of being tickled. After
talking with a college class in Washington, a young man came up
and thanked me for talking about tickling. "I now know what I did
wrong," he confessed. "I want to go home and tell my girlfriend
that I'm sorry and I know why she was angry." He went on to
describe what had gone on the previous night. They had not been
going together for very long. During the evening he began tickling her. She laughed and said stop simultaneously. He didn't stop
because he thought she was having fun. He didn't listen to her; he

didn't feel her pain. He had never been a tickling victim. She responded with a degree of anger that surprised him. He didn't understand; he felt hurt. They parted angry and frustrated.

Touch is a very powerful means of communication. What seems to us as a gentle, reassuring touch may be felt as an attack. A father once put his head down on the desk and sobbed during a class on play that I was giving when I spoke about tickling. After a few minutes, he wanted to share his grief with us. About a month earlier, he had tickled his teenage daughter to the point of anger. She cried, and since then had not let him touch her at all. He had not understood what he had done, and now he was desperate to find a way to reconnect with his daughter. Often a tickle spot becomes a literal sore point throughout one's life.

We often do not know what wounds we carry nor what may be reawakened in others. The sensitivities carried just beneath the surface of the men and women in these examples are not isolated experiences, but illustrate the result of playing the Duchess' Game.

Play-Fighting

"Play-fighting" is a term that succinctly expresses our confusion over the nature of play. Nowhere has the meaning of play been more demeaned than in the idea that it is something that one can win at. From the perspective of original play, play-fighting is an oxymoron, a juxtaposition of opposites.

The vast majority of our so-called play in which seemingly no one is hurt is called "healthy competition." Maria Piers and Genevieve Landau suggest, "If the aggression in children's behavior is not injurious to the child or to others, and if the aggressive play is not the main and only way in which a youngster plays, it is nothing to worry about." Children's war play is often thought of as healthy competition. Brian Sutton-Smith, for example, suggests "To ban war toys or war play only takes away a child's healthy response to his universe." Bruno Bettleheim takes a psychoanalytic perspective to defend children's war play saying that it is the necessary learning of the fight between us and them, between good and evil. But as children mature, their focus is "on the good feeling of comradeship against a common enemy." As if we can't feel comradeship without an enemy.

To argue for healthy competition is to argue for exactly what we have now. One must ask "healthy" for whom? "Fair" to whom? Our belief in "healthy competition" is dependent upon our notion of "fair play." From the vantage point of the game, to act out our fight according to the rules of the game promotes self-esteem. Good violence is civilized. This is precisely the belief necessary to keep the game going. But healthy competition and fair play are euphemisms enabling us to hide the truth that the game itself is destructive.

When I played marbles as a boy, it was very important to find out ahead of time if the game was for "keepsies." This changed everything. "Keepsies" meant that I would hold back my favorite marbles because I could lose not only the game but the marbles as well. Play becomes a contest when it is played for keeps. In the Gulf War, the U.S. Marine Commandant Alfred Gray, Jr. was reported to have told his troops in Saudi Arabia, "We're going to play for keeps if that's required."

Our "play for keeps" attitude describes our all-consuming efforts to make the world conform to our desires. One play theorist, Roger Caillois writes, "Competition is a law of modern life." Woody Hayes, former Ohio State football coach, emphatically sums it up: "I'd rather die a winner, than live a loser."

Adults, themselves confused about the nature of touch and play, adopt the term "play-fighting." Parents and teachers are frustrated by play-fighting which seems to begin with gentle wrestling and ends in punches, pain and tears. Not knowing themselves whether it's play or fighting, whether it's good or bad, adults tend to stop it before it gets out of hand. Then children see fights in professional sports and ask, "Are they playing?" In this way we pass on our illness to our children. Often children receive their first training sessions in the switch from play to contest during "play-fighting" or "rough-and-tumble" play bouts. In my play with young children, I find that often by the age of four children have learned how to play the game. They fight and call it play.

Mothers and fathers may have different perceptions of play-fighting. Often in a gathering, a father will say to me that he plays with his kids a lot. After he has finished boasting to me about the fun he has and wanders off, his wife will shake her head sadly. "He thinks he's playing, but every time he does our son gets hurt."

The following is a description of a particular family play experience. The same essential circumstances have been described to me by many parents and children.

Father comes home tired around six o'clock, feeling guilty about not having spent enough time with his ten-year-old son over the past weekend. He doesn't really want to play, but he feels obligated. The son, excited, runs out to play before his dad has changed his clothes. The boy wants to be with his father, but is ambivalent. He is afraid because he gets hurt when they play. They meet in the backyard a few minutes later.

They begin by throwing a football back and forth, then running and tagging are added. Soon tackling is added, and the ball seems to become secondary to the contact as they roll and punch and grab each other on the grass. At one point the father, using his weight, pins the boy underneath him and doesn't let him up. The boy squirms, wiggles and strains but cannot free himself. In frustration he hits his father's arm. The father, surprised by what to him is unprovoked aggression, pushes down harder. The boy cries. Angry and frustrated, the father gets up and yells at his son, "Sissy, you have to learn to play like a man!" The father storms by his wife and gives her a glare that says, "Don't baby him." The mother stands still, feeling caught between wanting to comfort her son and supporting her husband. The boy wants to go to his mother for comfort, but doesn't want to be called a sissy if he does. Here are three angry people caught in the tragedy of "constructive" play-fighting.

There are a number of misunderstandings and miscommunications in this interaction pattern. The father-son play was a contest in the first place. The interaction is about winning. First, neither father nor son really wants to play, but follows through out of obligation and fear of sharing their true feelings with each other. Both must try to play as if they want to. All of this has happened before they have even begun to touch.

Consequently, when the actual rough-and-tumble begins, neither is relaxed. Both carry the tension of their past bad experiences as well as the current double messages in their minds, muscles, and nerves. Neither knows the difference between contest and play touch. Their beginning touch is apparently gentle, but quickly escalates into retaliatory get-backs. This comes to a climax in the pin. The father maintains his pin, ignoring his son's kinesthetic and verbal messages to stop. Angered, the boy lashes out in kind — contest for contest. The escalation continues as the father gets back at him by pinning harder. The father plays to win, and further degrades his victim with name calling. The boy is incompetent because he cannot respond to his father's messages, insolent for his desperate acting out and unmanly for crying.

At each point in the interaction, father and son make decisions that seem to be common sense, only to find subsequently that their right moves make them wrong. Finally, the mother is drawn into the contest. Over a period of time, the father-son play becomes increasingly unwanted and competitive. The experience is one of pain and negation of self. It is a very widespread experience in our society.

The inability of the adult, whether parent, teacher or researcher to draw appropriate conclusions about play-fighting is not only evident in our ambiguous language, but even more evident when it comes to "play-fighting" or "rough-and-tumble" bouts in family living rooms and on school playgrounds. It may be easy for adults to differentiate between rough-and-tumble and intentional acts of aggression, but when and how one changes to the other is unknown, as is how play-fighting is conducted and built up. This is especially true where the children have been exposed to violent TV, movies and advertising. Imitating what they think they see, children kick and punch wildly.

Peter K. Smith doubts the value of rough-and-tumble play because he believes it provides practice for fighting skills and dominance relations. David W. Shantz says, "A growing body of research suggests that aggressive behavior and low peer status during childhood are both rich factors for serious maladjustment in later life." Dr. Marilyn Segal, on the other hand, suggests that it is in aggressive play that children learn to deal with such feelings. "Competitive games have an important place. They can be useful in teaching children about winning and losing," says child psychiatrist Dr. Charles F. Rich, Jr. Anthony Pellegrini and Jane Perlmutter add that boys especially, "seem to develop and learn in rough-and-tumble play those social skills necessary to be socially competent." Socially competent competitors, that is.

These opinions illustrate our adult confusion; we want children to be strong competitors, but not hurt anyone. In describing success to children as if there were no victims, we hide a significant part of the truth. Adult after adult asks me how they can tell when play-fighting turns to real fighting. They do not understand that authentic play cannot "turn" into fighting. There is no mechanism in play to turn. If it "turned" it was a contest in the first place which escalated as each player used get-backs. Caught in our own contests adults don't know what to tell children. Preschool teachers are often advised to reduce physical competitiveness; they consistently intervene to teach young children to share. But as the children get older, adults allow and encourage more competition. Fairness begins to take a backseat to winning. Children learn that sharing is sissy "child's play." A study of children in a suburban elementary school revealed that by second grade boys had to be willing to fight. Older children are supposed to try to win, but not yet at all costs; learn how to be good losers and not to cheat. All of this changes later.

The Embedded Contest

The barbaric law that has obtained throughout the ages is that he who wins is just.

Daisaku Ikeda

When original play was abandoned, life ceased to have meaning and we discovered purpose. When ethics arrived, we played fairly — to win at any cost. When kindness dissolved, we played for keeps.

Fred Donaldson

Contests are so embedded throughout the culture that it isn't necessary for one to want to hurt another. All that is necessary is for one to be able to separate oneself in such a way that differentiates the other as undeserving of the same rights as you. Since this adversary process has been an integral part of our upbringing, separation requires no effort at all. Then the desire to want something that requires an aggressive action that hurts someone is perceived as appropriate. The act that would need justification has not happened. We can disregard the fact of victimization in a sincere desire to obtain our goal. The fact of victimization is one step removed, which is a giant step insulating us from the fact that our actions hurt others who are just like us.

It is no small irony that the fear of differences, which is absent in the the play mind, is taken as the basic axiom of the contest mind. Only after becoming split within ourselves, do we have a reason to enter the external forms of the game, which are nothing more than manifestations of our propensity to see ourselves as essentially separate entities. Nothing outside of ourselves is attacking us, but from the viewpoint of the split, fearful self, everything and everyone is a potential adversary. Fear engulfs the mind so that the individual sees the world divided as the culture decrees that one should. Contestants are manufactured by a false industry of heroes and hero-worshipers, trinkets, trophies and tickets. As contestants, players are mercenaries. The tragedy is that we only feel safe by believing in fear.

Contestants define people in terms of their categories. As players of the game we can carry out actions against other players that would be otherwise unthinkable. What happens to "them" doesn't matter. The whole person is sacrificed to further the games. Contests are agglomerations of splinter individuals obliged to shun real human interaction, not because they are ethically callous, but simply because they have no personal sense of meaning.

Rarely has a contest been undertaken without some justification couched in sustaining myths. *Our* missiles are defensive; *theirs* are offensive. *Their* attacks are unprovoked, *ours* are in defense of our rightful privileges and possessions. The moral justification for competition — that it builds character, teaches teamwork, instills discipline, loyalty, decency, friendship, honor and "fair play" are openly avowed, assiduously cultivated and zealously carried out in all areas of our lives. It is common for adults to feel that the game is what brings out the best in them; without it they would not be able to excel. Our education, sports, political and business systems are based upon the idea that competition is our primary motivation for success and excellence.

The Chameleon Principle

Perhaps the first lesson a contestant has to learn is the "Chameleon Principle," that contests are not what they seem. Within the game players are to play as if playing to win is the same as playing fair. That this is an ethical problem embedded in the game is to be forgotten. While this is the first step toward contest mental health, it is simultaneously the initial step to alienation. Contestants must learn to disengage themselves from others; to believe that what they are doing makes good, logical sense and is the authentic expression of themselves. This disguise must be flawless; the last thing one must do is to admit to oneself that one's life-ways are false or without meaning.

Cut off from the wisdom of kindness, and unable with the experience of our own life to discern its underlying reality, we cannot seriously envisage the possibility of living a kind life. We don't know what such a life would look like. We conclude, therefore, that kindness is a sentimental fable. In place of kindness we are admonished to "play fair," that is, to select those elements that are in agreement with the patterns one is taught to be true and just.

Fairness is esteemed because it enables us to maintain an illusion. In our unremitting efforts to win, we are easily led to create fantasy worlds of fairness remote from direct awareness of others' pain. There is a vicious circle here: Ideas about fairness are derived from a failure to be kind. Failing to achieve kindness, we settle for fairness. Thinking that fairness is kindness, we exhibit fairness, which obstructs our attempts at kindness by encouraging egocentricity characteristic of personal and sociocultural games and competition.

At Any Cost

Playing by the rules provides the illusion that playing fair and playing to win are kept in balance. A cultural player is a world beater, where the world is defined by the game. The urge for more toys, control, power, money, land, prestige, thrill is well lubricated with natural and well-meaning intentions coupled with a lack of responsibility for any pain or destruction. Oppressive economic and political practices, group aggression and personal violence, destruction and persecution have been explained away as necessary and inevitable incidentals, accidents and appropriate defenses or revenge. Young children, sportsmen, gang members, convicted murderers, politicians, business people and soldiers give the excuse that it's a competitive world in which we have to fight fiercely for what we want or lose. Within the Duchess' Game is the same process which drives political, economic and medical fraud resulting, for example, in the destruction of wolves, rainforests and children. As Alfie Kohn so accurately put it, "In the case of competition, the root cause of abuses is the competitive structure itself."

When fair play is made secondary to "play to win," the measure of appropriate conduct isn't fairness but winning. Fair play is held hostage to play to win and play for keeps. This is commonly seen in political campaigns, divorce, and national defense. And even in family games. I recall a game of *Pictionary* in which an adult said to his spouse who was going to help her daughter-teammate, "No, don't help her, we're playing a game." The contest roles superseded family ties.

"Playing dirty" or cheating is part of the game itself. In their study of pinball players Conn and Marquez found that, "In fact, among regular players there are no cheaters. Cheating is part of playing. It is frequent and continuous." In a 1991 survey of American major college football coaches, 62% of those who responded said, "Some of their peers knowingly cheat." Like other skills of the game, cheating is condoned and admired. The player is constantly trying to get away with something or beat the system. The "tilt" in pinball is the referee. And like the referee in sports, pinball players expect there to be some "give" in the machine and in referees. Players and spectators get angry if every infraction is called. Fairness is an ethical system in which the weak exist to limit the strong. Michael Novak is clear, "Sports provide an almost deliberate exercise in pushing the psyche to cheat and take advantage, to be ruthless, cruel, deceitful, vengeful, and aggressive." The problem isn't limited to sports. Anne Strick said of our legal system, "Where polarity shapes thinking and winning is the orthodoxy to which men chiefly adhere, deceit is absolutely justifiable."

Cheating is not outside the game. Whatever it takes to win in everyday life, in sports, business or politics is still playing within the context of the game. Normally we think of cheating as outside the rules. This has been a delusion. Cheating is, in fact, part of the game itself. The cheat, says Huizinga, "pretends to be playing the game and, on the face of it, still acknowledges the magic circle," and Caillois believes "the cheat's dishonesty does not destroy the game." The cheater bends and breaks rules, but this is the way to play the game. The legitimization of cheating has to do with the hierarchy of value within the game itself. Alfie Kohn reports research that "regular sport participants become more committed to winning at any cost and less committed to values of fairness and justice as their competitive experience increases."

It is the function of adults, especially in their roles as parents and teachers, to con children out of original play and promote belief in cultural play. What is described as play by adults in time becomes experienced as play by children, if only because they are told, in effect, "This is how things are." It is crucial that this process appear as though what adults are doing makes good, logical sense and is an expression of being good adults. "To teach a young child to compete is just preparing them for the world in which they have to live," say parents and teachers when I suggest that play be substituted for contests in public school. We know no other way to relate. As Ernest Becker points out, "If everybody lives roughly the same lies about the same things, there is no one to call them liars. They jointly establish their own sanity and call themselves normal." Unable to see the contradiction, we continue to befuddle each new generation because we, having been so befuddled ourselves, know only the game.

The innumerable contests that make up the Duchess' Game are all futile attempts to mend the schism and splintering of the self. Individual contests are pseudo-events that we adjust to with a false consciousness adapted to experience these events as play. The primary question of "Who am I?" is subsumed and determined by "Who wins?" They are no more than particularized attempts to mend one tragic experience — the self split in two, as if cleaved by a master Samurai swordsman. We have been disenchanted and disembodied, and no amount of contesting can heal our splits. We live under the illusion that we can be made whole by medals, trophies and positions. When we fight against ourselves, we lose — even when we win.

With All Good Intentions

All things are connected. Whatever befalls the earth,
befalls the children of the earth.

Chief Sealth

We sat on a worn couch with a mother who seemed equally as worn out from her life. "After working and taking orders all day, I want to come home and have someone take orders from me," she wished out loud. She sighed as she glanced to see what her two boys were doing. Tom, a five-year-old who has autism, is climbing on the kitchen sink. She shows us around the house, pointing to the breakage resulting from Tom's outbursts. She has placed locks wherever she can to protect him and the few remaining family valuables. She is tired. Tom is tired too, I believe. He suffers from precisely what tears down his mother. He is given orders and restrained all day. The father is away much of the time. I play with Tom at school. He smiles and comes by for an occasional touch. I thought of things I might tell Tom's mother, but they seemed, however useful in my own mind, inappropriate right then. Instead, I was to listen to her. She seemed interested in sharing, in letting me know what it was like for her at home, managing most of the time alone day in, day out, with her two sons. She tries; I wonder if I would do as well. And clearly, she needs help. Many of us do.

It has been difficult to diagnose what the pervading sickness might be, though many try. The United Nations had a recent summit on children. *Time* magazine asked on a recent cover, "Do We Care About Our Kids?" New York City's Teacher of the Year, John Catto, told us that "Our Children Are Dying In Our Schools." Senator John D. Rockefeller, IV, Chairman of the National Commission on Children, writes, "As a society, we have lacked the vision and political will necessary to address these problems head on."

It's not the absence of facts that kill children, not even the paltry allocation of resources. It's a lack of relationship. Even in cultures in which adults say they love children, we are simply disconnected from our own children. What's happening to children throughout the world amounts to a slow, grinding process of attrition. When we read the statistics on the children whom adults destroy, the horror is beyond belief. To sit with a mother and son and witness the pain and despair is heart-wrenching. To watch women childcare providers who day after day sit and talk to each other and ignore children in their care is disheartening. Discounting and wasting of children is nothing new. In the early years of this century, the labor movement called for "a childhood for every child." The call remains unheeded.

The plight of children worldwide is difficult to understand. It doesn't seem to matter that we were all once children. It doesn't seem to matter that children are our only real insurance policy. It is not enough to write reports and convene conferences, nor is it enough to give money. A question needs pondering: How is it possible that with all of our knowledge, the adults worldwide would rather pay for weapons to kill children than give of ourselves to help them? To continue to destroy, on such a sustained basis, the beauty, imagination and creative power of children is not merely unimaginative, but deliberately cruel. More disturbing, more subtle and more profound still is the feeling that somehow childhood dies from natural causes rather than from our calculated acts.

Our contest consciousness makes wisdom and the ecological mind impossible, severing one's mind and way of knowing from the communication between oneself, other life forms and the source of life. As contestants we endlessly check to see if we must defend or attack. From such a viewpoint we are totally unprepared to be caregivers. Learning to be a contestant is learning to sacrifice life for no life at all.

The drastic and incalculably dangerous assumptions are that winners can be considered apart from losers and that winning may be conceptually separated from losing. We have not understood that in our quest to conquer each other and the earth, the longer "we" win, the more "we" lose. We must begin to understand that when we "play to win," every victory is a funeral.

We are continuing to live out an outcome of a way of life that is rooted in our past, but it need not define our future. "Some type of holistic or participating consciousness and a corresponding sociopolitical formulation," suggests Morris Berman, "has to emerge if we are to survive as a species." Wendell Berry is more specific, "Love one another or die, individually and as a species." Like the addict who "hits bottom" before recovering, we individually and collectively are hopefully "played out" and can now begin to mend the schism within. Healing requires that we face the truth that contests are the fabrication of persons afraid to love.

Play encodes a way of being on which the world has repeatedly turned its back, and in so doing, lost the key to the cipher. It is as if we carry with us a dreadful fear that in order to be all that we should become we must first abandon all that we have been. But we must see beyond that fear. My playmates have shared with me a vision of human possibility that tugs, like Cort, at my being. Our play is haunted by the spirit within each of us that strives to be born. Again and again that which has been denied its birth, like the monsters hiding beneath our childhood beds, stirs in the dark, as if to remind us that they are waiting to pull our covers off. We can run away and hide and disguise ourselves from the love of play; but in the end that which we believed to be a monster, but in reality is the love of Creation, is us.

How then are we to heal ourselves and our children? How can we extricate ourselves from the futility of winning and losing?

PART
THREE

Feeling The Heartbeat
Of The Universe

I cannot tell you what God is . . . I can only tell you that my work as a
natural scientist has established empirically that the pattern which men
call God exists in every man, and that this pattern has at its disposal the
greatest transformative energies of life.

C.G. Jung

Blake once led the painter Samuel Palmer to his window and, pointing to
a group of children at play, said, "That is heaven."

Stephen Mitchell

Boys and girls tumbling in the street, and playing, were moving jewels.

Thomas Traherne

Silence, O, brother! Put learning and culture away:
Till Thou namedst culture, I knew no culture but Thee.

Divani Shamsi Tabriz

It would be sad, and could be fatal, if we continue to allow all the clarity of childish perception to be clouded in this way. For there seem to be moments, before we become familiar with the house rules, when we are able to see right through the cracks in the cosmic egg and almost touch the truth.

Lyall Watson

6

Spoilsports:
Remaking Contest
Into Play

The spoilsport shatters the play-world itself.

Johan Huizinga

The game of "I" is up, no longer do I play it against you, fellow beings.

Frederick Franck

Stacy and I rolled on the grass. She pushed me onto my back and sat on my chest with her legs dangling down beside my neck. With a most intense concentration in her eyes, she bent forward, took my face in her hands, lifted it and kissed me, then gently placed my head down on the grass. Stacy and I shared an epiphany, a sudden manifestation of the essential nature and meaning of life. I paused not only to allow myself to feel my tears, but because so much and so profoundly had adulthood become a part of my life that, on these rare occasions when I am allowed to be taken in and to take in, I reel from the impact of her presence which momentarily washes away my categorical world.

Never is so much life compressed into so little space. Kindness, Stacy showed me, is not mere sentimentality; it is a basic law of the human spirit, an uncompromising manifesto of life. We who realize such an experience are charged by life itself to live in such a way that no evasion or aggression can be excused.

It may be that some people grow up without ever losing their playful consciousness, and so never know what it is to be a fully contesting, confused adult. There are also genuine playmates. Not many, but a few for whom cultural conditioning does not take. And there are those whom the culture decides do not need conditioning in the first place. These include children, who because of physical or mental differences are excluded from the normal cultural conditioning.

Our very notion of play is distorted, based as it is on the illusion of contest. We have implanted, like cancerous tumors, the seeds of a mutually parasitic winner-loser dyad into our acting and thinking. Ludicrously misled, we have assumed contests to be the basis of life, its moral order and cohesion as well as the source of its vitality and creative powers. A search for a new order of relationship requires a sabbatical from thinking and acting as if: (1) the world were a geography of adversarial systems; (2) we could stop violence with aggression; (3) contests provide the way out of contests; (4) winners are separate from losers; and (5) conflict is the basis of creativity.

Our quest for relationship, rooted in the shallow, arid ground of contesting, is a kind of cultural schizophrenia in which we effectively decouple ourselves from each other and our deeper ground of being. In the midst of such collective pathology, we must dare to ask ourselves if this splitting apart was a good idea in the first place.

We consider play to be childish, self-indulgent, self-centered, frivolous and even mischievious "kid's stuff." We tell children not to play with their food and not to play on the grass; teenagers are admonished not to play around. Children in the backyards of America throw ninja kicks at each other and run from yard to yard shooting their plastic guns. Adults smile and shrug, "It's just play. After all, we did it and turned out all right." Children in Lebanon are photographed "playing" with an abandoned AK-47. And the Los Angeles Times reported that boys in Belfast, Northern Ireland, played soccer with a suspected IRA bomb, thinking it was a doll's head.

Teenagers break some windows following a football victory in a small town in Texas and, "They're just having fun." Young men driving down a Montana highway pull out their Magnums and Winchesters and blast a stop sign into a piece of red Swiss cheese. It's about 11:30 P.M., a car with headlights off careens around a corner of a quiet street in east Los Angeles. Automatic gunfire sprays a house. A two-year-girl is dead. Our "play" is aimless, irresponsible, illicit and illegal. But, "We're just funnin'." Our playing for fun is for "keeps." We've been living in a cataclysm of contest that separates people while promoting the illusion of connectedness to teams, groups and countries.

Caught between the arbitrary alternatives of winning and losing, we are unable either to conceive or to develop the kindness necessary to remake our lives, and in the process we waste our own lives as well as our children's.

We tend to think of a spoilsport as someone who destroys the game. But the spoilsport as an authentic playmate plays *outside* the boundaries of culture's games. Such a spoilsport is like the child in the fairytale who has the courage to tell the emperor that he is naked. A playmate does not try to destroy the game. For the playmate it is not the rules or the game that is important, but the playmates themselves. Such play inevitably spoils the Duchess' Game.

Telling the truth robs the contest of its illusion, thus threatening the very existence of the Duchess' Game. It is for this reason that the spoilsport must be denounced and expelled. As Huizinga points out, from the game players' point of view, "He [the spoilsport] is a coward and must be ejected."

But underneath it all lies the unintelligible truth of play. The point is not to enter the contest or to substitute a new one in place of it. The playmate does not smash idols, but instead realizes that life is lost in the game's forms. The playmate's intention is not the destruction of the game; this is a waste of time and energy. Rather his or her intent is to give love—which itself, being what cultural players are surreptitiously seeking, destroys the fearful reason for the Duchess' Game in the first place.

To spend time relentlessly attacking cultural games is as much an attachment to them as participating in them. It is merely being bound by another contest. Ridicule and attack can easily become ends in themselves and can be exploited as justifications for the exact behavior they desire to halt. In this regard we often fail to make the distinction between nonattachment and either frivolous disregard or blind ignorance. The playmate recognizes the game for what it is and lets go of both the game and the necessity to attack it.

I-Tuan, a disciple of Zen master Nan-ch'uan, expressed the matter simply: "Speech is blasphemy, silence is a lie. Above speech and silence there is a way out." The way out is easier to write about than it is to live. It has taken a long time for me to realize that modeling play is more important than attacking contests. To only attack contest is to fail to comprehend the essential principle of play.

To be a playmate is life's way of superceding the games of culture. Cultural play is based on established rules and differences that seem to make a difference. Human differences are exaggerated and prized. Through love the playmate realigns these relationships. All the identifiable differences in cultural games are insignificant. Imagine, for example, a game of hockey or basketball in which there was no score and everyone wore the same uniform, with no identifying names or numbers. Categories like "us" and "them" begin to dissolve. Then players become playmates, shattering the contest.

The "game" of Chinese baseball is described by R.G.H. Siu:

Chinese baseball is played almost exactly like American baseball — the same field, players, bats and balls, method of scoring, and so on. The batter stands in the batter's box, as usual. The pitcher stands on the pitcher's mound, as usual. He winds up, as usual, and zips the ball down the alley. There is only one difference, and that is: After the ball leaves the pitcher's hand, and as long as the ball is in the air, *anyone* can move *any* of the bases *anywhere.*

The playmate does to relationships what Chinese baseball does to the American game. That is, we become unattached to our bases.

The spoilsport is likely to be considered foolish or mad. In engaging the world as a playmate, he or she may be shocked by the explosive force that this new approach elicits from other members of society, entrenched as they are in their games. Playmates are not likely to understand the nature of the threat they pose to the existing order of the game. As Simone Weil points out, we see this contrast between loyal contestant and playmate in the exchange between Creon and Antigone in the Greek play *Antigone.* Creon tries to convince Antigone that she outrages one brother by paying the same honor to both the brother who died trying to destroy his own country and the brother who died defending it.

She answers: "Nevertheless the other world demands equal laws." To which he sensibly objects: "There can be no sharing between a brave man and a traitor," and she has only the absurd reply: "Who knows whether this holds in the other world?"

Creon's comment is reasonable: "A foe is never a friend, not even in death." Antigone replies: "I was born to share, not hate, but love."

In 1944 J. Glenn Gray, then a second lieutenant in the U.S. Counter Intelligence Corps in Europe, wrote to a friend a remarkably similar realization about life and love. "Oh, you would have to see many things, Fred, to know why I should come to realize such a primitive truth as that I have only one alternative to death and that is to love, to care for people whom I as a natural man, want to strike down."

Antigone, J. Glenn Gray and Dennis, each did not know how to compete in a race; they played outside the game. They are unintelligible to players like Creon and the childcare worker who are within the game. Antigone, Glenn Gray and Dennis point to the truth that allegiance to life in place of human groups ceases to be an intellectual exercise. It is a very sobering, practical issue with monumental implications. It truly means that we not only must, but can surrender our allegience to the very groups that we believe define our status in the world. The experience of having our illusions stripped away is often a very painful process. It is also dangerous, because we believe the fabric of our security is threatened. Not surprisingly, we tend to resist having our contestant masks ripped off. Often under such attack we build stronger defenses against further exposure by hardening the underlying masks. If a mask is forced off, it reappears as another disguise.

To subordinate cultural allegiances is asking a great deal of a human being who believes that to do so would leave them adrift alone in a hostile world. Such a leap requires faith, without prior proof that there is indeed a safety net. In letting go we discover a much grander, more supportive playground. "It lands us," as Larry Dossey put it, "squarely in the lap of God." Only then will we experience that "God is at play with us." This is what makes play sacred.

Playing achieves the very result which we have painfully built our character over the years in order to avoid: It makes routine, competitive activity impossible. It makes unkind living in the world an impossibility. Playmates extend their identification of self until it includes the universe, thereby experiencing a sense of meaning beyond questions and articulation. Such people transcend fear, are moved by kindness, and become so vulnerable that they cannot help being touched by the world. The strength found in this playing self is what one wanted but couldn't find in contests. The

Bhagavad Gita says, "Weapons cut It not; fire burns It not; water wets It not; the wind does not wither It. This self cannot be cut nor burnt nor wetted nor withered. Eternal, all-pervading, unchanging, immovable, the Self is the same for ever." Kindness, as an aspect of play, is not an ethical judgment; it isn't about shoulds and efforts, guilt and self-righteousness. Jesus put this succinctly, "Whosoever will lose his life for my sake shall find it."

On Being Nobody Special: A Motley Crew Of Playmates

Fueled by innumerable fears, we have been like Alice afraid that we'd disappear. But our fears of becoming nothing are abrogated by the words of Julian of Norwich, when she found in the palm of her hand something small. "I looked at it with the eye of my understanding and thought: What can this be? I was amazed that it could last, for I thought that because of its littleness, it would suddenly have fallen into nothing. And I was answered in my understanding: It lasts and always will because God loves it; and thus everything has being through the love of God."

Russell Schweickart, the first astronaut to float unattached in space, also experienced wonder, seeing earth as a "small spot." Like Julian, the small object "contained everything that had any meaning for him — all of history and music and art and death and birth and love, tears, joy . . . And in that silence there were no frames . . . no boundaries." This is the meaning of William Blake's famous lines from *Songs of Innocence:*

To See a World in a Grain of Sand
And Heaven in a Wild Flower,
Hold Infinity in the palm of your hand
And Eternity in an hour.

The importance of their visions shows not the insignificance of each of us in our apparent smallness, but our significance. A realization of smallness can open our understanding to a much fuller love, one that embraces all of life. It is in this love that we feel the certitude of who we are in relation to all of life. As we feel loved and give kindness, we will no longer act like separate entities in a dangerous world. Steven Mitchell writes, "Eventually [we] will feel confident enough to disappear." Here we see the true meaning of sacrifice: *sacer facere,* to make sacred — "to rise up vertically in a single act from the profane world of greed and fear, up into the serene, still dimension of the sacred, and to transfigure one's whole life in one moment," as Piero Ferrucci wrote. And to do this repeatedly in the midst of ordinary, everyday life. Then we are playmates. This is the mystery of limitless belonging. The source is hidden from us, but its expression is a reality, a kind of aliveness within and around us that cannot be extinguished.

What we are looking for *really* is a new order of relationship in which a will to play replaces a will to power. Only the exercise of kindness, the energy beyond aggression, rooted in the authentic spirit of life provides our spent selves and worn-out societies with the necessary transforming energies to initiate the beginning of real reconciliation.

Perhaps this is why Meister Eckhart saw this kindness in a young girl who came to the preaching cloister and asked for him. The doorman asked:

"Whom shall I announce?"

"I don't know," she said.

"Why don't you know?"

"Because I am neither a girl, nor a woman, nor a husband, nor a wife, nor a widow, nor a virgin, nor a master, nor a maid, nor a servant."

The doorman went to Meister Eckhart and said:

"Come out here and see the strangest creature you ever heard of. Let me go with you, and you stick your head out and ask 'Who wants me?' "

Eckhart did so and she gave him the same reply she had made to the doorman. Then he said, "My dear child, what you say is right and sensible but explain to me what you mean."

She said: "If I were a girl, I should be still in my first innocence; if I were a woman, I should always be giving birth in my soul to the eternal word; if I were a husband, I should put up a stiff resistance to all evil; if I were a wife, I should keep faith with my dear one, whom I married; if I were a widow, I should be always longing for the one I loved; if I were a virgin, I should be reverently devout; if I were a servant-maid, in humility I should count myself lower than God or any creature; and if I were a man-servant, I should be hard at work, always serving my Lord with my whole heart. But since of all of these I am neither one, I am just a something among something, and so I go."

Then Meister Eckhart went in and said to his pupils: "It seems to me that I have just listened to the purest person I have ever known."

Some do escape the process of mask building. Most for just a few brief moments when the hard shell masks of adulthood are melted with a shift of awareness. I am reminded of Pablo Picasso's wonderful remark: "Don't blame me for those fantastic prices and possessings. I'm only playing." And Zen Master Sengai: "This play of mine with brush and ink is neither calligraphy nor drawing. Yet in the view of the common minded people it becomes mere calligraphy and drawing." It is very difficult to take a path that goes beyond one's culture, even if the culture itself introduces you to such a way.

Pu-tai and St. Francis of Assisi, for example, were becoming playmates in secular worlds. Of course we have their predecessors Jesus and Buddha before them. Pu-tai and Francis of Assisi are, however, a step closer to us.

Pu-tai

Without knowing it, you may have a statue of a famous Asian holy fool standing and smiling somewhere on a shelf in your home. This is the potbellied figure we see in Chinese paintings and as statues in restaurants and souvenir shops throughout the world. He is Pu-tai, or Hotai in Japanese. Historically, Pu-tai is identified with a Chinese vagabond priest named Keishi or Cho Tai-shi who died in 916. Legend has it that Pu-tai, which means "linen sack," refused the designation of Zen master and wandered the countryside with his sack over his shoulder, giving gifts to children. He was popularly believed to be an incognito appearance of Future Buddha, Maitreya, of the age to come. His religious life consisted of playing with and giving gifts to village children, "as if life had now come full circle, as if the end were in some way a return to the beginning, as if even children and fools knew what priests and monks did not," writes Conrad Hyers.

Pu-tai's gleeful, roly-polyness "is the full circle of existence and the completed vision of life." Not unlike Jesus, who pauses to play with children, he is the master returned to the streets. He is the ordinarily sacred playmate whose love as expressed in a Buddhist chant, "With his bag of cloth vast is he as the Universe," embraces all. In keeping with the concept of playmate, Pu-tai is not to be seen as a frivolous person out to have fun. He is not in opposition to discipline and order; his play emerges out of the harmony of spontaneity and discipline.

St. Francis Of Assisi

In the early thirteenth century, another man wandered the European countryside with a rough brown tunic on his body. Francis of Assisi could not resist the call of the open road. He is remembered for his gentle nature and his special kindness to animals.

It was difficult for Francis to live out his vision. "He would never be allowed to do things entirely his own way," writes Julian Green. His vision was continually thwarted by those with power both inside and outside the church.

Perhaps more important than the expansiveness of Francis' kindness is the fact that he remained human, with a seeming blind spot in his kindness. He stretched out his arms to embrace so many within his heart. The terrible wolf of Gubbio was converted and lived happily in cooperation with the village for the remainder of his years. After his visit in 1219 with Malik al-Kamil in the sultan's palace, then surrounded by the Fifth Crusade, Francis' notion of Islam had to be modified. He saw that the essence of faith, a belief in God, existed outside Christianity. He respected this. He could include lepers within his open arms. When he seemed to have limits, they were repealed.

One day Francis rebuffed a particularly repugnant leper but he was allowed in the house by John the Simple. Ashamed, Francis gave the leper a place of honor, food and drink and drank from the man's bowl where he had placed his oozing lips. But he seemingly could never include women within this warmth, except for Clare and Jacqueline.

Francis' upbringing, the emerging intellectual groundswells and the political struggles in Europe and the church were enormous difficulties that he had to deal with in proclaiming and living out his vision. I use him, as all other playmates in this book, to suggest that it is possible for *you and me*, however difficult this may be, to be on a playmate's path in the world as we know it. It helps to know that there are others who've shared not only the vision but the practice.

To fledgling birds, flight in the sky may appear incredible. They may with apparent reason measure the highest limit of their possibilities by the limited standard of their nests. But in the meanwhile they find that their food is not grown inside those nests; it is brought to them across the measureless blue. There is a silent voice that speaks to them, that they are more than what they are, and that they must not laugh at the message of soaring wings and glad songs of freedom.

Rabindranath Tagore

It is as if we are illegitimate adults, feeling unloved and of little value. This is the legacy we've inherited and pass on to our children. Like modern absentee agriculturalists, who having no weather eye, must call the weather bureau as they have lost the judicious ability to see and feel the weather coming, adults, unable to comprehend the children's play in front of them, must read books on how to play. This will never be sufficient. Neither will observing and remembering be enough. Children and our inner child need something more from us than memorials to play; they need our whole participation in the celebration of play.

The playmate is an archeologist of sorts, unearthing the childlikeness that has been buried beneath years of the accumulated debris of adulthood. In bringing what's hidden to light, the playmate cancels fear and makes obsolete or meaningless all divisions, thereby filling this intense longing for someone to come and say as Stephen Mitchell does: "Yes, you do belong to the human community. You are of infinite value, like every human being. You are my beloved child." This idea is very old, implying as Chang says the "primordial, immediate source of love, the secret root of all love and compassion."

7

Coming Out To Play
With The World

Someone said to Jesus, "Who trained you?" He said, "No one trained me.
I saw the ignorance of the ignorant man to be a blemish, so I avoided it."
James Robson

He is always acting in accord with his Self-Nature. His work is play.
Hui-neng

Recently I crossed the border from the United States to Canada. A Canadian customs official asked me to identify my occupation, and I replied, "I'm a play specialist." "What do you do?" he asked. "I play with children and train adults to play with children." He looked puzzled and began scanning a large black notebook. Not finding a category "play specialist," he asked if I was a psychologist, a physical therapist or an occupational therapist. When I said no, he went into another office and brought back his supervisor. The three of us went over the whole story again. He, too, could not find a category for me in the black notebook. He waved me on and suggested that next time I bring a letter from the U.S. government verifying my occupation. I smiled to myself. My suspicion is that I do not have a category in U.S. catalogues either.

Vocation-Questing

yes,   It takes intelligence to be playful after one is no longer a child!
                                                        Elizabeth Gawain

Most people make do with jobs and careers in which they find refuge and reassurance in place of meaning. They may contemplate meaning, but their lives do not reflect it. Although I never thought about it at the time, this was the nature of my university teaching career. In retrospect I can see that it took a good many years before I was to realize that the play in which I was being initiated was very different. Play is a vocation, not a job. I'm not at all sure how one goes about finding a vocation. You can't use effort at all, at best you can only be open to its presence. Only in hindsight, after slowly being pirated away from adulthood by young children, did I realize that my vocation had found me.

One day I read a definition of vocation as "that which the gods call upon you to do." I suddenly realized that I didn't have a job or a career; I had a vocation. Not knowing how different vocations were from careers, I decided to get another Ph.D. So I began to investigate which university would be the best. I soon found there were none that clearly specialized in play as I was beginning to understand it. I narrowed down my list to the two that I thought would provide the most suitable training.

I visited one, a major university in the Midwest, and spent a day looking over the campus, investigating the program, and talking with faculty. As the day was drawing to a close, I met with the Dean of the school. After hearing me describe my experience, plans and needs, she replied, "You don't need us. Oh, you can come, we'd love to have you here. But you already know what you want. You're beyond our help. We'll make you take courses you don't need just to fill our requirements."

I drove home that evening disappointed, comforted and frightened at the same time. I thought they would be able to help me. I didn't understand that vocations don't fit job slots. I am independent of the boxes and codes, and by this independence I am free to honor a deeper code or devotion that culture cannot express.

Questing

Such a quest is personal; it is not a collective experience, nor can it be taught or assigned. As a quest, vocation speaks to us as individuals, since only as individuals have we the power within — as we must learn, sooner or later — to discover the highest possibilities of human nature. This means that each of us is required to take back to ourselves the responsibilities we have delegated to leaders, teachers and systems.

Martin Buber said, "What is required is a deed that a man does with his whole being." It is at once exciting and frightening to find that my future rests on *my* quest for self.

Questing is education at its most intensive, at the depth where the self dissolves, and expansive at the width where the self merges with the world. Within such octaves of meaning, the real interests of the universe are met, and not the superficial, narrow interests of a self and society. There is an urgent need to discover such a

belonging consciousness — an awareness of our connection with
and participation in the larger world, which can be accomplished
with an intimate grace in our everyday lives. Such a sense requires
intellectual humility, fearlessness and direct insight of the heart.
This is what life expects from us, nothing more, nothing less.
God   Questing might be characterized as a life fully lived, being true
to the love that is the inexhaustible well from which we draw life.
Its fruits include a passion for living and a compassion for all life.
The restorative function of questing draws its energy from an
epic memory, a sense of kinship of the mind/heart in collusion
with the hand and the spirit. The extraordinary power of questing is that it provides a link from the most fleeting moment of
immediate experience to the highest abstractions of science and
the profound richness of human experience expressed in poetic
and spiritual insight.

Pooh's Paradox

Play would not be "playful" if it were not for paradox.
                                                    William F. Fry

Winnie-the-Pooh knew that if humans were better than animals, we would take greater care of life on earth. We have missed
our way. But what way are we looking for? How will we know it
if we find it?

Play isn't a sentimental nostalgic trip through an attic of old
dusty, broken toys with which all living relationship has disappeared. It is about a flight of fancy and a whit of wisdom. The
psychic as well as the physical distance between ourselves and
play must be eliminated. Unless we change our direction, as the
old Chinese proverb says, we are likely to end up where we are
headed. In playing, compassion collaborates with wisdom and
opens the door not only to a different order of understanding,
but also to a profoundly different level of participation.

In the memory of our cosmic childhood play, we can find the
nucleus of a playmate who remains at the center of the human
psyche receptive to any opening through which to burst. This is
Lila, the divine play of Hindu mythology, which like the heat

latent in firewood, is a creative energy poking around and rummaging about in the life history of each adult.

In spite of its tensions and contradictions, playmates receive life and play with it as it comes. This play with life is not a cultural activity that we try to do, nor is it a moral obligation that we have, it is not even an activity that we want to do; it is beyond the artificiality of commandment, license to do as we please or tension between duty and desire. "The spiritual goal is not a giant step backward into a personal or primordial infancy, but the regeneration of one's Original Nature," writes Conrad Hyers. It is something one merely is.

Wu-wei, an idea expressed in early Chinese thought and emphasized by the Taoists, fits here. It is translated by a variety of English words, including nonassertiveness, nonaction, unselfconscious responsiveness. Chuang-tzu describes this:

Joy does all things without concern;
For emptiness, stillness, tranquility, tastelessness,
Silence, and nonaction
Are the root of all things.

The spontaneity and apparent effortlessness of harmonious activity inherent in *wu-wei* is neither naivete or indifference, nor is it assertive and defiant. We see this concept in motion in the Japanese arts of judo and aikido. George Leonard's description of Richard Heckler's black belt ceremony in aikido is one that establishes the confluence of the ordinary with the extraordinary in a playground. Gathering impressions from others as well as himself, George creates a marvelous picture, making me wish that I had been present to share Richard's gift. He describes the event as "Something achingly beautiful and inevitable, an enactment in space and time of how the universe works, how things are." At one point in the routine, "It was as if Richard's hands were reaching beyond the four walls of the *dojo* to a point of balance in the cosmos." And "For his part, Richard was beginning to get the feeling that he was not 'doing' anything at all, that the movements

of his body were 'just happening' without thought or effort." It is
an expression of internal stability from which one can naturally
be in accord with all that is. *Wu-wei* is not a retreat from the
world, but full participation in the presence of life as it is. Only
then is one capable of becoming the ground of kindness.

Perhaps Pooh could, in a roundabout way, help us find our way.
If we thought for a moment of our current notion of relationship
as a "pit" and a new order as "home," we could then follow the
lead of Pooh, who suggests since we are not finding home, we
could look for something else like a pit and, not discovering it,
which would be fine because we would then surely find something else which we were not seeking, which could be what we
were really trying to find in the first place.

Cultures do not teach play, they can only allow it. It is as if a
presence subsides into you such that you know you are not just
physically and historically whole, but mysteriously whole. This
is a kind of innate, unconscious intelligence of the whole organism. The point is that understanding play is a matter of getting
the point intuitively, not from the practice of a discipline. One
does not learn play by reading books or watching children, but
by playing. It is a sense of belonging to something so large in
scope that it is invisible as a community, so large that there are
no outsiders.

Don Quixote and Dr. D.T. Suzuki, Werner Heisenberg and
Alice have known that there are realities that transcend the ability
of language to describe or explain. The nonsensical wording of a
Zen koan, the dual nature of electromagnetic radiation, the reality
of Wonderland and the disciplined chaos of play are impossible to
penetrate with logical reasoning. These are processes designed to
stop thinking. They must be grasped in terms of another awareness. The most important step in this process is being open to the
possibility. Not a given possibility, but any possibility.

What mystics have always known, some physicists are discovering, and most of us still find very difficult to grasp: to feel
comfortable with the notion that surprise and paradox belong to
the intrinsic nature of our own daily lives as well as belonging to
atomic physics and Zen.

How are we to rediscover original play? We can't try, and we
can't try not to try! Both of these efforts are counterproductive,

leading as they do to a situation in which the anticipated result cannot occur.

As Matthew Fox points out, "That is the question that sages of the world's great religions — Islamic and Buddhist, Hindu and Christian, Jewish and African and Indian tribal religions — asked themselves and which they devised deliberate methods or strategies to achieve." There is an inherent paradox here. How do we use cultural strategies to go beyond culture?

In play, we re-experience the paradox that occurred at birth: Life is both intoxicating and panicky. The transmigration from the womb — our first matrix of possibility — through the four inches of birth canal, writes Ashley Montagu in *Growing Young*, is the most hazardous journey a human being ever takes. It is also the most creative. Joseph Chilton Pearce describes paradox as the threshold to truth, an entry point from one way of thinking into another. The simple yet difficult truth of the paradoxes of play is that a change in viewpoint dissolves the paradox. Once experienced, we can smile and put a question mark after the supposedly firm reality of our logical statements and irrefutable, sophisticated reason.

The learning necessary in this quest does not happen willy-nilly, simply by sitting and waiting for it to come. On the other hand, it doesn't come from striving. This quest is paradoxical: We must first give up our efforts to find what we are looking for. This is sort of like trying to find a dim star in the evening sky; it disappears when you try to focus on it, but as soon as you give up that focus, you see it peripherally, knowing it to have been there all along.

We may try hard and compete to get a job and rise on the ladder of success in our careers, but a vocation is different. It is not won. It is not a limited good. There's no one to impress; there are no leaders, no followers. To seek it is to preclude the idea that you already have it. And if you already have it, there is no need to go about looking for it, "as if it were elsewhere, alien, but to acknowledge, use, and *be* it. Hence the act of seeking and striving must itself be turned into the non-act of not-seeking and not-striving," says Conrad Hyers. We have to be careful not to misinterpret the idea as one of laziness, passivity or intentional caprice. This would be to miss the point altogether.

This paradox is descriptive of play with wolves. Once I gave up control, I found that it was unnecessary. When I entered an enclosure to play with seven cavorting, anxious three-year-old wolves, there was no question of who had control inside. They were much faster and stronger than I was. So I let go of the fear that would require that I be in control. I walked in and felt comfortable. Standing up, I kept the wolves somewhat away from me. I decided to sit down and get closer to them. All seven were alert to the message I was giving. I was the only one who wasn't ready for the play bout that was about to happen. All seven of the wolves trotted up and converged on top of me. Underneath that pile of fur, paws and jaws I felt a tightening spread across my shoulders, signaling some tension. Here was the nonplay message that contradicted my play message of sitting on the ground. Hambone, the dominant male wolf read my tension and placed his jaws over my head. His lower canines went in one of my ears; the upper canines went in the other ear. He clamped down his teeth just enough to firmly, but gently, hold my head, which he ever so softly placed on the ground. I recall thinking on the way down that Little Red Riding Hood was right, wolves do have very large teeth. As soon as I relaxed the tension in my shoulders, Hambone let me go. He was very careful; I was unhurt, and we continued playing.

Once I released my need for control, I found that the "need" was inside me. This is not building up courage to be with wolves, which would merely be another form of contest between human and animal. Then I would be back in the realm of trying to control either my fear or a wolf. In play there is no contest, no control. The trust of play remains both a healing relationship and a wonderful mystery for me.

I told this story to a group of junior high school boys following a play session. Later I learned from a counselor that during the week following our play, one of the boys argued heatedly with a teacher and was thrown out of class. Both teacher and student were righteously angry. The boy returned to his counselor, who reminded him of the importance of being centered and not using get-backs in conflict situations as he had heard from Fred in play and the wolf story. He listened, returned to class and is now passing a class he had been failing.

The Play Way:
Letting The World Tickle Your Heart

Play is a vocation and a quest requiring trust, fearlessness and action. Play is being aware and taking care without appearing to do much of anything. This integration of spirit and practice in useful and effective action is described as a "way" in Eastern thought.

A "way" consists of principle and practice. With the perfection of form through endless repetition, a person approaches the formlessness of principle. Combining them we have the play way. This is a repeated breaking through to our true nature, a repeated dropping of our ego disguises so that we can truly *play* our worldly roles.

I recall hearing a maxim attributed to Miyamoto Musashi, the Japanese master swordsman and artist: "All ways are one in the end." It is also true that all ways are one in the beginning. Play is the common ground of the universe. To commit oneself to play is to be molded, nourished and connected by this ancient, childlike wisdom, a ground of compassion, gentleness and grace that exists as a potential within all life. To realize such a potential, according to Mencius, is to dwell in the wide house of the world. As the oldest of the ways, play is our body/mind training before we are taught our cultural ways.

A delightful story told by T.P. Kasulis illustrates the relationship of form and spirit, principle and practice in play:

Walking along a mountain path in Japan, we come upon a rudimentary hermitage with a large temple bell suspended from a simple wooden pagoda. Unlike Western carillon bells, the Japanese bell has no clapper and is struck on the outside much as one might strike a gong (in this case by a small log suspended from the pagoda by two ropes). Admiring the excellence and the obvious age of the engravings on the casting, we hear the footsteps of the temple priest and turn to ask, "How old is this extraordinary bell?" Touching his palm to the massive casting, he responds, "This is about 500 years old, but" (removing his hand to point into the black void within the bell) "the emptiness within — that's eternal." He then proceeds to swing the striker back and forth, holding it lightly but firmly, with his two hands. Almost indiscernibly he releases it, letting it swing freely so that it strikes the metal casting. The even tone permeates the area from the distant mountains across the valley, beyond the tops of the cedars, back to the very foundations of the hermitage. It seems as if the bell had rung itself, as if even the leaves stopped rustling in the wind to attend to its music. Smiling the priest looks at us and asks, "Now, please answer my question. Where did the sound come from — from the metal casting or from the emptiness inside?" Taken aback, we are dumbfounded. Still smiling, the monk turns, walking back to his hermitage.

To refine the analogy: Think of the casting of the bell as form or practice, and the hollow center as principle. The bell's function, the ringing of its unique tonal quality (play), is located neither in the casting (form) nor in its emptiness (principle). Without the hollow center (principle), the bell (play) would be a metal slab (body) that might clang (move) but certainly could never emit music (play). On the other hand, the hollowness (principle) without the casting (form/practice) could only produce the rushing echo of silence. For the bell (play) to resound, both the Being (form/practice) and the Nonbeing (principle) of the bell (play) are necessary.

We might have raised the log and let it go, sounding the bell. Our response to the monk is the same as in play. Don't think. Just play. To play too softly is to be afraid of the other. On the other hand, to be too forceful is also to be afraid of the other. For the bell to ring and for play to happen, there must be a harmonious blending. But to allow life to happen without our interference is much more difficult to actualize than to talk about.

The quest itself, wherever and however it is undertaken, is universal; for while we are certainly a part of a culture, we are undertaking an adventure that is truly metacultural in scope. In our personal quest we are extending the influence of the source of all order.

Regardless of culture, quest training and discipline contains three elements: (1) an openness to experience life's mystery, (2) a capacity for fearlessness to meet the unknown and (3) a willingness to practice steadfastly. Fearlessness moves one to all.

Openness moves all to one. Without openness there is no ground of potentiality to support fearlessness. Without fearlessness there is no means of actuality to reveal mystery. Through practice, openness and fearlessness become kindness. In questing, we are continually attempting to reach within and beyond ourselves; and in striving within the limits of our finite works, we overcome our earthly nature and generate the promise for which we long. Questing, then, is about ordinary people, through commitment and warmth, fearlessness and humility, living extraordinary lives.

To rediscover the code we have to be immersed in play, there has to be a genuine experience; then the mind reflecting on it gets to subtler and subtler dimensions of its inherent kindness. It is only then that we can release the child who wants to come out and play with the world in a truly open way. Share yourself; you will not be required to do anything beyond what you are able.

Just be present and play at this very moment. If you can play with the harassing, bedeviling and boring reality that is in front of you moment by moment such as diapers, food spills, phone calls, attacks — constantly failing, accepting failure and beginning again — this perfectly ordinary day might become extraordinary. Play then becomes a sanctuary; when this happens, you will no longer think of play as leftover time, but as an indispensible part of your relationship with life.

"Getting Down And Dirty:"
Playgrounds As Divine Territory

True places are not found on maps.

Herman Melville

Out beyond ideas of right doing and wrong doing, there is a field.
I'll meet you there.

Rumi

Oh, what a joy to clamber there,
Oh, what a place for play,

With the sweet, the dim, the dusty air,
The happy hills of hay!

Robert Louis Stevenson

Playgrounds are geographic artifacts of cultural play. Fields of grass and dirt, courts of hardwood, asphalt and concrete are demarcated by lines of paint and chalk. There are sand areas with plastic, steel and concrete structures created by planners. Such playgrounds are subject to the whims of society's evaluation of children's play.

During my graduate studies, I submitted a proposal to the Seattle Model Cities Program for small neighborhood playgrounds that local children would help design. The proposal went to Washington, D.C., where it was cut because it was too expensive. I asked a planner how they were going to plan playgrounds in the Model Cities area. He said they would drive up and down the streets, and where they could find land cheap enough that was not planned for anything else, it would be made into a playground. When I mentioned that such planning was exactly what put them in the unacceptable position they were in now, he shrugged his shoulders. He knew it as well as I; children and play are leftovers in the minds of adults.

These habitual models of play space are useless here. We must allow ourselves to be stripped of all cultural categories. An original playground is beyond geography. Geography and planning cannot hope to comprehend, much less outline an original playground. Trying to demarcate an original playground is like laying the European system of geographical land measurement on top of the Native American sense of earth as Mother. Original play has an extra dimension that enables a bit of earth to be a bedrock, firm enough to support life itself. It is divine territory, so vast that we can go on exploring it forever and never map its dimensions.

The way to play is nowhere and everywhere. Life's playgrounds are available anywhere on earth, a place and time of refuge from turmoil, strife and predatory beings. Places that evoke interior resonances based on real experience are sanctuaries.

These cozy playgrounds are easy to recognize; we have all spent time there — attics, lofts, ponds, trees, fields, streams. Indeed this is a rich sense of belonging. All infinity can be contained in an overstuffed chair comforted by a teddy bear, a quilt and a dream.

The playgrounds of original play require less of us and give more. The rolling of waves, the smell of hay piled to the eves of the barn, the flickering of golden aspen leaves — how remote from cultural play space these may seem. Sense impressions of childhood playgrounds are ciphers of welcome, belonging and well-being, all invitations to abide. Play combines landscape and "inscape." Landscape being those patterns, forms, surfaces and movements that are external to the self. "Inscape" is the dissolution of such boundaries and a merging of personal horizons with the other. In this process we are led from the outer nature of things to the inner spirit of life.

Finding A Playground

A playground is a geographic convergence of life forms, a warp and woof of being and environment. We indeed can find playgrounds anywhere. This is the way things are on earth.

Each playground has qualities found only by being there. Some places feel better than others, some will entice you, some offer a kind of intimacy, others a personal identity. It may be a place for visions or simply a rest. I cannot tell you where this will be; you will know when you open up to the possibility of such places. Here are some clues.

1. Finding a playground takes time. Don't rush. Wander about. If you are new at this, watch a dog or cat search out a place to take a nap. They understand that everywhere is not the same. Sit down like a child and be prepared to let go of all your preconceived ideas. When you forget everything, everything becomes a teacher. Playgrounds enchant, teach and astound; follow humbly or you shall learn nothing.

2. Finding a playground is a mutual choosing; it chooses you as you choose it. Find a place that feels good, a small place; not a mountain or a lake, perhaps a tree, a rock or a pile of leaves — someplace you fit.

3. Once adopted, a playground becomes more than landscape; it is a "heart/mindscape." It will be a place you can ask hard

questions, ones that take a while to answer. Listen. Its
wisdom is older than you. Be patient. You need to take time
for something this important.

4. Treat your playground as an old friend.

5. Playgrounds are not owned. Never say of them, "This is
   mine to do with as I please." You are responsible for the
   path you leave behind.

6. Something of yourself is left behind. If you are aware, your
   playground will give you special gifts — a feather, a little
   rock, a feeling. And you, too, may wonder like the Kiowa
   elder Ko-sahn: Will I become in my sleep "that old purveyor
   of the sacred earth, perhaps, that ancient one who, old as
   she was, still had the feeling of play"?

Playmates As Guides

There are children playing in the streets who could solve my top problem.
They have a dimension of knowing I have lost long ago.

Robert Oppenheimer

What we give to animals [and each other] at the moment of giving is
the fact of our relationship. If we give them respect and honest attention, that is how they know us, and that is the bridge we travel toward
one another.

Joan McIntyre

Like the abandoned hulk of a rusty car left by the roadside,
childhood is in a general state of neglect. On recent trips to
South Africa and the Cheyenne and Navaho reservations, Zulu,
Navaho and Cheyenne elders complained to me that children in
their tribes no longer speak of what is first and oldest in the spirit
of their respective peoples, but only of modern things. To play
with the world is a quickening of life making "young and immediate what is first and oldest in the spirit of man," in the words of
Laurens van der Post. This is precisely the reconciliation between
the individual and the life we have abandoned.

Do you recall what it was like to first discover and play with
your toes, a leaf, water, a star?

Remember play's summons? I recall my friends' sing-song voices calling my name from the front yard, the light from the morning sun reflected by a mirror on the kitchen wall and horses' whinneying from the barnyard.

Do you recall what it was like to return from play to the world of adults?

Adult: "Where were you?"

Child: "Nowhere."

Adult: "What were you doing?"

Child: "Nothin.'"

Adult: "Who were you with?"

Child: "No one."

Children often go out to play nowhere, to do nothing with no one. Trees, clouds and rocks do the same. Actually the child is doing what the cosmos is doing — being. It's not that he or she is purposefully deceitful or evasive. But the child knows that it is impossible to inform those who have not taken or who have forgotten the adventure.

The playmate and the adult do not often have the same idea of play. Adults approach play out of fear, with the authority of those who *know*. For children, on the other hand, play is written in their hearts. That is why they can play with authenticity.

The ninth-century Zen Master Huang-po described this distinction:

This pure Mind, which is the source of all things, shines forever with the radiance of its own perfection. But most people are not aware of it and think that the Mind is just the faculty that sees, hears, feels and knows. Blinded by their own sight, hearing, feeling, and knowing they don't perceive the radiance of the source.

For an adult, coming out to play with the world is like Alice meeting the unicorn in Lewis Carroll's *Through The Looking Glass:*

"I always thought they were fabulous monsters!" said the Unicorn. "Is it alive?"

"It can talk," said Haigha, solemnly.

The Unicorn looked dreamily at Alice, and said "Talk, child."

Alice could not help her lips curling up into a smile as she began: "Do you know, I always thought Unicorns were fabulous monsters, too! I never saw one alive before!"

"Well, now that we *have* seen each other," said the Unicorn, "if you'll believe in me, I'll believe in you. Is that a bargain?"

"Yes, if you like," said Alice.

A child is born through the rending of the womb, a playmate is born through the rending of the dimensioned world. Within each of us there is a guide, an inner playmate, a Pooh, an Alice, a Peter Pan, an Odysseus anxious to undertake a journey and bring new worlds to light. To play again would be to know truth in the original, pre-Socratic sense of *atathia,* to be ripped out of darkness and born into the womb of the universe. To become a playmate is to participate in original play, which is prior to the distinction between self and other, holy and profane, cosmos and chaos, prior to the knowledge of guilt and shame.

There is more than a little bit of terror here — a terror that is a counterpart to wonder. Going into play requires that I let go of my adult habit of discriminating. We are beginners again, face-to-face with the infinite mystery of life, reborn into a world we didn't create and don't comprehend. We must make the unknown a playmate.

In play I leave behind a world where everything is prisoner captured in a cage called a name. Adults, for example, are always asking me what it's like to play with South African or Hungarian children compared to American kids. Or, how do I play with a child with autism or cerebral palsy? The answer is that I do not play with their cultures, diseases or "special needs." I play with an essence that exists prior to culture or disease. The playmate relationship carries with it none of the obligations, duties, dignities or rules of cultural roles such as parent-child, teacher-student, therapist-client, observer-observed or winner-loser. Only then is play able to teach, astound and enchant us, revealing the most ingenious resemblances and relations. The doors are opened. The richness of life pours forth. Everything is fantastic, disquieting and sublime. And frightening! The opening of my mind continues to be a subtle yet painful process. But stripped of all its predictability, every perception becomes a discovery; and free of all I believe and know, I find kindness.

As green makes red "sing" in a painting, a playmate brings grace to an adult. The French novel *Renee Mauperin* provides an image of such a blend. In Renee Mauperin's garden a horticulturist makes rose bushes climb the entire length of a spruce, thereby the old tree can "wave roses in its green arms." Like the horticulturist who had the kindness to put roses into the arms of an old tree, should we consent to it, the playmate puts the grace of a child into the body of an adult.

If you want to learn how to play, go to children and play with all your heart. It seems that it was no accident that it was young children who literally tugged on me until I joined them. Sages from many of the world's traditions, including Jesus, Lao-tzu, Black Elk (the Dakota holy man), Zen Master Takuan, Saraha (the Buddhist saint and sage) and Sri Ramakrishna remind us that in order to reclaim the wisdom and love we yearn for, we must again become as children.

It is important to be clear about what is being recommended. Erich Fromm suggests that:

Basically there can only be two answers. One is to overcome separateness and find unity by regression to the state of unity which existed before awareness ever arose, that is, before man was born. The other answer is to be fully born, to develop one's awareness, one's reason, one's capacity to love, to such a point that one transcends one's own egocentric involvement, and arrives at a new harmony, at a new oneness with the world.

It is not a return to a second childhood per se, but a recovery as a sage of the lost characteristics of childhood: simplicity, unity, innocence, immediacy, spontaneity, naturalness. Infants have the mind of nonattachment because they have never experienced it. The playmate comes from experiencing a life of success and failure and still chooses to love in the world as it is.

Finding A Playmate

Finding a playmate can be difficult, especially if you have had
little practice. I cannot teach you, but I can give you some clues
that have been shared with me by my playmates.

1. First, you'll need to believe that, like love and faith, Santa
   Claus and quarks, playmates exist. A playmate can be
   anyone or anything, real or imaginary.
2. They may arrive when you least expect. If you listen
   attentively with your heart, you will hear the faint, gentle
   stirring of a playmate amidst the rush and uproar of your
   daily life. If you make your mind very silent and stop
   talking to yourself, close your eyes and really see, you
   may, if neither your eye nor your mind is already focused,
   come upon a playmate.
3. Don't let anyone else choose your playmate or tell you
   who it should be. You don't need to tell anyone about your
   playmate.
4. Finding a playmate takes time. Don't try too hard. Trying
   doesn't work. You'll know when you find one. Don't read
   about playmates. You will not find the playmate before
   you, face-to-face, in a report or a file or an abstract. Humbly be present and know nothing.
5. Have alone time with your playmate. Getting to know
   your playmate requires 100% attention. If this seems difficult, trees, rocks, kittens and young children can help
   you with this. You need to be together without others to
   disturb or distract you. Play takes place between individuals not crowds.
6. You do not own or possess your playmates. Like butterflies
   and dolphins, summer winds and mountain streams, they
   don't stand still for holding on to.
7. We often have a residue of fascination after playing with
   an "exotic" animal. It is tempting to think, for example,
   that a grizzly is more exciting than a child, that dolphins
   are more playful than other forms of life. Always remember that in their specialness, each playmate is nothing special. All life is of only one kind.

We are all faced with the same choice: to explore life's mystery. Deciding to set out as a playmate is a crucial event. Life becomes a playground offering unimagined possibilities for kindness. To accept the cosmic invitation to "come out and play" is only the beginning. So too the final hexagram in the *I-Ching*, The Book of Changes, is the symbol of the not-yet-complete suggesting a parallel to spring which leads out of winter's stagnation into the fruitful time of summer. As Chuang-tzu has Lao-tzu respond to a disciple who inquires about being like an infant:

"Is this perfection?"
Not at all.
It is only the beginning;
This melts the ice.
This enables you to unlearn
So that you can be led by Tao,
Be a child of Tao.

8

Reenchantment:
The Mind Of Play

It is emptiness that makes possible all forms of play.
Michael Adam

One does not dream with taught ideas.
Gaston Bachelard

When you walk across the fields with your mind pure and holy, then from all the stones and all growing things, and all animals, the sparks of their souls come out and cling to you, and then they are purified and become a holy fire in you.
From an old Hasid Master

The Seeds Of Mystery

"Long Ago, when wishing still could lead to something . . ." This something — this numen or regenerative life force which we were born feeling — exists around us throughout our lifetimes. Although it seems to elude us, we must reexperience it if we are to move beyond contest as our measure of survival on earth.

It is difficult to write about this sense of "something," so it is best to acknowledge my participation in a mystery about which I seem to know less and less as the years go by. I do best if I remember that mystery reveals itself to those who have a "long youthfulness of heart," as Maurois says. The world is transformed, not through sleight of hand or deception, but rather by unknowing. Albert Einstein knew this: "The most beautiful experience we can have is the mysterious. It is the fundamental emotion which stands at the cradle of true art and true science. Whosoever does not know it and can no longer wonder, no longer marvel, is as good as dead, and his eyes are dimmed."

We were christened with this sense of wonder. Insofar as we play with the world, wonder is naturally present. I remember a game that David taught me. We would lie on our backs on a small hill, tilting our heads so that we were looking at the horizon upside down. He told me that if I looked upside down, I could see the roundness of the earth. I tried it again. I was giddy, with no sense of being on a flat surface. I craned my neck back further; I could see only a curved reddish line blending into a blue-purple sky lightly sprinkled with faint twinkling blue-white stars. Like an odd-shaped barnacle, I felt stuck to the surface of a big blue-white agate, spinning through space in a cosmic game of marbles.

This sense of wonder is not perplexity or puzzlement that is something to resolve. Wonder is something to savor, like gazing at a star-filled night sky. If we see with our eyes, we can only see what's there; but when we see with a sense of wonder, we are not limited by what is there.

For play to enchant it must have the reality for us that Shambhala has for the Tibetan yogi who seeks it, or that secret friend in a secret place you had when you were four. The mind is as pregnantly open as the blank backgrounds in a traditional Chinese or Japanese landscape, in which most of the background consists of "nothing." Such a picture invites play by presenting emptiness out of which to create forms. In the same way, play's emptiness is not nothingness, but fullness with which to create. Then, as composer John Cage put it, "Each something is a celebration of the nothing that supports it."

Within us, then, there remains a spark of light that can dispel the shadows cast by our fears. We create our fears, but the source of light, like the sun, comes from beyond us, transcending not only what we know, but what we are able to know. This is the playful mystery that evokes the divine from the profane, the extraordinary from the ordinary.

Play informs, nourishes and heals, like the protoplasm of life beginning to quicken within tree buds in March. Play comes with the gift of life and is a response to the source within each of us that seeks to join with life's wisdom. Play's power is deeply physical, poetic and mythical, penetrating sinew and spirit far below the conscious levels of thought, returning us to our origins, joining the beginning to the end, the child and the old one, the curious and the wise. To play with the world is to be seized by it, just as your mind is when captured by a flight of fancy or awakened to ecstasy. It is a time of not-knowing. It is asking questions with no answers.

Where does rain begin? How high is the sky? It is having a discussion with your teddy bear. It is a child building sand castles or Henri Poincare discovering Fuchsian functions or Lao-tzu wondering about a butterfly. It is Albert Einstein at 15 wondering, "What do you suppose it would be like if you could sit on the front end of a light beam and travel with it through the night?" It is Copernicus' playful imagination of what he assumed to be a more beautiful scheme from a stationary central earth to one that moved around a central sun. It is the Wright brothers flying against conventional knowledge. It is the violins of Antonio Stradivari made from discarded, broken, waterlogged oars he found on the Venice docks.

Most of us need reminders of play's mystery. We must allow children and nature to take us by the hand and heart; then the imprint of God is tangible in the simple treasures and small wonders of our everyday lives, which contain the seeds of mystery. I believe each of us is in some way potentially receptive to this transcendent mystery. Often through some very little thing — being kind to someone, experiencing a moment of nature's beauty — without quite realizing it, we make contact and are enchanted.

The first essential in play practice is to realize the "Ah!" of Life. And what better guides to the vast storehouse of earth's wonders and imagination's delights than children and nature? To be within their realms is to feel the contagion of something deep within the human heart. It is humorous, sorrowful, wistful and whimsical, quiet and rambunctious.

Some playgrounds are communal, time-spaces of understanding and sharing with others on their own terms. Like feeling the tickle in my hand and in my heart when a chickadee explores her perch on my finger. Like feeling the tingle of excitement in the back of my neck and the heightened sense of awareness when I find fresh grizzly tracks in river mud.

Rilke reminds us that life is not a problem to be solved but a mystery to be experienced. Then, unadulterated, we are free to play. Ferrucci tells us that Tchaikovsky heard a deep bass note, which he imagined coming from earth's movement through space. Debussy heard mermaids in sea waves. French painter Eugene Delacroix saw tiger's markings in tidal patterns. William Blake saw a fearful presence in a knot on a log.

Dennis and I were out on the school lawn one day, just wandering, open to everything and not worrying. We lay down on our tummies, separating blades of grass with our fingers. Dennis saw a friend in a ladybug. He put his finger gently under her and lifted her up to his eyes. He was so excited he shivered all over as he talked to her.

Some playgrounds are solitary — a nest for dreaming in the branches of an apple tree, a pasture with a hill for watching the summer clouds float by, a cliff for perching to watch hawks spiral upward. Alone spaces are not merely geographically private places. There is an opportunity for harmony here. Anthony Storr relates how Admiral Byrd on his daily walk at 4 P.M. recorded such an experience:

"Harmony, that was it! That was what came out of the silence — a gentle rhythm, the strain of a perfect chord, the music of the spheres, perhaps.

"It was enough to catch the rhythm, momentarily to be myself a part of it. In that instant I could feel no doubt of man's oneness with the universe."

I often wandered the mountains of Montana searching for such spots. Hiking is too goal-directed for me when I'm in the mountains; I wander here and there, going wherever my intuition guides me.

One summer day I found a niche on a serrated summit, near Big Sky. I was just another sky-shouldering bulge on the ridge. Could I sit as quietly as the centuries-old petrified stump nearby? Could I be a form existing apart from any classification? Just aware. A being. Well, I didn't do as well as the stump or the pink moss campions in the crevices. Rock waited quietly, flowers bloomed calmly and I squirmed restlessly.

Play transforms earth from the commonplace into heart-warming spaces. These are places of grace where reality opens up and one knows that he or she is at home. It is a most indefinable thing to speak about the feeling, yet it is decisive because in the end it is what defines a sacred playground.

I remember walking among the ruins of Glastonbury Cathedral in England with Jan, Des and Catherine. It was a cool, rainy day. Every so often the sun would splash some warmth on the rolling countryside. I touched one of the cathedral walls and felt something. It was like the sun's warmth on the ancient stones, but it was more than that; it was a deeper warmth coming from inside the stones. Each of us felt an energy there.

Perhaps just once in a lifetime we ought to experience how space becomes sacred. We ought to give ourselves up to a particular patch of earth, to look at it from as many different possible perspectives as we can, to wonder and be. We ought to touch it and play upon it. There is such a special place for me in Montana. I remember the colors of the blue Montana sky, the red-orange of Indian paintbrush, the sepia brown of the stream, and the pungent odor of grizzly, bison and elk. This is what I call the bear-point place.

One summer day I was wandering the mountains north of Yellowstone Park. Seeing a fresh grizzly track in the mud of a streambed, I felt the heightened sense of awareness that comes when you realize that the landscape in which you are wandering has wildlife bigger than you. Nearby I found a daybed and some elk remains. I chose to leave the area and began walking down an elk trail through some lodgepole pines next to the stream. I stopped for a moment and looked around. Down on the ground, just in front of my feet, I saw something shiny — a fully formed obsidian spear point about six inches long and over an inch wide in the middle. It was beautifully made. I was so excited that I could hardly contain myself. I wanted to leave the mountains right away and show everyone my treasure. But I also thought I should leave it. I couldn't decide; I took it with me to my campsite and slept with it. When I awoke, I knew what I must do. During the night I realized that I had been given a gift from the Grandfathers; but the gift wasn't in the keeping, it was in the sharing. I was allowed to hold the spearpoint and share in its spirit. Now it was time for me to give it back so the next wanderer might find a treasure. I returned to the spot where I had found it and placed it in the cavity of a small tree stump next to the trail. I burned some sage and had some quiet time.

Play is an invitation to unlearn, to be a beginner. The greatest obstacle to my play is thinking that I already know how. In play, "non-knowing is a not a form of ignorance but a difficult transcendence of knowledge," says Gaston Bachelard. To arrive at the simplest understanding requires not activity, not thinking, not reasoning, not calculating nor busyness of any kind. One must simply bear in mind what it is one needs to know. This is being empty. It is allowing for natural pauses. It is a presence of absence, not an absence of presence.

When I first began playing with young children, I had no idea what I was doing. I just lay down on the ground, watched and listened. I noticed that their movements weren't random or chaotic, but simple with a kind of elegance; they were a visible expression of an invisible grace. Their hands didn't grab or hold on tight to each other; instead they seemed to caress with a relaxed lightness. They hugged as they moved into and rolled over each other. I felt them take rest periods that were so brief as to be virtually unnoticable. They invited me to play with quick, smiling glances and open-handed touch. Their care with me was obvious and sincere. I didn't want to interfere or stop their play, so I suppressed the urge to talk or to ask questions. This allowed me to take direction from and follow them. My emulation of them caused a great many unabashed but not condescending smiles. It became clear to me that learning to play was going to require more than reason and imitation.

I continue my apprenticeship with many children, including Christian, the four-year-old with cerebral palsy, with whom I play each week. Each day we play together is a new day in which we unfold with each other and explore new possibilities of motion and touch. He lies on his back, resting on a mat in the classroom. I whistle softly and call his name. He turns his head and smiles in recognition. I move slowly to his side, saying his name. He giggles and extends his body in excitement. I touch his hand, yet I am careful not to encroach upon him. I whistle. He squirms and smiles. I put my head within the range of motion of his arm and move in concert with his motions. I roll him over on top of me and he laughs out loud.

Our play is a continuous process of the unfolding of new activity. One day I sat him in my lap and began to slowly rock back and forth. His excitement increased as I extended our range of motion. Eventually I did an aikido back roll with him nestled in my lap. *Aha!* We had a new movement to share. Now when we get into our back roll position, I say to Christian, "Ready?" He excitedly presses his back into my chest and we roll back. We laugh together as we come up.

Christian's giggle reminds me of Nietzsche's famous aphorism: "If it be granted that we say Yea to a single moment, then in so doing we have said Yea not only to ourselves, but to all existence." Here, between Christian and me, lies the "magic stuff" of the universe, an alchemical transformation in which I am altered from a common, leaden adult into a precious playmate.

In the personal history of everyone in whom the playmate has survived conditioning, schooling and training, there are influences like Christian who help to keep us fully alive, who have encouraged without even trying, just by being. Other essentials may be acquired by study, but this mysterious, graceful spirit is an inherent quality and no amount of skill can reveal it, nor will the passing of time make one its owner. It is invisible and unfathomable, beyond the reaches of discursive thinking. If it — an inner presence not to be explained by its outward form — is found at all, it is found in the silent spaces of a clear, kind heart.

Other playgrounds are the legendary landscapes and secret lairs of our childhood reveries, which we cover over with the heavy snows of adult indifference. My friend Kevin Kemper, an arborist, told me when we first met that trees are special places. Hermann Hesse describes them as sanctuaries that preach the ancient law of life. "A tree says: A kernel is hidden in me, a spark, a thought, I am life from eternal life."

As a boy I had favorite trees on my uncle's farm. I used to climb up and sit eating apples in the orchard behind the chicken coop. Years later, I had walked past the troll tree many times, thinking it to be merely a large cedar with a cavernous hole in the trunk. Later my young friend's secret transformed the beautiful, old cedar into a magical tree. There is another such tree named Michael Angelo Sanzio Raphael. Opal Whiteley jumps off of the barn roof into his arms. As she says, "It is such a comfort to nestle up to Michael Angelo Sanzio Raphael when one is in trouble." He is a grand fir tree with an understanding soul. Bernard Berenson writes about losing himself in "some instant of perfect harmony" in a lime tree. "I remember — I need not recall — that I climbed up a tree stump and felt suddenly immersed in Itness, I did not call it by that name. I had no need for words. It and I were one." Sometimes we need a child's imagination and wonder to approach the playgrounds of the natural world. Such a playmate knows very well that clouds can be tickled in a quiet pond.

Play issues from the preconscious intuitions of one's whole being. As such it is not a matter of effort but of grace, not a matter of morality, but of vision. A playmate has nothing to teach, rather a presence to share. A playmate has no doctrines to preach, only the gift of kindness. The playmate does not try to be graceful, only to play with any of the 10,000 things that reveal it — a child, a dolphin, a butterfly perhaps. Then, aware of grace, we feel that we belong; we are of infinite value. Can we imagine that we are participating in the creation of the universe?

We miss the point and the play if we strive to play as a symbol of something grander like God or Tao. We must play with the being who is with us. The Zen exhortation to do spontaneously with all one's heart and mind what life presents is the living of the playful way. Every life form plays according to its own nature, and in this individual play is a universal understanding. The form and energy of my individual play is but a mirror of the universal soul wrought particular. When I play with a child, I play with a particular child and every child. This is the ground upon which compassion rests, expressed in Sanskrit as "*tat tvam asi*, thou art that." So, we play with a butterfly, and yet. . . . It is this "and yet . . . " that haunts us.

During a t'ai chi workshop at Esalen, I stood on the cliffs watching the grey whales swim south to Baja, the otters floating about amidst the kelp and the monarch butterflies fluttering among the trees. Chungliang Al Huang told us that if we moved as one with all that surrounded us, a monarch might alight on us. During a break in our sessions I took my *bokken* (a wooden sword) out on the lawn and practiced t'ai chi and aikido. A butterfly landed on the sword's tip and stayed as it sliced through space. It glided down and walked up and down on my arm. I put the *bokken* down and resumed t'ai chi with the butterfly. It stayed with me all afternoon, moving from me to Hillary to Al and back again. To watch Al move with the butterfly was truly to see two beings move as one. As dusk approached I placed the butterfly on a bush, said goodbye and left. In the morning I couldn't wait, I ran to the bush before breakfast. I'm not sure what I expected, perhaps to see the butterfly once more. The bush was empty. I glanced to the ground below the bush and saw four monarch butterfly wings in a neat pile. These wings are as Lynda Sexson writes, "precisely the stuff of the sacred."

Our play with an ordinary butterfly revealed the graceful whole that links and accords with all that is. This is an enormous leap from psychology, beyond geography and ecology to cosmology. It wasn't just that a butterfly and I were together; for a time the barriers between myself and others vanished. Kindness existed as a witness for the powerful love which lies beyond the fabrications of culture and species. Through play we have access to kindness which gives playmates their "supercultural" power.

Play is about experiencing "first times" again and again. "A good artist always feels the work anew" is as true of playmates as it is of Pablo Casals and Arturo Toscanini. In Japanese this concept is called *Ichigo, ichie,* meaning, "one time, one meeting." In play, I never play with the same playmate twice. This is much more difficult to actualize than it may seem. This means that I must be prepared to give up every preconceived notion and follow humbly wherever I am led. This is as true of children I see for the first time, as it is for those with whom I play every day.

Etienne taught me a very important lesson early in our play together. She, Anthony and I played all over the house and yard. One day on the front lawn in the midst of our play she ran in the house crying. I thought she had been physically hurt, so I ran after her. It was true she had been hurt, but not physically. When I asked what was wrong, she said, "You don't play with me like you do Anthony." At first I didn't know what she meant. Did she mean that I was to be as physical with her as I was with Anthony? No, that wasn't it. She felt that I didn't blend my play with her abilities. I wasn't present for her. I wasn't playing with Etienne, but whom she had been; whom I thought she was. I am continually practicing this lesson.

I must play with the person who is in front of me, not the person I played with yesterday nor the one with whom I want to play, but with the one who is actually present. I do not read charts or files, nor do I read about childhood diseases. I remain as ignorant as possible of the categories to which a child has been assigned by adults to fit society's needs. I play with the person, not her or his illness, disability or culture. These latter designations are categories assigned by others. Ferrucci reminds us that French physiologist Claude Bernard, British biophysicist Francis Crick, Charles Darwin and Louis Pasteur all shared this view of letting go of knowledge in order to approach life afresh with an openness of mind that allows everything in.

For the mind to begin to play, to become reenchanted with the world, we must relinquish allegiance to what our cultures say is true. To "play by heart" is to give up one's isolated intellect for the intelligence of the entire universe. But this shouldn't worry us because, as Joseph Chilton Pearce asserts, "Children are driven by millions of years of genetic encoding to follow intuitively their only road to survival and intelligence — which is play." We must leave that which we know for that which we do not know. This is just what is required of any explorer, whether it is a young child learning to walk, Columbus taking a trip away from southern Europe, an astronaut exploring space, or you and me exploring play with children, animals and each other.

As the higher powers of grace can dispel those of lower states of being, so too can the removal of fears evoke play. If we are to "come out and play," we must open ourselves "to the wonder, at once terrible and fascinating, of ourselves and of the universe of which we are the ears and eyes and mind," says Joseph Campbell. Sainte-Beuve described grace as "an inner state which before all things is one of love and humility." This grace is a readiness or emptiness in which to receive the gift of what is already existent in the nature of things. The graceful emptiness of original play contains all: the sun and the cyclone, the lion and the lamb, the dewdrop and the ocean, and you and me.

9

"And To Him Who Knocks." Trusting The Spirit Of Play

Trust is power.

Lao Tzu

Understanding is the reward of faith. Therefore do not seek to understand in order that you may believe, but make the act of faith in order that you may understand; for unless you make an act of faith you will not understand.

St. Augustine of Hippo

In love there's never a pure identity because love involves two and yet the two become one. That's the great mystery.

Fr. Bede Griffiths

We are seeking the experience of being alive. This seems easy enough. The difficulty is that in order to find it, we must not be afraid of life. Play requires a profound fearlessness with which we can expand ourselves trustingly into the unknown. If we let go, we find in play a source of trust more profound than we had previously imagined. But to perceive its inner essence, we must be empty. John Keats put this idea well in one of his letters: "The only way to strengthen one's intellect is to make up one's mind about nothing." This apparent self-forgetting is really cosmic remembering. There are no experts in play. There are no ranks, no prizes, no champions. In the mind of the expert there are few possibilities; in the mind of the beginner the possibilities are limitless. As remarkable as this kind of trust seems, it is nothing special to playmates.

The trust of play is an invitation to a mystery, and within the original mystery is a deeper mystery — and the gate opens, again and again. Such a great mystery demands equally great patience, fearlessness, surrender and love. It is only with these that we can hope to dissolve what appears to be a Gordian knot of paradoxes that seem to block our way.

The first of these was mentioned as Pooh's paradox in Chapter Eight. It is well put by Abu Yazid al-Bistami: "This thing we tell of can never be found by seeking, yet only seekers find it." There are more: A focused unconditional love for one encompasses every one; determined practice achieves that which cannot be practiced; thinking doesn't work, doing doesn't work, not thinking doesn't work, not doing doesn't work; there is only one "right" move and no "wrong" moves; the quest that appears to be of the highest spiritual attainment is here amidst our everyday situations;

letting go of trying to know brings about the most profound comprehension: knowing by heart.

The trust of play is a natural wisdom, a bond that saturates one's life. It is like a seventh sense, enabling one to detect what is far away, hidden and innermost. As Harvey Cox points out, faith is really a form of play.

As playmates we must trust the relationship to go in any way, unencumbered by our desires. To play without conditions can be especially difficult, but it is the only way. Teilhard de Chardin told us:

Some day, after we have mastered the winds, the waves, the tides and gravity, we shall harness . . . the energies of love. Then for the second time in the history of the world, man will have discovered fire.

Fearlessness is living this realization in everyday life. As playmates we are no one special, yet we are committed to a practice that is a lifelong training of spirit. As playmates we experience an unconditional state, if only momentarily, in which all winning and losing is impossible, for we have nothing to prove, hide or lose. We feel the great relief of letting down our guard to become a conduit for an empowering, inexhaustible source greater than we can imagine.

Rabindranath Tagore writes:

When Buddha said to men, "Spread thy thoughts of love beyond limits," when Christ said, "Love thine enemies," their words transcended the average standard of ideals belonging to the ordinary world.

Drawn from our inner depths, from a realm beyond culture, this wisdom is available to all humans.

"Come to God," said Madame Guyon, "as a weak child, one who is all soiled and badly bruised — a child that has been hurt from falling again and again. Come to the Lord as one who has no strength of his own."

We certainly have been badly hurt; violence, abuse, aggression not only seem endemic, but so many are resigned to living and bringing up children as if such a state were inevitable. In a conversation with Najagneq, an Inuit shaman, Dr. Knud Rasmussen learned of the strong spirit, Sila, who is the "upholder of the universe," and whose words come not through ordinary speech but through such forces as "small innocent playing children who understand nothing."

And what does Sila say?

"*Sila ersinarsinivdluge:* Be not afraid of the universe."

Madame Guyon and Najagneq set out the parameters of the trust required in our quest: Let go, there is nothing to be afraid of. Children, even after being so badly hurt can demonstrate a fearlessness in their play that is utterly disarming.

The quest to be a playmate is demanding. How could it be otherwise? Developing and exercising this compassion is the great adventure; to do less is merely to go on vacation. The only way to draw oneself out — to be educated — is to sacrifice oneself. If we do not abandon the self, there is superficiality and self-expression which is insufficient for the continuation of the adventure.

Trust provides the recuperative energy source — psychologically, physiologically and spiritually — for authentic play. A playmate says, "I trust. " Period. There are no conditions, no obligations. What or who are we to trust in? Self? Other? Country? Play-trust is not housed in something tangible like money or a husband or a country. It is a relationship we have with the universe.

Robert helped me feel trust in my tummy, not my head. Robert and I met in the mountains east of San Diego. He was directing a lamentation experience I attended with my friend Ed. Robert placed me alone for 24 hours in my sacred circle with great sincerity and kindness. After the experience I was so taken by Robert that I called and made arrangements to visit. I discovered in the intervening time that he was internationally known in his field. On the drive up the coast to his home, I felt embarrassed about inviting myself to see him. I felt that I had nothing to offer, I just wanted to share time with him. I kept trying to come up with important topics to discuss. When I arrived, he graciously invited me in. I still had not come up with anything to talk about. He turned and said to me, "You know, Fred, I knew you were coming up here today, and I didn't know what to talk about with you." He knew exactly what I was feeling!

He introduced me to a trust game, which is utterly disarming in its simplicity. It is a game of giving and receiving played between two people. Robert's gift to me that day was a deep blue lapis lazuli that matches his eyes. But more than that, he gave me the wisdom to feel trust not in my thought-filled head, but in my empty tummy, which, he told me, knew about the stone before I arrived.

Sometime later I was to respond to a feeling in my tummy that reinforced Robert's lesson. In the mid-1980s, I had a delightful correspondence with Jean, a "mountain man" living in Switzerland. Jean and Nicole lived in a tepee. We shared poems and stories. In early February 1986, I received a small package including a letter written by Nicole and two gifts from Jean, a small knife and necklace made of Catlinite, antique glass beads and elk ivories. During the previous months I had written a story about my relationship with an "old one," a composite of the elders I'd experienced in my life. I knew right away that the story was for Jean, and I sent him a copy immediately. About a month later I received a letter from Nicole. She had received and read my story to Jean the day before he died peacefully in her arms.

The expansion of the heart can come in as many ways as there are life situations. It is in the invisible, nothing in particular and everything. We must trust in the new way before we are able to see its benefits. Of course, this is precisely what trust means. I learned this most important lesson in play from Paul.

Paul was in my kindergarten class. He had leukemia and his parents were afraid that physical play would hasten his death. For a number of months Paul and I touched in a variety of ways, but we avoided rambunctious play. He snuggled in my lap to read stories, I carried him on my shoulders, I lay down on the floor when we played with the blocks.

One day Paul came to me and asked if I would invite his parents to school for a meeting. The following afternoon the four of us met in the classroom. Paul began quietly, "I want to play with Fred. I know that I am not going to live as long as the three of you, but I want to live as if I were." His sincerity was powerful. There were tears in our eyes as we all agreed that he could play. When he came to school the following day, he was so excited and he played so fully that he was exhausted and had to stay home and rest the next day. The pattern of coming to school for a morning and resting the next continued. About a month later Paul died of leukemia.

Paul and I talked about death a number of times during our months together. He talked and I listened. Paul trusted in something beyond human beings. I'm convinced that Paul, at five years old, chose to play, knowing that it would shorten his life. I don't have any formula for what we shared, its power and certainty are ineffable. Paul shared with me not a content, but a presence. The mystery remains, but the question about play's meaning has vanished.

As remarkable as this trust is, it seems to me that Paul treated it as if it were nothing special. The more he trusted, the more unremarkable it was to him and the more extraordinary was his difference from my normal reality. Like breathing, play is a life-support system that says, "If I hadn't trusted it with all my heart, I couldn't have played."

Ferrucci retells a story from India that illustrates the intensity which is both a prerequisite and a consequence of play. A disciple asks his master what he needs to reach true realization. Taking him to a lake, the master pushes his head under the water, holding him under until the disciple can endure it no longer. The master asks, "What did you long for?" "To breathe," answers the disciple. "And how intensely?" inquires the master. "With all my strength," replies the disciple. "When you feel the same desire to reach the divine, you will be on the right track."

A dolphin dream reinforced the trust in play that Paul demonstrated. After returning home from Australia, I was bothered by continuing reports of whale and dolphin killings by humans "for fun." I learned that Old Charley, the first dolphin to become a friend at Monkey Mia, had been shot and killed. Two dolphins who became friends with humans in New Zealand were shot and killed. And in the spring of my return from Australia a beluga whale who trusted humans was shot and killed off the east coast of the United States. Cetaceans, like wolves and many other animals, should be brimming over with hatred and revenge, yet they continue to exhibit a remarkable trust toward us. As Jim Nollman put it in writing about an encounter with a dolphin entangled in a fisherman's net, "We reached the inescapable conclusion that this battered but quite aware animal trusted us humans more than we humans trusted each other." I just couldn't explain the apparent discrepancy between dolphin trust and sensitivity, and our killings. Then in a Sunday morning dream a dolphin told me that at their level of love there simply was no room for hatred or mistrust, only space for yet more trust. Such a powerful love — trust is immune to erosion either by suffering or fear. Paul knew this.

Where paths that have affinity for each other intersect the whole world looks like home, for a time.

Hermann Hesse

In Budapest, Hungary, Jan, Des, Catherine and I had the opportunity to play with a group of 15 children from 18 months to 11 years old. In the midst of our play session, a young boy held me at arm's length and hesitated for a moment. We were silent. He peered with gentle intensity, not at me, but beyond, somewhere within me. It was as if he threw open a door and asked, "Who is in there?" His eyes looked around as if he were exploring and fully taking in a place he hadn't been before. I was not wholly conscious, keenly aware of a fire between us. It was as if we were a unit and our bodies were only experiments for something much larger to work with. He tilted his head and smiled as if to say, "Yes, I am at home here." Reassured, he fell down on top of me and we continued playing. Two playmates had taken each other in. I had no knowledge to help dispel the mystery. I knew more deeply that God is at play with us.

Following a play session with Navaho kindergarten children, an elder who had stopped to watch, said to me, "Watching you play with children is like watching flowers grow." Playing in this way, we come to know the wonder of all things.

A child's grasp of my finger, a dolphin's touch, the trust felt in the nuzzle of a coyote are all such invitations to play. One autumn day I rested on a sun-warmed carpet of sycamore leaves in an enclosure at Wolf Haven. I was enjoying the large yellow leaves as they drifted to the ground, trying to guess which one would let go next. My reverie was soon shattered by Little Guy, a young coyote, pouncing on my chest and nibbling my beard. Suddenly, like the sweeping strokes of master swordsmen, we rotated together entwined in a tight spiral of motion. Then nothing, he left as suddenly as he arrived. He peered at me, flashing from tree to tree like the rapidly moving projections of a tachistoscope. I was reminded of the little girl who surprised me with play at Monkey Mia when I expected Holly. As is so often true among playmates, I never found out her name. These are instances of trust when so much life is compressed into so small a time/space. Such is the way of play.

A playground is a "trust area," an invisible magic circle surrounded and sealed off in such a way that whoever or whatever enters the field is embraced by it. In the trust area the anxieties and fears built up from our lives are temporarily bracketed. "It is almost as if nature, in its playfulness, was attempting to [pierce] through the barriers of logic with its synchronicities and moments of illusion," writes F. David Peat. The playground then becomes an exceedingly rich source of sacred experience.

I experienced this sense of sacred space when I was invited to play with children in Navaho country. I lived with a Navaho family and felt privileged to stay in their hogan, a few steps behind their home. It was an eight-sided structure made from logs and adobe and a hard red sand floor. In the center was a small wood-burning stove. I could feel as I entered that it was more than a house. This was especially true as I listened to the high desert winds swirl around the smokehole at night or awakened to the sun's warmth coming in the east-facing door. As I slept in it, I felt the truth in Trebbe Johnson's words, "Navaho people have nothing to fear, for they are in a holy place of 'long life and happiness.' "

On the school campus was a small building built like a hogan, with a skylight where the smokehole would be. When I wanted to play with just one or two children, I could use this space. I realize now that this was the appropriate place for Jenny and me to initiate our play together. In our play we experienced the sacredness of the cosmos.

I first met Jenny the day before, when my friend Eleanor brought me to the school. Eleanor and I were in her classroom when Jenny came by. But Jenny doesn't just come by. She's an amazing synthesis of sandstorm and stillness.

"Fred plays with children. Would you like to play with him?" Eleanor asked. Jenny glanced over, but didn't seem interested in me at all.

Then Eleanor added, "Fred plays with wolves." I thought this might be an opening, so I pulled out the photos I had and put them on a desk top. She gave them a cursory look and said, "Wolves eat you. They're mean."

"No," I responded, "you can play with them." She left as she arrived. I don't think she believed me. Eleanor smiled at me. "That's Jenny." I had no idea what was in store for me.

The next afternoon I was in the hogan on campus, waiting between play sessions. During these times I liked to open the door and lie on my back watching the clouds through the skylight. I felt someone watching me and looked up to see a young boy peeking in the door. I invited him in. Following him, to my surprise, was Jenny.

"What do you play?" Jenny asked.

"I'll show you." I crawled up to them, tucked my head and began lightly touching it to the boy's legs. Right away he leaped on my back. He knew what play was. Before I could turn around to crawl back to invite Jenny, she was on top of me too. We played, crawled and rolled with each other for an hour before they had to go. I walked them back to their classrooms. Jenny got permission to return, so we walked back. On the way we stopped to swing. When her peers began passing between classes, she hurried me on, obviously not wanting to be seen by the other teenagers. We went to the hogan. She wanted the door closed, worried again about being seen by her peers.

Jenny and I played all afternoon. She sat on my back; we tumbled around the room and we rested on each other looking at the clouds pass over the skylight. I knew she had never experienced play. Every man who had ever touched her before had hurt her or had wanted something from her, but this was sacred play, innocent and loving fun. I smiled in awe at the power of play to unite a 15-year-old Navaho girl and a caucasian male who had just met.

The next day Jenny jumped on my back as I was leaving the hogan to go to lunch. Later in the afternoon, as I walked through the school on my way to get my ride to the airport, Jenny was waiting for me. She was standing against the hallway wall with a number of other students. It was difficult for me not to bump her or give her a tussle, but I knew from everything that she had shown me that she didn't feel comfortable playing with me in sight of her classmates. We shared a wonderful look and a smile, undetectable to all but us. I left smiling at the difference between her first look and this one. In the traditional dome-shaped hogan, Jenny and I played and created sacred space attached to the earth and yet free to be taken with us.

Jenny, I and the hogan are blended and remembered by my body and soul. It is from such a warp and woof that a subtle natural tapestry is woven. And like the spider in a Navaho weaving, we leave an invisible trace.

I remember looking down on the vast expanse of desert and mesas from the small oval airplane window. Tears flowed as I thought of my play with Jenny. I feel enriched by Jenny and the trust that united us. I am reminded again of Paul's trust in life.

The following year I returned for another series of workshops and play sessions. Jenny was no longer in school, but she had heard about my arrival. She had two young sons. As my initial afternoon talk to the staff was about to end, I noticed her head bob around the door. I was delighted. When she looked in again, I ran out and chased her into the room through the back door. For a few minutes Jenny and I crawled under the tables and around the desks of the classroom. I hugged her and finished my talk. If the adults could only comprehend that our hug was the origin of my words. Without first loving, one cannot hope to restore balance, meaning and kindness to our lives. As Jenny and I walked back toward Eleanor's office, I pointed off beyond the homes clustered about the school toward the mesas turning purple in the late afternoon. "Do you ever go out there?"

"Sometimes, to be alone. When you come next time, you should come with me out there."

"I'd like that."

We walked in the school and began shoving each other down the empty hallway. Then we had a one-on-one play time in the lobby of the school. That evening we had a playtime in which we set out mats in an open space and anyone in the community was invited to attend. Jenny gave me a special gift. She brought her young sons to play with me.

Any environment can be a sanctuary for play. In South Africa I visited Patrick's House, a center for street kids in Capetown. When I arrived, the director thought that I was there to talk with staff and arrange for a later visit. I had to return to Johannesburg the next day and really wanted to play with children. So her assistant quickly went around the building collecting boys. It is important to be ready to play in the place that you have. The boys began to gather around us in the hallway. Some had just come from school; others came right off the streets. Their clothes were too big or too small, worn and tattered in a nondescript muddy brown color that comes from constant wear. Marian, Liz and I gathered together a group of boys to go out and play. A social worker, the house mother and a psychologist from child welfare wanted to come along, just to watch. We were a strange group as we moved down the block to a small park — three white women, two white men, a black woman and 15 black boys.

"What do you do about violence?" the psychologist asked me as we walked in front of 15 boys, aged eight to 18, careening down the street yelling, punching and kicking at each other. "You know, these kids live with it. Do you know the kind of lives these kids live?" Of course I didn't. I might be able to imagine some of the external conditions of living on the streets, but not the daily wear and tear on one's body and spirit.

The psychologist seemed unsure about what would take place at the park. I didn't tell him, but I was unsure too. I had to maintain an openness that allowed me to respond to whatever conditions we found. When we entered the park, I saw some young children playing on equipment. In the other direction I saw a sprinkler watering an area of grass. Suddenly, I ran through the spray of the lawn sprinkler toward a grassy area away from other children. The boys followed. I purposely fell down; they hurled themselves on top of me. We launched ourselves at and over each other like tumblers in a circus act. In the midst of our loud play were moments of silent rest when our bodies would lie across each other like strands of spaghetti. To my delight their house mother laughed heartily and bowled me over just like the boys. We all delighted in her laughter and energy. Then from underneath a pile of boys I motioned to Marian and Liz to join us. They crawled right in. The boys loved it. They were very physical, yet there were no punches or kicks. And they knew how to blend their play with each of the adults.

Laughter often erupted from us like so many active volcanoes as we tumbled and chased, hugged and rested. It didn't matter that we spoke different languages; we were beyond the use of words. Much too soon a maintenance man told us that he had to lock the gate so we had to leave. We were all disappointed. As we untangled I saw Liz sitting on the ground holding one of the boys, who was about 11 and dressed in a tattered shirt and shorts. He was snuggled in her lap as she rocked back and forth.

We were different on our walk back to Patrick's House. When we first went to the park, we walked separately like so many discordant notes, now we blended with meaning, like a chord. Tired and lighthearted, we walked slowly with our arms around each other, sharing quietly, enjoying each other's closeness. I walked with Marian and Nazeem, the tallest and one of the oldest boys. Marian acted as interpreter. He told me, "I would like to make a living playing too." Liz and the little boy were walking back with their arms around each other. Our tangible connectedness was evidence of something deeper. We had taken each other in. A "between-ness" existed that eclipsed words such as trust and love. I had sensed this before, but still I had no knowledge to help dispel the mystery I felt. This was play undistorted by culture.

As we left Patrick's House, one of the older boys, about 16, came out and stood on the sidewalk near the car. Our eyes met.

There was a connection that transcends lesser moments, where-in all differences are rendered unimportant. Single hearts changed, canceling out personal and private conflicts, thus pre-venting misunderstanding, hatred and revenge from spreading further that day.

The trust relationship is most powerful when all concerned are unburdened and independent. For it is only when one's cup is empty that it is able to hold the greatest possibilities, when it is most receptive for either exploration or as a reservoir for the trust of others. Only when this trust is neither hoarded nor bound does it continue to grow. Another's trust is not meant to possess as if it were a medal or a trophy. When we lose this sense of trust, we create self-righteousness.

When I moved to California, I was interested in surfing, but my fear of sharks was stronger. There was just no logical way it seemed that I could let go of my fears. Then I met Brian.

On a cloudy, fall day I pulled on my rented wet suit and looked down the cliffs at the few surfers bobbing up and down on the waves. I really didn't know why I was doing this. We walked down the cliff trail to the cold grey water. Brian didn't talk to me about what to do. I was to follow his lead. He held his board in front of his body, jumped off the rock into the outgoing water and began paddling out. I waited for the next wave to recede, jumped in and immediately began paddling. I wasn't prepared for the shock as the first wave broke over me and the cold water rushed through my wetsuit. It seemed to take forever to paddle out past the breakers next to Brian. "Just go with them and don't try," Brian suggested quietly. I was caught, thrown and tumbled off my board many times that day. A seal nibbled on my toes; I fell in the kelp. I even stood up ever so briefly.

Standing up on the board was wonderful, but what was so remarkable about the day was not what I did, but what Brian did. We shared a wonderful lesson about trust. I didn't trust myself, so I silently placed all of my trust in Brian. He served as a reservoir for my trust. He accepted all of it without a word or a sign of self-congratulation. He received and gave with wide open arms. Never did he try to hold on to it. The flow of trust was effortless. What Brian evoked naturally and what I strived to acquire coincided and something more was revealed. Brian knew how to allow trust to do the only thing it can do: flow without obstruction. I felt as if I was receiving it from beyond both of us. *The heart of the teacher and the heart of the apprentice are suddenly one.* At the end of the day we smiled, knowing that I had surfed, yet knowing also that *we* had surfed.

Brian knew that it was only by allowing me to retrieve my trust that I would have the energy to explore the possibilities of surfing. He trusted in a web of relationships. He showed me an open mind with no fixed opinions about me, the ocean or surfing. Nothing distorted the flow of information that came in that day. He did not rely on information gained solely through his senses, but looked beyond with an open heart and mind. In this way he shared surfing, infant-like, without unbalancing himself or me or the waves. Such trust is extremely powerful, freeing us from the physical and mental constraints that come from our being too full of fear to explore and too full of knowledge to grow.

Don't keep searching for the truth;
Just let go of your opinions.

Seng-Ts'an

Play develops a tolerance for ambiguity in which we must expect nothing, yet be ready for anything. This requires an open, flexible mind with no fixed ideas, no rigid plans, no expectations. In practice this means spending a great deal of time in quiet time. Play requires much patience to allow it to develop without trying to make things happen as we would like them to. In play we learn to share the richness of the apparently empty time/spaces as we do the rambunctious moments. In practice this means letting go of our impulse to control everything around us.

The universe, for all its vastness and complexity, is a wondrous harmony of which we are an integral part. Likewise our everyday lives are composed of many possibilities and unpredictable relationships. We can choose whether to live with this knowledge and participate in its grace or not. To approach such an environment with tension and stress upsets the mind, limits the perception of potential, and narrows the ability to respond. It is only by learning to see the whole picture that we can move with the greatest love, sincerity and calmness. This requires intense focus combined with absolute openness. To play is to interact with the world as "one," rather than as "won."

Play, then, is an act of trust in life, which was given in trust. One doesn't ask "Why?" to this kind of trust; it just is "so." Until one realizes this "just so-ness" of life, one is stuck in perpetual contests. Defy gravity and you break your neck; ignore play and you break your heart.

10

Being In Touch:
The Craft Of A Playmate

To play means to devote oneself so completely to the psychic process that one becomes its body: the psychic finds its fulfillment in the physical, and becomes form.

M.C. Cammerloher

It is clear that the decisive form of our intercourse with things is in fact touch. And if this is so, touch and contact are necessarily the most conclusive factor in determining the structure of our world.

Jose Ortega y Gasset

Reach Out And Touch Someone

(AT&T advertising slogan)

Once in a while, when everthing is just right, there is a moment of magic.
People can live on moments of magic.

Sarah Caldwell

Touch. There is no more

Arthur Dobrin

When you think you've reached the moment of truth, you've lost it. It is
in the wordless not knowing, the moment before thought begins.

Marie Tavroges

An Inuit carver sits in the translucent light of his igloo and turns the unworked walrus ivory lightly in his bronzed and gnarled hands. He whispers, "Who are you? Who hides within?" He turns it slightly and then in a moment of stillness breathes, "Ah, whale!" He carves lightly with respect.

The carver helps the whale to come forth; it is not created, but released. The Inuit doesn't control the ivory, but blends with it; he participates in whaleness. The ivory whale embodies the essentials of a pattern that connects his senses, intuition and traditions. As Edmund Carpenter explains, his and other Inuit carvings were not made with a flat surface because they weren't made to be viewed from a stationary perspective. Then one day a European trader arrives and collects the whale. Upon his return home, he finds that the whale doesn't stand on his shelf. It rolls about clumsily. Since this won't do, he files the "bottom" so it will be stationary and stand up on his shelf as a showpiece.

By filing, the trader made the whale something the carver never intended. What was known from all one's senses plus tradition and imagination is now something to stand apart from and observe. A whale, who could once assert its own form by rolling about unhampered by a fixed position, is now stuck.

The trader did to the whale what we have done to play. That is, our innate wonderful, wobbly, roly-poly orientation to life has been filed in an effort to be more secure As a result we are continually "on edge."

The Crafting Of A Playmate

The child Jesus made clay birds just as the other children did, but touched his and made them fly.

Lynda Sexson

We touch heaven when we lay our hands on a human body.

Novalis

Rub some sunlight on my face.

Linda (a four-year-old who is blind)

Twenty years ago, like Pinocchio hidden in his piece of wood, I was waiting for someone to hear my song. I have been fortunate to have played with children who, like Geppetto and the Inuit carver, use the simplicity, gentleness and genuineness of their touch to summon life from within. I am keenly aware that I am the material being worked. In children's hands I have been crafted into more than I was, more than I thought I could be and perhaps, more than I can put into words. Through their sincere, careful and loving touch, many, many children have made me someone new.

Kit, a two-year-old girl with Down syndrome, shunned adult touch because of the poking and prodding she had received as a result of her bout with leukemia. At one point in our play, I lay on my back and she knelt by my head. She reached out and caressed my face with eager tenderness. Maybe, I thought, I'm feeling how a cat feels when she nestles in my lap. If I had known how to purr, I would have. She touched me as if her movements expressed the lifelong training of a tea master; she gracefully and slowly bent forward and kissed me. Her seismographic kiss reminded me of the "art of leaving out" exemplified by the tea master who with no distortion or tension brushes the tea bowl with the feather-like touch of the whisk. This bringing forth of life is the craft of play. I realize now that I am both Pinocchio, the puppet come alive, and Geppetto, the craftsman answering the call.

In order to be made whole, the word must be made flesh. It is only by being in touch that the playmate can create. The craft of play is not merely discursive, not merely a head full of abstractions; it is first and foremost sensuous, derived as it is from bodily participation. In playful touch the subject-object distinction breaks down; the hands, muscles, joints and skin all transmit the language of the womb.

Like the ivory of the Inuit and the wood of Geppetto, our bodies, minds and hearts are touched in play until all that is unnecessary is removed. This is practicing; it is how we become playmates.

The Meaning Of Practice

Thus, the first and most vital practice in everyday life is to learn effectively to value those moments in which we are touched by something hitherto undreamt of.

Karlfried Graf Durckheim

The initiates strive toward mastery and even at this stage should have the taste for play on the way, pleasure in the *dharma*, the *samadhi* of playing.

Karlfried Graf Durckheim

It would have seemed silly as a child to go out to practice play. I never thought about practicing; I simply played. I practiced other things, like baseball, drums and public speaking, activities with which I could win approval. Practice meant drudgery to me and discipline to the adults who encouraged me. Play is entirely different.

Playing is about changing our practice. Within each of us is a spark of play — like a nightlight in the darkness of adulthood — that reminds us of the boundless mystery of life. We are caught in a contradiction: practicing a life of contest while being, if only so very faintly, aware that authentic life is beyond all these contests.

We know how to compete. We know how to have fun. But we don't know how to play. The methods of adulterated play do not accomplish authentic play. As play is adulterated from Creation to culture, its concerns and patterns are transformed from intimate connections to performances. Playing the game becomes more worthy than to play with someone. Being good becomes more important than being together.

I once asked a friend, "Did you ever play one-on-one basketball or football with your father in the driveway or on the front lawn when you were a kid?"

"Yeah, both games," he said. "We played a lot. I always lost. Every time. Finally, one day in eleventh grade I beat him. That was the last time we ever played."

Play practice is simple, but it isn't easy; it demands commitment to a different way of being and doing. Play practice entails a fundamental alteration in our notion of life. Play is not conditioned by expediency. This commitment is not about a job or career. Play practice is not an abstract care for children as expressed by social services and countries. The connections are both more intensely personal and, consequently, much broader than that. Play practice implies a responsibility arising out of a love that is exact and particular. Only through such practice of love for the being at hand do we discover a much richer and larger concept of intelligence and kindness.

We recognize that in any skill or craft, beginners need help from masters, but we may not be comfortable acknowledging the mastery of children who retain the love and fearlessness inherent in life. There is no substitute for young children or wild animals. Adults who practice only with other adults live the illusion that we really already know what play is. We must keep in mind that play practice is a process in which increasingly more life is embraced within our playground, thus opening the barriers formed by cultural categories. This is why we must go to those children and animals who have not been adulterated, not only as our playmates but also as our masters.

"Come on, Fred!" Tiffany invited me along as she handed me her lunch box, took hold of my fingers and led me outside. We didn't talk as we walked outside to wait for her bus to arrive. Sometimes it is their nature for two playmates to enjoy each other's company in silence. She held onto my fingers and slowly swung my hand as we watched other children come and go. Our communication took place effortessly, spontaneously and silently. Like the coming of the seasons, it comes in its own time. There was power in this simple act of holding and being held.

I had seen grizzlies many times in Yellowstone Park, sometimes up close but most of the time through binoculars as small furry brown bags of marbles rolling around the landscape. As an instructor at the Yellowstone Institute I was privileged to go on early morning and evening bear watches with Gene, Rick and Steve on the slopes of Mt. Washburn. I learned a great deal about grizzly ecology being with them. This time was different.

On a special summer day, I had the feeling of truly being present with a grizzly. We first saw each other from a short distance. I judged the bear to be three years old. It was alone. I sat quietly as the bear wandered about sniffing and clawing logs. It seemed to keep an eye on me and sauntered toward me. There was no aggression in its look or walk. The moment when we touched gave me a glimpse of a shared eternal kindness beyond form. When the bear wandered off, I felt awe at the gift that had been given to me.

That grizzly bear and Tiffany shared with me the paradoxical equation that exists among playmates: One plus one equals one. What makes play possible comes from within. Play's touch is a deeply interested sense of kinship in which the soul is allowed to express itself. This is a strange kind of learning. While it is the most real, it remains the most difficult to speak about. I know it better than my years of book learning. And yet it is as if I know nothing at all.

Play is restored with long years of training in the art of self-forgetfulness. Dolphins, wolves and children are very good at this. Returning to play after so many years away is like humming along when I've forgotten the lyrics. I keep trying to remember what I've forgotten. This is the mark of an apprentice, whose practice is threefold: (1) forgetting everything that adulterates play, (2) endless practice and finally, (3) forgetting even this. The reality is that the playmate apprentice is doing things and not doing things, consciously and unconsciously, which if he or she were playing would happen effortlessly.

Trying to comprehend original play all at once is like jumping into the ocean without first learning how to swim: We'll drown in our own efforts. Play is only truly practiced when we feel that we can do nothing else. For some, play may overcome their lives like a flood. For others, it may gently seep into everything one does. It doesn't matter. Allow yourself to join it however it comes. Practice provides us with continual opportunities to live a kind life. I can't play to improve myself or help a child. It's wonderful when this occurs, but I can't play in order for it to happen. I must, not as a command, but as a simple condition, play each moment. Not only when I'm on the ground with children, but when I drive my car or stand in a line, the kindness is called for each moment — all life is play practice.

I cannot strive to play. Play is a universal privilege, not a selective reward. Practice isn't a contest of self against the world; neither is it a war of wills. Play practice is not an intellectual exercise. The real practice — this is a very difficult task — is to risk over and over again, letting go of what I think I know about play. Practicing is playing right now with my situation at the moment.

My play practice continues to be a forward and backward process, learning and relearning, forgetting and remembering. Many lessons I learn repeatedly, all over again, for the first time. I often have a day full of high energy, after which I feel as if I've shared and learned a great deal. Then I have discouraging days in which I am fearful or preoccupied and not fully present; I move too slowly and get a bloody nose or I use too much pressure with a child and he cries. The awareness required in play is not a state of mind that is reached once and for all without daily effort. It is a continuing process.

The patterns and techniques of touch which I share are not based on a theory about how I believe play should be, but rather they are drawn from my actual play with young children and wild animals. Obviously play occurs as a patterned whole, a time/space in which energy flows are transmitted, received and transformed. Play's vision requires so much from us, and the movements are so different from how we have learned to play that I've found it safer to present play to adults slowly, in a step-by-step process. This helps to allay fears and soften bodies, healing mind, body and spirit along the way. Play then can be shared, but not taught. When I work with others, my attempt is to share the patterns of play piece-by-piece, until each one feels ready to go out and play. Knowing full well, of course, that I too remain an apprentice.

There is only one way to share play — heart to heart. The real work is done within, going deep into the inexhaustible wellspring from which each playmate draws their vision.

Not Too Soft, Not Too Hard, But Just Right: The Craft Of Play/Touch

The playmate's practice is to "get back in touch" with ourselves, each other and our world. Play's touch is an awesome little thing to share. Jesus said to Thomas, "Reach hither thy finger, and behold my hands; and reach hither thy hand, and thrust it into my side." Thomas could not believe that Jesus rose from the dead until he touched him. I am reminded of the outstretched dynamic hand of God reaching out with immense potential to the limp and lifeless hand of Adam in Michaelangelo's "Creation." Touch provides the emotional highlights of such popular movies as *E.T.* and *Gorillas In The Mist* with scenes in which connection is made between human and nonhuman life. In Tolstoy's *The Death of Ivan Ilych*, Ivan, tormented and wracked by pain on a lonely deathbed, suddenly becomes aware of his son's hand and for the first time feels a loving touch that dissolves the fear of death. I can feel it in the gentle strength of an infant's grasp of my finger. The immense potential energy implied in these examples of play/touch creates a bridge across all the categories that separate us.

Touch is the parent of all our other senses says Ashley Montagu. We are born to love, to connect and be connected with. Touch is how we make these connections. Just as a plant cannot thrive without the sun's energy throughout its life, play's touch is fundamentally necessary for the healthy behavioral and emotional development of the individual. As Bertrand

Russell pointed out, "Our whole conception of what exists outside us is based on the sense of touch." We must be able to feel in order to connect.

Touch is the Rosetta Stone of play, with a large vocabulary communicating a directness and honesty unavailable to language. Through touch the ineffable language of the heart is made tangible. In play we know that we belong to a larger continuum. We feel a tremendous reassurance in the reciprocity that we are both capable of nurturing and worthwhile of nurturance. Through play/touch we experience in a myriad of lives, one life.

Play Principles

Relearning play becomes a series of physical and mental principles or koans, each being quite literally a touchstone of reality in which a key issue of practice and realization is experienced. "The mind simply becomes as it was in the beginning when he knew nothing and had yet to be taught anything at all," says TaKuan Soho.

These koans of play are dynamic, childlike principles of playful experience. For the adult they are mental devices to help unlearn and put the notions and motions of play into coherent practice. Techniques associated with principles are not ends in themselves; they are ways into play, like Pooh's 100-acre wood, Alice's discovery of the rabbit burrow and Dorothy's heels clicking. In Zen these are known as upaya, or "skillful means," used to shock us out of delusional states that distort our interactions. In play these learnings conduct us across difficult thresholds of change away from the contest patterns we know in both our conscious and unconscious life. To recover the characteristics of childlikeness, the basic principles must be mastered. But mastery is only the beginning, enabling us to unlearn.

Here are the six Play Principles:

1. Be not afraid of life.
2. All life is of one kind.
3. Touch is our primary language.
4. Be a beginner.
5. Smooth moves follow a clear heart.
6. Expect nothing, be ready for anything.

These tenets of play are neither fortune-cookie sayings nor rules to be memorized. Six principles, six ways of viewing the same thing; the unity of mind, body and spirit. To understand fully, one is to know them all. To misuse one is to misuse them all. Intellectual assent is useless if feeling and action are not in accord. The principles and forms serve as hangers on which to place your mind and body so they won't get in your way.

In actual play practice these principles can be translated into interaction as follows:

1. Get down.
2. Be quiet.
3. Pay attention.
4. Let go.
5. Table thoughts.
6. Be in touch.

We must feel it with our flesh and bones. We must touch and be touched. Then we will earn the integrity and wholeness of our lives by every act we do.

When I first began playing with young children, I was surprised by their trust and the patterns of gentleness, power and reciprocity in their touch. They didn't teach or even talk to me about play. Day after day they simply shared it with me; thereby, patiently drawing play out of me. A permanent yet hidden force had suddenly been released, freeing me momentarily from the restraints of my culture. Suddenly, one day I experienced a leap in consciousness. I knew something more about play and touch. I realized that there was an inner pattern of sharing within their outward pattern of touch. In the ultimate mastery of form, the playmate is released from the adherence to form. To be a playmate is a reciprocal relationship in which a new "we" is born, which is something more than either of its component "I's." What began as connection hand-to-hand, then from body-to-body became direct from spirit-to-spirit or heart-to-heart. A fundamental door opens, which, ever since humans have existed, has helped them to derive meaning in their lives. When we are awakened to the possibilities, we begin to see that life can be more open and joyful than we thought possible.

Playing With Angel

I first met Angel, a girl with autism and Down syndrome, on a sunny afternoon on the grassy playground of a school in California. As I walked around the corner of the building, I saw Angel sitting cross-legged, rocking back and forth against a cement block wall. She was stroking the right side of her face in short rapid motions with her slightly closed hand. Her eyes rolled around as if encompassing the entire scene, yet not seeming to really take or allow anyone in.

Our play was to be simultaneously ordinary and special. Special in the sense that it is a unique relationship between Fred and Angel, and ordinary because it is a relationship taken for granted by adults who don't understand its importance and by young children because it is the only way to play.

All of my years of playing with children, dolphins, bears and wolves haven't made it any easier as I think about approaching Angel. Part of me "knows" that I never play with the same playmate twice, that it is always a first time. Perhaps I'm insecure because I know that I don't control what is about to happen. Maybe it's knowing that the upcoming encounter is going to require me to be fully present. Perhaps it is feeling that I am about to meet a master. I wonder if I am up to it. Suppose she will not play with me?

All of my past training stampedes through my mind as if I were supposed to search for and instantly catch the right move. It is not that I must remember what I know; it is more subtle than that and more powerful.

I cannot hold back any part of myself; play does not permit this. It is imperious in this regard. Play can only occur through one's whole being. In this reciprocal relationship it is not particulars that are known; it is everything at once. I search her for a hint; she doesn't rush to reassure. She is taking my measure. I feel a tingle of excitement in the back of my neck and a heightened sense of awareness, like when I find a fresh grizzly track in river mud.

Angel is in front of me. My thinking and worrying disappear. I walk over and lie on my side about three feet in front of her with my head propped up on my hand. I try not to encroach, leaving her room for some infinitesimal advance or retreat. Even with such care, there is a chasm in the three feet of space separating us; across we will build a bridge. There is an almost painful deliberateness in just being present, aware, vulnerable.

Play includes both our bodies and the space between them. This "between" space is to be used and shared rather than possessed or controlled. It is not empty, but full of potential energy. Both playmates help to create it by movements of withdrawal and invitation — pauses, glances, leaning back and slight approaches — all done with the utmost gentleness and barely perceptible by nonplayers. In this mutual dance of playmates, each learns from the other.

In the beginning, I provide a secure space from which the child can explore and to which she can return without clinging. Angel, meanwhile, is teaching me the art of touch that engages with love without restricting movement. We weave patterns together in the unspoken syntax of play, flickers of eye contact and circles of arm movement. Eyes, hands, arms and bodies act as links, not controls or threats. Patterns of movement always leave room for each other.

An intensity of silence filled with more not-doing than doing inform these initial moments of play. This reverent intensity with which playmates attend to the initial bonding is carried on with the utmost care and reverberates back and forth with warmth and trust.

We use very little language, exploring and sharing with slight movements of hand or head. We are not merely watching each other; we are keeping fully aware without conscious effort. Every nerve and muscle becomes another eye. We do not guide our bodies, we trust them. I put my hand out on the ground between us, and she increases her rocking or shifts away. If I think about inching forward, Angel lurches backward, her body sensing my thoughts. I tilt my head and stroke my beard as she does her face.

Initially, play/touch is tenuous, exploratory and gentle; advances are made with eyes and fingertips. This is a kind of a dance in which playmates are unusually alert and explore each other, looking or feeling for positive signs of mutuality, feeling the differences in the pressure, intensity, rhythm, duration and firmness of each other's touch. This is an important phase. It often requires much patience to get below the fears and cultural masks.

Like the arrival of spring in Montana, Angel is cautious. If you know where to look, you'll see furtive signs of connection, but only a few. Every so often, for example, our eyes catch each other's for an instant and then rapidly let go. At other times she hesitates briefly and looks intently at me. Then an almost imperceptible smile flicks from her eyes. Something — a fragile turning point — is happening between us; we are opening like buds unfolding in the spring. There is a promise in this play, a reassurance in a force sensed but not seen, that we make to each other. It is that play's trust outlasts all uncertainties.

Often eye contact is the initial touch, the hand at a distance, between playmates. It is a way in, so that who is there may enter "as a guest in my house," as Joan McIntyre puts it. There is no hesitation in this play look, yet it is not an aggressive, penetrating stare. Neither are the eyes cast downward in submission. If the eye is clear, it functions properly and promptly. As it connects, it is free of fear. Fear begets doubt; doubt begets thought; thought blinds the eye. There is no hesitation in the play look. Only then is the play message transmitted with precision.

Change has come and it will slowly accelerate in the moments ahead. Suddenly Angel stands up and hurriedly walks out onto the lawn. I follow and begin to run, jump and skip around Angel, as if I were a frisky foal. Angel smiles more openly, beginning to chase after me. We share a sense of mutual quickening as we frolick around the lawn. Our mutual animation is a wonderful connection. We both begin to laugh out loud.

My movement around and up and down emphasizes circles, loops and figure eights. I run backwards and stop with my arms outstretched as an invitation. Angel trots up to me smiling, slows down and pulls her arms into her body so as not to touch me. Gradually, Angel begins to touch me lightly, almost as if in passing. Later she runs into me as I stop. Then we undo our physical connection and begin running around again. I stop, kneel, smile and extend my arms to her. She runs into me, turns around and fits herself backwards into my lap. I pick her up, twirl her, tip her upside down, hug her, rock her, fall with her on top of me. She gets up, goes around me, pulls my hands up and pushes on my

back to do it again. Angel walks around, lifts my feet up in the air
and lies across them, holding on to my hands and instructing me
to hold her in an airplane position. She likes to sit on my back. I
give her "horsey" rides. She walks toward my head and sits on it.
Then I lift her upside down on my back.

The powerful mutuality in our relationship is not a result of
technique, but a *forgetting* of all technique. Because we trust our
bodies, we move as if slashing like a sword, as finely as a silk
thread being pulled from a cocoon or gracefully like a dolphin's
dips and swirls.

In the midst of our romping on the grass are periods of gentle
soft, ephemeral embraces, like a snug hearth during a howling
winter storm. These moments are perishable, like shooting stars,
and virtually imperceptible to the uninitiated. When Angel sits, I
sit down next to her. If I don't sit right away, she reaches up and
pulls me down by the hand. She doesn't make any moves to turn
or get away. During one of these sitting times, Angel wets her
pants. As the puddle flows out onto the cement, she begins patting
her hands in the wetness. Before I know it, I too am patting the
wet cement. She smiles, holds my hand and pulls me up. Laughing
she runs onto the grass and motions me to get down. I drop to my
hands and knees. Angel rides on my back and neck.

We walk to a large red toy car mounted on giant springs stuck
into the ground. Angel gets in and moves it rapidly back and
forth. When I reach out to slow it down, she pushes me away
saying, "No!" I am amazed at her perception. A few times I reach
toward the back when I think she can't see me. She reaches to
stop me just as I touch the car. During one of these stops, Angel
slowly turns to me and leans out of the car, touches me lightly on
the face and kisses me. She gives me the very love that I sought
to give her.

She continues rocking until it is time to see her mother. She
slows her rocking and reaches for my hand. I help her out of the
car and holding hands we walk to the school.

Approaching Touch

We often approach the subject of touch as if only the child
gains from the experience. Touch is reciprocal; both partners

receive benefits that contribute to their optimum functioning. The fact is that nurturing touch is important for everyone. We've assumed that only the child benefits from touch: strengthening the structure and inter-related functions of the nervous and immunological systems; strengthening bonds between self and other and supporting exploratory behavior. Each of these benefits is equally important to adults. Through play/touch, playmates learn that they are supported not suspended, that they can initiate their explorations into the outside world.

Lavish touch may be crucial in cooperative, egalitarian and consensual relations. Animals who are gentled and touched respond with an increased functional efficiency in the organization of their body systems. Premature babies who received touch from caregivers were more responsive, alert and able to go home six days sooner than others, according to Ashley Montagu.

If touch is rushed or undertaken too harshly, however, skin may become a barrier that shuts one in. Then touch becomes an assault upon our integrity. In addition to the obvious and violent examples of attack, rape and other forms of manhandling, there are also many more subtle forms of intrusive touch.

Adults, for example, often touch children whom they meet for the first time on the top of the head. To the adult, of course, this only seems appropriate. It is, after all, the easiest, most convenient place to touch a child. It is more common than I realized for men to do this to short women. I have learned from children, dolphins and wolves not to touch the head without having established a great deal of trust. The head is the last place that I touch. I've witnessed dolphins and wolves bite and hold a person's hand for making this transgression.

In a third-grade classroom, after showing slides of my wolf and dolphin play, I mentioned that it takes a long time and a great deal of trust before I touch anyone's head. I decided to ask them how they liked it. I was surprised by the energy in their responses. Hands shot up. Everyone wanted to answer. They told me their stories about how uncomfortable, small and bad they felt when adults touch them on the heads.

I allow each child to approach me in their own time without external pressure. Some come directly and quickly. Others are hesitant and may take from a few minutes to a number of hours.

Still other children may take even years to actually play. The
length of time doesn't matter. A few children have taken three
years to fully engage in play with me. During this time they have
watched me play with their friends three to five days a week. I
don't know what keeps them away, neither do I know what finally
draws them in. One particularly hesitant girl's first touch was to
step on my hand. Following months of shying away from me, she
repeated this three times in a few minutes. I was so excited that I
told the staff that afternoon that I was happy because Alice
stepped on my hand! It took a few additional months for Alice to
play fully with me. Regardless of the time involved, there is a
pattern of alternate approach and retreat from the time children
first identify me as a potential playmate to our full engagement. I
trust that when the child is in control they make the necessary
decisions about joining play in ways that are meaningful to them.
I don't need to know the basis for these choices, I need to be
patient enough to allow them to be made.

The play-look is an invitation and a gift. It does not seek to
extract information, to "take" from the one looked at. There is a
gentleness of seeing in this look that acts like both an invitation
and a bond. I am amazed at the depth of trust transmitted so
quickly in the play-look. It is an awesome little thing to share. The
look is not planned ahead of time; intuition takes over. The play-
look bypasses our cultural meanings and analytical definitions,
and in so doing, the mind is allowed truly to see. The play-look is
one of those aspects of play that can be learned but not taught.
Don't try to do it. Forget it, it will come of itself as you begin to
play. Once you've shared it, you will know what it is.

Robert, Danny, Vanessa and Lydia are teachers in the art of
looking. Their looks touch me inside first, then seem to open me
from inside out like a chrysalis. The result is an extraordinary
metamorphosis in which I emerge as a playmate, someone more
than I ever expected to be. Their faces hold so much joy. I realize
in sharing looks with them that as Bachelard says, "The eye is the
projector of a human force." I believe this to be the power that
the traditional martial artists recognized as being present in the
eyes. Such eyes, according to Morihei Ueshiba, the founder of
aikido, are spiritual eyes that transcend the selfish ego and in the
emptiness echo the universe.

In play, touch is as open as the eyes. It begins at or near ground level and moves upward toward the head in somewhat regular stages from lower legs to hips to shoulders. At first children watch me and my interactions with other children. They cautiously venture into the "playground," edging their way near me. I may touch them on the foot or lower leg. Usually they giggle and run away until they are just outside the "playground." Turning around, smiling, they briefly wait and watch, then walk in again. I repeat the previous touch. If the child stays, then I can proceed to the next stage of touch. If the child retreats, we continue touching at that level until it is comfortable, which is signaled by remaining in the "playground." I do not chase, grab or otherwise force children to play. On the other side of the imaginary line is a "time-out" place. This pattern of approach-retreat continues until playmates are fully engaged or they separate for any reason.

Enfolding

Once both playmates are comfortable with touch, the enfolding process continues. Like traditional swaddling, this requires skill. If done poorly, a playmate will feel dependent, captured or too loosely engaged. Hands and arms are used to support, so they remain open, fluid and circular. Touch now may include hugging, cuddling, caressing, snuggling, resting on or next to each other, carrying, hand-holding, cooing and listening. I listen more than I talk. When I talk, my voice is as soft as my touch.

Play/touch can be very rambunctious and roly-poly with fast, large and energetic movements. When I see videos of my play with a group of children, I am reminded of photos of spiral nebula. Bodies twist and tilt in every imaginable position — downside up and upside down. A playmate is only lightly conscious of another's presence. There is a delicate balance here. On the one hand, I constantly move my arms and hands so that they lie along the spine and back of the neck of my playmates to help them make their spiral falls and rolls safely. On the other hand, I know my playmate shouldn't be robbed of their right to feel the outcomes of their motions. The movements of play provide the child with a view of the world from virtually every possible position.

As we roll over each other, children find themselves on top, looking down at an adult. Then we are sideways, looking in each other's eyes side by side.

When I have wanted to run, leap and shout, hills and haylofts, wolves, dolphins and children have echoed my joy. The sun draws the coolness out of the early morning as I walk toward the enclosure of six two-year-old eastern timber wolves. Morning is their active time; they converge on me with ardent and boisterous greetings.

After I am finished with my introductions at the fence, I slip in the gate. All six jump up on me in turn to get in their affectionate licks and nips. After a few moments of romping around me, they settle down somewhat so that I can move around their territory. I drag a long stick behind me; in pairs and trios, the wolves follow and pounce on the stick holding it down with their paws as they try to grab it with their teeth. We engage in a brief "tug-of-peace." It is clear to all of us that they could just take the stick away, but they blend their pulls to my strength in a matched give and take. Hambone escapes with the stick trailing from his jaws, trots over the low hills and glances behind to make sure we are still in the chase.

When in doubt, be a circle! Why? Because in the words of Vincent Van Gogh, "Life is probably round," and as Black Elk said, "The power of the world always moves in circles." A ball is a wonderful paradox. It is always perfectly on balance and off balance. It can move to any other point on its surface and retain this paradox of balance. Such roundness permeates the motion of play.

When playing with children, wolves or dolphins, I often have the sensation of being surrounded even when I have only one playmate. They seem to be sinuous Mobius strips, weaving a three-dimensional yin-yang symbol in which there is no up or down, no back or front, no left or right. In these circles movement and stillness are blended. The essence of one is born in the extreme of the other. I seem like a stick figure compared to them. I am relearning with their help that the energy of the universe moves in curves, circles and spirals.

I was not surprised to experience this circular movement-balance from Holly, my dolphin friend. I assumed it to be her nature. But I was surprised by the sinuous nature of my wolf playmates. Sybil and Livia explode off the ground and surround me as if I were a pole and they were tether balls entwining me in their twirls.

Livia, Sybil and Holly are teachers and yet they do nothing special, just move in their own way. The result is a gravitational field that holds me in a dynamic, meaningful relation. Unlike the centrifugal forces of contest, play maintains a delicate equilibrium between the self-assertive tendencies of individual playmates and the integrative tendency of a group. The result is a seeming "superindividual," whose movements are synchronized like integrated flocks of birds in which there is no wave-like motion indicative of a time differential between leader and follower.

Energetic play sessions are often interrupted by periods of recuperative stillness. Stillness is to play what silence is to sound. Much of play time is quiet time; time spent just being together. These are the invisible intervals of play.

Before going in a wolf enclosure for the first time, I spent two weeks of long eight-hour days on the outside of their enclosure. I sat next to the fence so the wolves and I could get to know one another. I touched, groomed and watched; they licked, sniffed and watched. It was a time for building trust.

Much of my time with wolves is spent quietly. Sybil, Nero or Hambone will walk by and rest their heads on my shoulder or stand in front of me for some touch. I spend much of my contact time with Holly, Puck, Holey Fin and Nicki, the dolphins at Monkey Mia, Australia, simply touching gently. The same is true with children. They come by and rest on top of me for a while and then dart off. Sometimes they go to sleep on me. There are children who can sense when I need some quiet time. Kim, Tracy and Vanessa, for example, will come and get me, sit quietly on my tummy and gently touch my face, beard or hands.

Such still-points are not formal conveniences like time-outs in sports. They are an integral part of the action of play. There is a great deal of reassurance in this kind of handling. As with any explorer, reassurance is extremely helpful in taking the next step into the unknown. In the midst of rambunctious rough-

and-tumble play, it is common for a playmate, who is otherwise very physical, to rest on my back or chest or ask to be picked up and carried or simply held. Such rests are often invisible to nonplaymates.

Today I met a new playmate. Sally is not yet a year old. This was her first day at school and she was in the midst of an initial evaluation by a physical therapist. I was on the floor playing with A.D. and Christian. She looked over at me and I smiled. After about ten minutes, she was put on the floor and began crawling directly toward my face. Our eyes connected again and maintained their link as she advanced. She crawled right up to within a few inches of my face. She hovered over me and looked intently into me, beyond my eyes in a focused effort to make and explore a connection. It seemed as if she never blinked. As she moved closer, I whistled softly and she moved her lips. I rolled to my back and put her on my chest. She propped herself up on her arms and peered again straight down into my eyes. After a couple of minutes, she nestled her head into my neck and rested quietly, getting up every so often to look at me and change head positions.

After summer vacations to far-away places, it is somehow reassuring to take a short walk just down the road. Summer is past. I know that because I can read September on the calendar; but autumn is a change I can taste, smell, see and hear. I try to match my rhythm with that of the autumn sun and the breeze and the creek where there is no haste, no frantic activity. Slow, measured change is all about me.

Sitting quietly on a grey, granite boulder, my fingers play in the water of Strawberry Creek as if literally to touch its pulse. The creek's pace has changed from the frothy bounce of spring's fast water to the slow rolling and meandering of autumn. Instead of bouncing over boulders, the creek now takes an easier path around them. But there remains much sparkle as patterns of sun and shadow dance on the gold and sepia water rolling around the rocks. Miniature fir, cedar and pine trees stand just barely above the forest litter of previous seasons. Within the flimsy branches I see the glimmer of spider filaments, for this is gossamer season. Above me green and brown pine needles bow and curtsy gracefully like stick figures dancing in the autumn breeze.

> How we are educated by children, by animals! Inscrutably involved, we live in the currents of universal reciprocity.
>
> *Martin Buber*

Years of play experience lie behind the touch present in the above encounters. Mutual support and freedom between playmates illustrates the paradoxical nature of play. It is a sense of the power within limits. Like Goldilocks finding the little bear's bed, "It is not too hard or too soft, but just right." We learn to play within life's constraints, which are flexible, soft and firm, and which Doczi writes, "As limitations they open doors toward the limitless."

There is no restless, anxious striving, but an effortless, tranquil harmony. I had a dream recently that depicts the skill inherent in play's touch. I am in a building, watching Japanese martial arts classes. In one room calligraphers are writing and in another bodies are moving in very elaborate *katas*. I am escorted into a smaller room to observe and then participate in a ceremony. The master, an elderly man, smiles. He holds a sheaf of rice grass, about which is wrapped a narrow band of silk. The bundle is about as big around as my thumb. The bundle is perched on the fingertips of his left hand. In his right hand he holds a sword. He sits so calmly, I almost don't see what happens. In one deft clean movement, he cuts cleanly through all the rice shafts without touching his fingertips.

He motions for me to come forward to repeat the cut. I know if I cut too softly, I will leave some grass blades uncut. If I cut too forcefully, I will slice off my fingertips. The room is very still, pleasant and reassuring. There is no fear or apprehension present. Then I awaken.

The natural spontaneity and effortlessness of play's movements are difficult to attain. Conceptually it seems easy to move naturally. Yet it can take an amazingly long time to regain the spontaneity of childlike motion after so many years of forced contrived movements. It is time spent letting go, not technique, which gives play its focus, fluidity and spontaneity reminiscent of the beginner's childlike mind.

I must have the patience to forget my expectations, reflections and worries and face the present moment simply and purely. At such a moment I am at one with myself; all my forces are concentrated unreflectingly, unselfconsciously on the play. Organismically I can live only in the present, but intellectually I seem to live everywhere else.

Practicing play is getting in touch. There is no other way, no shortcut. Becoming is the nature of apprenticeship in play; one that I consider to be a lifetime in length. The craft of being a playmate is not done by special people; it is simply the kindest way of living. Then your trace of life lingers on in others touched by your hand. Play is an immersion in life experience in which I try to make myself available both to life's energy coming through me and to that within all other beings.

As playmates we are engaged in a sacred craft, a collaborator with Creation. We engage life in its everyday, ordinary state and bring to it the possibility of becoming something more, "a channel of power for the reciprocal flow of human and divine energies," as stated by Paul Jordan-Smith. Such inter-relatedness is expressed by the Maoris as *mana*, which is "a direct experience of the sacred force that permeates existence." This is referred to in Sanskrit as the system of energies called *Prana*, "the organizing factors that underlie what we call the life process." It is not surprising then that a playmate is an instrument of play's energy, not the source. To be touched in play is to be "filled with God."

Play practice lasts a lifetime. Through play/touch we become aware of the life in all things. Aware, we are ready to "go out and play" with an open, boundless, compassionate heart. It is not kindness in the abstract that makes a playmate, but such love toward everyone with whom one comes into contact, that anything less than kindness is impossible. Play practice is demanding. As playmates our quest is to increase the playmates within our personal playgrounds until we can unequivocally exclaim a joyful "Yes" to Einstein's question: "Is the universe friendly?"

11

Kindness:
The Magic Circle Of Play

When we look with the eye of nonjudgment — that is, with the eye of
love — our vision includes all of humanity.

Stephen Mitchell

Communion between mortals is immortal.

Boris Pasternak

185

As a child growing up in Michigan, I remember running outside without my winter clothes to greet the first robin of spring. I ran with my arms outstretched, as if I could embrace the robin and spring itself in my small hug. Seeing the first one was an event worthy of dinner table discussion. Even if we had more days of snow and cold, which we often did, this lone robin was a promise, however tentative, of warmth. I knew that spring was on its way. I did not know this by reading the calendar; I could feel and smell it.

On a crisp February afternoon in Montana, when all things seem brittle with the cold and the winds as straight and piercing as arrows, I hold out my hand with some seeds and smile as a jaunty little ball of feathered energy we call a chickadee descends from a fir tree and alights on my glove. This chirping, perky, gregarious black, white and grey fluff of life seems to provide a lesson in kindness — a sense of welcoming kinship of human and chickadee.

On a sunny, late spring afternoon in a mountain meadow north of Yellowstone Park, I wander about looking for playmates. I come upon three young male elk grazing on the slope of a small hill. I sit in the warm sun to watch and be watched. One of the three shows an interest in me. Staying in their view, I slowly walk in front of them to a place along a path where I think the elk might meander. Two scamper by to graze beyond me; the other stays behind. He wanders and grazes in a zigzag path toward me, maintaining his slow pace until he is directly in front of me. He nibbles the grass near my legs. I feel embraced by his antlers curving around me. I can smell his pungent sweet-sourness, see his rib cage swell and hear his munchings. I feel that he has come to me, as I have to him, on purpose.

It is the day before Nelson Mandela is to be released from prison. I am in his hometown, Soweto, South Africa, to visit a girls' orphanage. We arrive a little late, park outside in the drive-way and walk into what appears to be an old school building. I have no idea what to expect; perhaps we will take a tour. My hope is that I can play with children.

We walk along the edge of a grassy courtyard where 100 girls are assembled. Most girls are in dark blue jumpers with white blouses. As we walk to the front of the group, they sing a wel-coming song. Although I don't understand the words, the meaning is clear. They steal my heart, and I am ready to play with all of them at once. I walk out onto the grass and into an incredible playground. I briefly introduce myself and what I do. This needs to be translated, so I decide to get right to playing.

I touch and play with many playmates this morning. In between our rambunctious play sessions, the girls teach me their tradi-tional songs and games. When it is time for us to leave, one girl who speaks very good English tells me that her friend, who doesn't speak English, would like to sing me a goodbye song. Her friend comes forward and begins to sing alone to me. A few others join in, and then some more, and then more, until they surround me with the rounds of their song. In the center of their song was a wonderful place to be.

After our play session, we have lunch with some of the staff. They tell me that they didn't know what to expect. They had never seen the girls play; they didn't know that they knew how. One woman asks if I understand what happened this morning. For most of those girls, I was the first white person whom they had ever touched, much less played with. Although I still remain at a loss to describe my feelings, I know that we belonged for a time to something greater than the categories limited by our sex, race and nationality. Within our play there was none of the con-tests that so many of the world's adults wage against each other, which these children and others will inherit one day soon.

This afternoon I join a group of five preschool children on an exploration of the hills around our school. We scramble up and down small slopes, pick up dried mud polygons, jump rivulets, slide down a steep hill, find treasures. I have joined countless children on such escapades. Yet each time I am drawn anew into the world by their curiosity. Playmates show me how to be someone I had forgotten how to be.

So much of life is ready and waiting to make us aware of epiphanies when we can feel all boundaries between self and others dissolve, as if the world were opening up to greet us. Life's greeting is a time of generosity and belonging, of remembering and extravagance, and a certainty that kindness transcends difference. This sense of kindness is a connectedness through individuals to the cosmos as a whole. It is a sense of deeply interested kinship reflecting the truth that there is only one kind of life and we are all it. Albert Einstein called our experience of ourselves as something separate from the rest as a kind of optical delusion of consciousness. Our task as playmates is to free ourselves from this prison by widening the circle of kindness to embrace all living creatures.

This is what I believe Gregory Bateson was seeking when he asked, "What pattern connects the crab to the lobster and the orchid to the primrose and all four of them to me?" Francis of Assisi, Pu-tai and Pooh knew the answer. But such knowing is not limited to fictional characters and saints.

Play's love and fearlessness are available to everyone. This is the most powerful message of this book.

Play belongs to the child of spring within each of us. It is a time not of ownership or competition, but of belonging; a time of openness of heart in which we sense more than we know. Kindness is not brought about by either human striving or supernatural intervention. Kindness is a remarkable, natural uncontrived wisdom that does not partake of artificialities. Kindness is more than "doing kindnesses." It is *being* kind. Kindness is a fundamental of life, not an ethical activity. I believe this is what Rabindranath Tagore meant when he said, "He who is too busy doing good finds no time to be good." We do not obey as a child to a parent, but we are engaged in and embraced by love. It is in realizing kindness that play becomes not only alive, but most difficult to explain.

Play mingles past and present, myth joins with fact, old with young in a tangle that is to be enjoyed, not analyzed. We do not know this as we know other things. Play is communion, available to all life forms across all barriers. This is what St. Paul was referring to in Corinthians when he said, "Then shall I know, even as also I am known." At such a moment of connection, we feel known by the self, by others and by the stars. Like the Bushman who believes that as Van der Post writes, "When he died, a star would fall from the sky to go and tell life everywhere else that something which was once upright had fallen down."

Jung speaks of the unconscious as unending; it can reach anywhere. Our unconscious is only part of that which extends throughout life. Fools Crow, the Lakota Holy Man, experiences the connection directly:

Since the quest of 1965, I am able to talk freely with pheasants, eagles, owls, prairie dogs, coyotes and wolves. All of these animals speak to me in Lakota. If another person who believed was there with me, he, too, would hear them, but I would be the only one who would know what they were saying. Unbelievers will see the animal's mouths move, and will hear the sounds and the creatures laughing. That is all.

Throughout this book I have provided examples of sages and scientists, mystics and children, all of whom opened themselves to be in touch with the creative source of all life, not merely as an intellectual idea, but in a tangible, real way. Playing by heart, they understand what was written in the fourteenth-century manual *The Cloud of Unknowing,* from which Mitchell quotes, "By love He [God] may be received and held; but by thinking, never."

This playful pattern of sharing remains a delicate mystery, not one to be solved, but rather to be lived. The moment I doubt or explain, it is gone. Play indicates that a connection can be made from each of our forms and this field of time and space into that transcendent formless source out of which life emerges. This is an enormous leap out of the confines of normal relationships. This is play that arises when we abandon our artificial categories and emotional attachment to their qualities. As we detach from our hold on things, we enter into a state of "weightlessness" that allows us to be increasingly open to life. Play is a divine reverberation through time, space and form, creating a resonance of love and kindness. There is a bit of heaven here. Is it real or metaphor, or both?

Yesterday I walked over to play with the older children at our school. I walked through the gate that separates the building and playground used by the older children from those of the younger children. Angel, the young girl with autism and Down syndrome, was lying on her back on the cement sidewalk, her feet propped up on the building. She was obviously agitated. She had a scrape on her arm. Her hands and face were very dirty. She had been striking out at both staff and other children. Children were taunting her. Staff were exhausted and frustrated.

When I knelt down beside her, she seemed to recognize me but made no movements to come to me. I leaned over and put my head near her. She swung her arms out at me. Then I put my head inside her arms and lightly on her chest. She hit the back of my head a few times, then suddenly popped up to her feet. I rose to my hands and knees. She sat on my back and leaned forward, lying on my back with her head resting on my shoulder. I moved around a little. Angel sat up and seemed to want me to stand up. I rose with her on my back. She laughed as we moved over to the grass. I could clearly feel that her agitation and frustration had melted away. We played horsey, intermixed with a game in which she pulled me to a sitting position and pushed me over.

Angel then sat down against a fence and made the sign for ball. I returned the sign and asked her if she wanted to play ball. She said, "Yes." I got a large rubber ball and we began bouncing the ball back and forth to each other. Within a few minutes, four other children joined us. Angel bounced the ball to each child in turn. When it was time for me to leave, I crawled to Angel, took her head softly in my hands and told her I was going home. I leaned forward, hugged her and waved. She seemed at peace, quietly looking directly into my eyes, and waved back. Each time I play with Angel, she gives me the gift of sharing the loving presence behind her aggressive posture.

One morning I had a delightful time playing with Little Guy and Little Girl, two coyotes at Wolf Haven. We played hide-and-seek around the trees, chased each other in the stick game and romped over each other. After a couple of hours, I said goodbye and left the enclosure.

I walked over to be with Windsong. I hadn't had as many opportunities to play with her as I had other wolves. I sat outside the enclosure getting reacquainted, while Jack and Steve went in with her. Windsong's greeting to her friends was very exuberant. She was excited, jumping up on Jack and Steve, darting back and forth between them and her hidden places in the bushes. When it felt right, I joined them. At first Windsong sniffed and brushed by me. I felt recognized, but she paid little attention to me. We all sat down. She meandered over, flopped down next to me and put her head in my lap. I petted her tummy and she mouthed my hand. Suddenly, she became excited and moved my hand to the back of her jaw. The pressure on my hand was excruciating as she seemed to be crushing it with her back teeth. My pain and tears suddenly disappeared, replaced by a feeling of calm. A minute ago it felt as if my hand was being chewed off; now it felt as if nothing were happening. Maybe I'm in shock, I thought.

Steve and Jack managed to get her off my hand and we left the enclosure. Once outside, we looked at my hand. I didn't know what to expect. There was some purple mottling on the back of my hand, and it was a little sore, but otherwise it was fine. Nothing was broken, no first aid was necessary. I could move everything. We agreed that it must have been the coyote smell that aroused her. That seemed like a logical explanation. But I still couldn't explain the lack of injury to my hand. I had been mouthed many times by animals, but I had never felt anything like this instant pain, immense pressure and sudden calm. I let it go and went in to wash and change clothes before continuing my play sessions with other wolves.

During my evening quiet time, I went over the experiences of the day. I was still troubled by Windsong. Suppose it wasn't the coyote smell at all or it was merely a trigger. Then what? I had a difficult time allowing in the thought that was trying to hold my attention. I was afraid. It was as if I knew something inexpressible that I didn't want to know. Once I said it, I would have to allow for its possibility as a guide to the nature of reality. Windsong had given me a lesson in the way the world plays. A lesson in physics and metaphysics. Her teeth merged with my hand. I wanted to dismiss it, but I couldn't.

The mystery remains, but I smile and accept Angel's and Windsong's gifts as moments of living wonder when I was able to touch my own roots, the point where heaven and earth intersect. Such play depends on being in touch with the source of life. Play was not an academic theory or a remote philosophy. I *felt* play as a tangible expression of kindness in the same way that Heloise spoke of her love for Abelard: "To God, in species, but to Abelard as individual."

The Magic Circle Of Play

Man has the capacity to love, not just his own species, but life in all its shapes and forms. This empathy with the interknit web of life is the highest spiritual expression I know of.

Loren Eiseley

It is not always easy to be a playmate. Going out to play is risky. Being kind seems foolhardy in such a dangerous world. I've been told that playing with infants is cute, playing with children with disabilities is nice, playing with a dolphin is interesting, playing at all for a man is suspect, but playing with a grizzly is stupid. As cultural beings, we make value judgments about all forms of life. Our cultures and social groups tell us who are insiders and who are outsiders. We are allowed certain behaviors in specific circumstances with certain kinds of people which are not allowed in other places with other people.

Parents may spank their child at home, but in accepting a job at a preschool they realize that they have to let go of spanking at school. If they carry behavior that they feel is appropriate for normal child development from their home into the school, they may be reprimanded, fired or prosecuted. This is how we live. We take all of this for granted. We know that we may make different judgments from people in other places, but we assume everyone is making such judgments.

Play has been thought of as merely another activity in which we learn the particular values of our culture. In cultural play we learn to do all those things that are listed in the cultural sphere in Figure 11.1, like compete, judge and retaliate. The games may be different, but everybody plays. Within our culture it is all right to discriminate and judge, coach and parent. This is no more than what is expected of us.

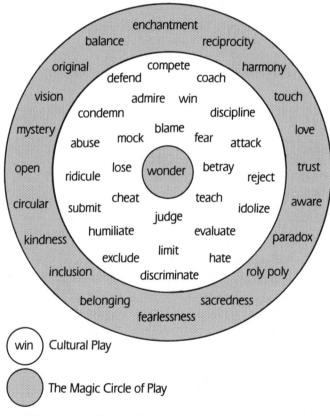

Figure 11.1. The Cultural Sphere and the Magic Circle of Play

Throughout this book I've been suggesting that there is another kind of play. I've called this "original play" because it originates outside the cultural sphere. All of the incidents I describe in this book take place in ordinary everyday life, but there is something else that transubstantiates them. It is this "something" that creates the "magic circle of play."

The magic circle of play is a psycho-physical space/time. When we enter it, we are thereby transported beyond the cultural sphere. Cultural realms and the magic circle of play are mutually exclusive. To remain in culture is to choose to abide by the rules that culture has established for whatever game you play. In cultural play there are accepted exclusionary rules. We make decisions and rules about others — who can and cannot play, how to play and who is against us. These are differences that make a difference. It may be team, or clan or tribal membership that determines playmate status.

I once had a discussion with an Olympic athlete about this point of exclusion. She felt that she was a playmate because of the companionship and love she felt for her teammates. I asked her why she didn't include the opposing team in the same comradeship. She said she couldn't because then they couldn't have won the event. She had to exclude in order to be a group. This may be expected, but it is not being a playmate.

Being human makes it extremely difficult to let go of the weight of social gravity. Play's vision is very grand, but as George Leonard has pointed out, "Every master is a master of vision."

The magic circle of play includes everyone. This means that in play we have to give up our allegiances, whatever they are. For most of us this will seem like a minor request until we are faced with what it is that we have to give up. For some it is easy to play with aggressive children, but they leave play's circle when children who are not of their group want to play. Some people can be a playmate with their own family members, with their teams, clans, tribes, races, nationalities. Some preschool teachers have a problem playing with children whom they feel are dirty. Others can play with any child except those who are intentionally aggressive. The list of exclusions we can make is endless.

To step into the magic circle of play is to step beyond culture and all of its categories.

To be a playmate means being committed to engage in practice that continually enlarges one's circle of playmates to include those who are presently excluded. Not by changing others to become more like us, but by working on oneself to be able to embrace more of life's diversity. Playmates work on themselves not on others. We eventually are brought face-to-face with a playmate who mirrors our deepest fears. Normally we retreat to the protection of culture. But as Albert Schweitzer pointed out:

Until he extends the circle of his compassion to all living things, man will not himself find peace.

Adults are afraid to step into play's magic circle because they believe it is a leap into an unknown pit from which they will be unable to escape. It is frightening for adults to think that they'll have to live their lives as playmates and not as parents and teachers. This is not, however, the way of play. There are times in which I play, and many others in which I live as a friend, husband, parent, teacher or consultant. I practice and practice. I find that play slowly begins to seep into my other roles, making me more open and accepting when I inhabit them. I don't worry about this and I don't have to try to make it happen. Also, once captured by the vision, I find life exceedingly more fulfilling and safer inside play's magic circle. I want to grow so that my circle will include the entire world of beings.

When It's Tough To Be Kind

Kindness cannot be taught by harshness.
Raymond Smullyan

How does one play in a world of fear, judgment and contest? How do I play when no one else is playing? There are many times when it's tough to be kind, to stay inside play's circle face-to-face with what we fear. But this is the discipline of play requiring us to think more deeply about becoming playmates. What seems so wonderful when I give love to a child with cerebral palsy or autism seems irrational when I give love to a child who kicks me in the face. I believe there are times when being human requires that I have enough love to embrace others who have been so deeply depleted.

Being kind means giving up our allegiance, not just to our groups and countries, but to fear. As Jiddu Krishnamurti wrote:

So a man who is seeking to understand violence does not belong to any country, to any religion, to any political party or partial system; he is concerned with the total understanding of mankind.

This can be extremely difficult, even seemingly beyond our capabilities. Like Jesus who ate with disciples and sinners, consorted with mothers and harlots, our love must be deep and clear enough to make contact with that which is common to all life. "And of course," says Thomas Merton, "in so far as a man returns to his own roots, he becomes able to resist exterior violence with complete success and even, after a certain point, invulnerability." It seems to me that the important point is that each of us has to do the returning ourselves.

It is one thing to be propelled by a vision; it is quite another to be pushed by a theory or reason. We cannot do it for each other, for to do so would turn the visceral into the vicarious. Knowledge misses its mark if it is not felt as union. Only by making the effort ourselves do we become Real. This is what I believe the Skin Horse, in Margery Williams' *The Velveteen Rabbit*, meant when it said, "When you are Real, you don't mind being hurt." This is crucial, because there are going to be hurts along the way and only authenticity sustains the vision through the difficult times. This is a very different emotional and physical experience than the hurt felt in contest behavior, which is, as Richard Heinberg says, "The suffering of separateness and alienation, arising from the mind's attachment to its own artificial categories of discrimination and its projection of those categories onto the world." The hurt from play, on the other hand, "should be ascribed to" what Rabindranath Tagore describes as, "the beginning of our entrance into a new plane of existence to which our vital nature has not been completely adapted nor our mind thoroughly accustomed." There is wisdom in our pain as it is the birth-throe through which we are freed from the habitual and arrive naked into the arms of a wider world.

I do not believe that it is possible to play with someone else's vision. Blaise Pascal, the seventeenth-century physicist and mathematician, put it matter of factly:

> Those to whom God has imparted religion by intuition are very fortunate, and justly convinced. But to those who do not have it, we can give it only by reasoning, waiting for God to give them spiritual insight, without which faith is only human, and useless for salvation.

Stephen Mitchell expresses this point with regard to Jesus and his apostles. He suggests that:

> We need to be aware of the *quality* of the transformation. It was what I would call a religious rather than a spiritual experience. That is, although it took the apostles from doubt and despair to faith, it didn't take them into the kingdom of God. "Every disciple who is fully taught will be like his teacher" (Luke 6:40). But they were nowhere near being fully taught. They only believed in, they hadn't experienced, God. And they still didn't understand Jesus' teaching.

To put these ideas into terms of play, I can only give ideas, reasons, methods and techniques to another. If this were all, if training ended here, it would be cultural play, useless for the kindness required in original play. It is not sufficient to believe in play. "Belief has the instability of yes and no," writes Mitchell. If an apprentice's play is based on belief in a master, it is a hostage. To be fully taught is to experience the vision or insight oneself, which comes only through playing. It may not come when we want it or think it should, but it will come. Then we learn to play by heart and not by the book.

Thomas Merton, Blaise Pascal, Stephen Mitchell and the Skin Horse have provided us with a profound truth of play. As playmates we do not have the choice of playing with what *should be,* with what we *would like*, we are asked to play with what *is*. We are not given the luxury of keeping our vision separate and apart from our actions. A playmate does not say, "Well, I agree with the philosophy, but the world is so aggressive that I need to respond in kind in order just to survive. I wish it were otherwise, but I must live here now." As a playmate I agree that I must live here, now, but that doesn't put off my vision. Vision, if it doesn't lead to play, is dead. In play, the vision is the practice.

I must play with everyone, not just cuddly infants, willing wolves and gregarious dolphins, but with the mass of humanity who has been repeatedly abused and hurt and therefore is desperately unloved, unloving and afraid. Most of the people, including children, with whom I play are not playmates. They are afraid. They've been taught to be victims and to lose or to "take care of themselves," to fight and to win. To most, play *is* fighting. People lash out, even in safe environments. It is all they know.

In our play sessions, young children ninja kick, older children karate punch, teenagers use wrestling pins and adults try to beat me up. All try to get back at me for whatever the world has dealt to them. I must learn not to become engaged in their contests. It will not help to become another victim.

Three women have tried to take out on me what men have done to them. After throwing me down, one said, "I've never been able to do anything to a man." Another repeatedly hit the side of my head and then shoved me away, accusing me of not playing. Later she admitted trying to hurt me. A third woman jumped on my back, because "of what all men have done to me."

I'm not a perfect playmate. I'm on the path, nothing more. There are times when it hurts to get kicked in the face. I am attached and vulnerable. I've had bloody noses, black eyes and cracked ribs. Some days I wonder why I play. I wonder to myself if I know what I'm doing. Adult violence toward children and their aggressive responses seem endless. To be a playmate under circumstances like these is not the invitation to aggression as it may seem. It is essential to understand that what is at issue here is acceptance of a person, not condoning violence. I don't say that violence is all right. I do not allow children to attack each other in any way. I do say that as a playmate there is a place in me where I will open up and give you love face-to-face, no matter who you are or what you do. This is not a psychological gimmick. It is the magic circle of play.

Giving love at the point of attack is very difficult to practice, much less master. In this regard it is important to reemphasize that play, as I practice it, does not arise from morality, but from vision. We've lived our lives as victims and aggressors. We don't know anything else. Many men have trouble understanding that play isn't aggression. Many women find it difficult not to be victims. These are the roles men and women have accepted in much of cultural play. Neither is appropriate or necessary in authentic play.

Being kind is not throwing oneself away. Being kind is not letting someone else do whatever they want to you. These are the other ends of the aggressor-victim continuum. When I model kindness in the face of the attacks, my entire presence, including my spirit and my movements, must be clear about being neither aggressor nor victim. This inner clarity must be very strong because most people are afraid. They do not know what to expect. From an observer's viewpoint, I seem to allow children to beat me up. My intention is not to attack or defend the child's aggression, but in changing myself to present a surrounding trust within which the child will find it unnecessary to attack. No matter who steps in the playground, a playmate keeps it safe for everyone. This can't be accomplished if you throw yourself away. You cannot keep others safe if you cannot keep yourself safe. Be as responsive to yourself as you are to others. Playmate practice requires continual growth.

Paradoxes lie like land mines in the fields of play. Here is another. The only way to bring about a result is to give up my efforts to make it happen. But I can't not try either. The point is not to interfere.

The safety of the playground depends on both your mental and physical state. I learn through experience what I am capable of. If, for any reason, you're not ready, it is best to wait.

Once I was at a school and I wanted to play with every child who wished to join me. I didn't want to leave anybody out. I maintained a pace for two-and-a-half days that exhausted me to the point where I became too sick to play with the last groups on the third day.

Safety is a difficult issue, because it means that we must examine ourselves first. Keeping safe means that I check what I'm wearing and how I'm feeling before I play. Before going in with the wolves and coyotes, I was very deliberate about both my mental and body check. If my mind was somewhere else, if I clearly wasn't present, I waited. Having passed my mental check, beginning with my head, I ran my hands down my body, checking for anything leather or wool that needed to come off. If I left my keys in my pocket some of the wolves would bite my pocket to get at the leather piece attached to the ring. Once I wore a heavy wool shirt on my early morning greeting rounds. As I was petting two arctic wolves, they grabbed the sleeve pinning my arm to the fence. They tugged until the sleeve ripped off, then they ate it. I made a note about no more wool.

I learned from experience to take everything out of my pockets. Once I wrote a list of possible photos I would like. I put this piece of paper in my chest pocket for handy reference during the morning. Once inside and down on the ground, Hambone unfastened the pocket and picked out the paper with his teeth. He carried it around like a stick. I tried to retrieve it, but he kept it just out of reach. At one point in our game he stopped, turned his head to look at me and swallowed it.

Everything that seems to be an obstacle — aggression, contests, misunderstandings — becomes an opportunity for a further degree of opening up on my part. As I open up, I allow what was present from the beginning to shine through. Only by constantly letting go and opening up can that part of me who feels defensive and attacked be forgiving. Then both I and my attacker can feel loved and nourished so that neither will any longer feel like a separate entity in a dangerous world. Eventually we come to trust in the kindness of the world.

We are like a stray line of a poem, which ever feels that it rhymes with another line and must find it, or miss its own fulfillment. This quest of the unattained is the great impulse in man which brings forth all his best creations.

Rabindranath Tagore

Playing is another way, entirely outside of our ordinary values of self and other, win and lose, blame and fault. Play is neither an adjustment to nor a refuge from the contests of the world. Play is without attack or blame, just love. That's all. An absence of love cannot be healed by another absence of love. What is needed is an even more encompassing love, one that is able to embrace the attack until it is no longer necessary. This love empowers from the inside out.

The crafting of a playmate is like the making of a fine Japanese sword. Saotome writes:

In making a fine sword the iron is continually stressed. Forged in flames, it is softened by the heat of aggression so that shaping and refinement may take place. It is beaten, pounded, folded back upon itself, heated, pounded until all the impurities are driven away. Plunged into water the temper is set, the fires are controlled and wisdom prepares to sharpen its edge. The process is very complicated and no part can be omitted. Its hidden layers number more than a million. But the finished product is simple and pure of line. It is strong, yet flexible, and its surface reflects all which is around it.

Like the sword, only through the experience of playing many times in the heat of all that life has to offer is a playmate forged. Each time I play with those who lash out afraid of life, it is as if they are purifying me with each strike. I am tempered by a hug or a held hand.

Play is a relationship of kindness — a realization that we are of one kind. The common ground of play expresses the "Tao of the ancients," with roots not in shifting cultural values, but in the deepest source of our being. Kindness is not an ethic at all. It is a way of living. Something within us, perhaps a primal energy of the essence of life itself, responds to the message of play as compass needles turn toward the north magnetic pole. Our entire being takes comfort from such consciousness of roots.

In my play with older children and teenagers, I may introduce play as the oldest of the martial arts, already in existence before cultures felt the need for defense. Play turns the normal need for martial arts on its head. While traditional martial arts are often seen as means of self-defense, protecting the individual from the ravages and attacks of the external world, play is the system of spirit and form that protects the outside world from the self. This is Abraham Maslow's "way of the scrutable":

Love for a person [which] permits him to unfold, to open up, to drop his defenses, to let himself be naked not only physically but psychogically and spiritually as well. In a word, he lets himself be seen instead of hiding himself. In ordinary interpersonal relations, we are to some extent inscrutable to each other. In love relationships, we become "scrutable."

Cultural play is eating from the Tree of the Knowledge of Good and Evil; original play is eating from the Tree of Life.

It is an axiom that what applies in one "Way" has application to the others. In traditional arts and crafts, it is not the material or the weapon but the self that must be mastered. In uniting the inner world with the external, play has a great deal in harmony with Japanese *budo*, described by Morihei Ueshiba as "invincible since it contends with nothing." He adds, "Real *budo* is a Path of Peace."

Manfred Clynes speaks of Beethoven's last works as achieving a fusion of being that eliminates struggle and "is replaced by a projection of a 'peace that passeth all understanding.' " What is important in kindness is not belief in the correct doctrine, but authentic experience.

Ultimately, kindness springs from personal experience, which moves inward to come to terms with what Jung called our "shadow" selves and outward to encompass what is strange and frightening. "To choose life is to affirm our existence. To choose death is to continue the cycle of violence," writes Richard Strozzi Heckler. Our dependence on violence has been the coward's way out of not facing up to the love we fear. Play gives us no such out. Individually we are required to face and to touch what terrifies us. Practice, love and fearlessness are just the beginning. We must, each of us, be hit in the heart.

Being human means being confronted continually with surprises, each of which is simultaneously an opportunity and a challenge. I don't know why three-year-old boys who have known no violence feel compelled to use aggression in a play session, any more than I know why 15 teenagers straight off the streets of Capetown knew exactly how to play with white strangers.

As a result of this inner and outer quest, we become increasingly capable of self-transformation, thereby going beyond the boundaries that separate us from our world. The experience of kindness is a broadening of feeling due to the emergence of a deep metaphysical insight, a grasp of infinitude unverbalized and yet momentous in its sense of connectedness. In our secret core, we realize that we are far more than we are normally aware of being.

I do not see that contests are bringing us one step nearer to anything that really matters to me: peace, ecological well-being, kindness. Nuclear disarmament will never be achieved unless it is considered as part of a larger vision that eliminates spanking children and bullying in schoolyards. As Laurens van der Post wrote, "It is the fission in the modern soul which makes nuclear fission so dangerous."

In kindness all human energies, formerly used for contest, acquisition and defense, are liberated and redirected into a timeless, powerful force propelling us into life's mysteries. "I" no longer belong to myself, but to one and all. Nothing's changed and everything's changed.

With each new birth, life sends a new playmate, a new possibility. A playmate is the actual medium for the continual process of creation which takes one past all the contests, defeats and glories. Past even, Laing says, "Chaos or emptiness, into the very mystery of that continual flip of nonbeing into being, and can be the occasion of that great liberation when one makes the transition from being afraid of nothing to the realization that there is nothing to fear."

Questioning

I went to the Owl because I heard he had the answers.
I found him at home, and it seemed to me that he,

sitting silent in the utmost concentration, must
indeed have the answer.
"It is said," I spoke, "that you alone have the answer."
The Owl replied, "My friend, as much as is said of me is true."
And so I asked the Owl the Question.
He answered me carefully, with infinite patience.
"You must find the answer yourself."
Thinking I had been deceived, I spoke angrily.
"Did I need the Owl to tell me I must think for myself?"
"But, my friend, that is the answer."

Questioning is often a way of avoiding the real answer, which is known already. Every person is enlightened, but wishes not to be. We all know how to *play* our parts on earth. But we don't want to know this, so we continue to masquerade as contestants and hide in ethical quandaries. Everyone knows we must be kind each moment, that we must give love with all our might, but we don't wish to know it — so we ask questions. Should wolves, whales, mountain lions and rainforests be saved? Should ancient cultures, babies, homeless people survive? Only contestants ask such dangerous, foolhardy and unkind questions.

The very fact that we began life as players is fraught with significance for the future of our universe. We are individually and collectively faced with a problem of birthing a new world paradigm. Like birth, coming out to play may be painful, but it is the only way to live. Jiddu Krishnamurti raised the question:

Is it possible for a human being living psychologically in any society to clear violence from himself inwardly? If it is, the very process will produce a different way of living in this world.

Yes, in providing us with its gifts of fearlessness and love, playing by heart is this process. We are back at the beginning. Love is *the* survival benefit we are able to confer upon each other.

Epilogue

Playing For God's Sake

"I am an earth child," she said proudly, "and this is a planet I live on. I would like to play with all its children for I, too, am its child."

Lillian Smith

The first day or so we all pointed to our countries. The third or fourth day we were pointing to our continents. By the fifth day we were aware of only one earth.

Sultan Bin Sulman al-Saud

A playmate sees God in everything. When categories vanish, that which is beyond all categories is found in the smallest aspect of life. Belonging to the whole is experienced by playing with particular individuals, which entails the responsibility of making that relationship divine. Having undertaken the quest, I find that I will never again be absolved, even for a moment, from the responsibility for the way in which I am present at any given time. I will ceaselessly pursue this adventure, knowing that, no matter what may be achieved, it will always be inadequate compared with the inner image of the quest itself. Above all, I realize that whatever greatness is achieved, it is never me who has created it. All I can do is allow and let go, transparent in the sure trust of that which abides within.

205

Playmates share two gifts: *You are lovable,* and *There is nothing to be afraid of.* These gifts may be easier to share with cuddly, curious infants than with aggressive, despairing adults, but the gifts and the need for them remain the same. The real obstacle in giving love lies not in the nature of the recipient, but in the heart of the giver. Cultural selves continually make judgments about such gift-giving. The playmate allows such decisions to dissolve. There is nothing we must do to earn these gifts; then they wouldn't be gifts. Quite unlike the Duchess' Game, the supply of love and fearlessness is beyond all imagination. Surprise! These gifts are already ours, our birthright, given by the grace of God.

Do we dare to be playmates? That is the question that counts. Play is an intensely personal act of insurrection in an unkind world. The era of contest can end; we can each choose to end it in our own lives. For this to happen, an alternative must be learned, understood and felt in the particular lives of particular people carried beyond abstraction into the specific relations between each person and their place in the world. To perceive the world differently, we must be willing to change our belief system, release our desire for revenge, be patient enough to allow an expanded sense of kindness to dissolve the fear in our minds and demonstratively support and sustain the potentialities in others for being.

Pause for a moment. Can you love with all your might? Can you allow yourself to trust, with all your heart, in these two gifts from the supreme intelligence of the universe? They touch what is true in all of us — the fear that I do not exist, which is the last thing I want to know; the acceptance that I am who I am; a sense of independence and a need to belong; the desire for security and the wish to explore. Pass the gifts on, for they are not for holding on to. The point is not that these gifts are available, that such encounters described in this book are possible — but that *they are possible for you and me.*

These gifts, which speak to the core of human loneliness, must be shared, thereby adding to the spiritual wealth of humanity from which we have been so estranged. Then play sustains all life. The invisible connections are carried forward and outward beyond a single lifetime. Play's energy flows through all forms and patterns, transcending all boundaries between mind and matter, physical and spiritual.

"In some strange sense," as physicist John Wheeler said, "this is a participatory universe." As playmates we are being initiated into the most expansive circle of relatedness possible. Here lies our source of identity and meaning. Then we truly play our parts and become part of the whole.

What we are discovering and feeling is original play, the heart-beat of the universe. The question is not whether nations are prepared to find an alternative for contest, but whether you and I, as individuals, have the wisdom to formulate a newly evolved process based on new assumptions and are prepared to live it. Our individual challenge is to comprehend and express in our daily lives the grace into which we are born. Heart and reason must blend so that we can be unfettered by fear. As playmates we invest in life as a covenant of faith in a future we will not likely see.

This is what all our practice, fearlessness and patience add up to. The gifts tell us that not only is the universe fundamentally all right, but that more specifically, we, *you and I*, are lovable. The wisdom to make the choice to love with all our strength may well be our ultimate divine gift.

Appendix

The Playmate Project

The Need: Children Without Love

What do we share with our children?

The Scope Of The Problem

The love of life is the most precious gift adults can share with children. We know that healthy human development depends on spending time together and sharing nurturing touch, not only in the early months of infancy, but throughout life. Far too few adults invest the personal time and effort needed to share the wonders of life with children.

We function in a world of accelerating change and ever-present conflict. We habitually view people and events as separate and engage in superficial, ritualized and contestant relations. In this fast-paced world, children are neglected or are sources of worry, guilt and even contempt. We concentrate on their material needs and give insufficient attention to their emotional and spiritual needs. As the U.S. Commission on Children put it, "A poverty of spirit touches every child." In our headlong rush toward material progress, not only do we give up being playmates to our children, we increasingly force them to give up their childhood at a very early age to feel our fears and continue our struggles.

Behind the facade of adulthood, we remain, in our essential humanity, unvisited, unpracticed in giving and receiving childhood's gifts. Although we speak and write about being close to our children, we, bogged down as we are in the general gravity of life and the seemingly serious task of making a living, have no experience of such a reality. Our interactions with children have become mere posturing. Though we may wish for something different and brood about our loss, we spend, on average, only ten minutes a day with children and during six of these we are being critical of them. We have no time for childhood or our children.

This is unnecessary. "Love suffers long," wrote St. Paul. But how long is too long for our children to wait? We have lacked the vision and the know-how necessary to address these problems. We need to find a means of relating to our children that commits ourselves to loving them. We will only begin to become fully aware of our own identity when we can touch and be touched by childhood's flashes of energy, whimsical outbursts and depth of feeling, thereby embracing the child within and joining with the children surrounding us. To truly share with our children we must learn a language of mutual empowerment, connectedness and trust. Fortunately, such a language exists within us. We only need to embody it.

The magnitude of the task is extraordinary. Many have called for a return to fundamental cultural values. That is not enough. In many cases it is these very values that cause aggression. We have called for a streamlining and increased cooperation of our complex system of services dealing with children. This, too, is insufficient. Marginal changes in existing systems will not provide our children with the necessary love. There is also a need for additional funding of childcare services. More money alone, however, is ineffective.

Instead, we need a fundamentally new approach. The way to save our skins is to get in touch with each other.

A Solution: The Playmate Project

In response to this need, the Playmate Project hopes to make a significant contribution to a kinder world through the encouragement of the playmate relationship. Because the plight of children cannot be overcome only by addressing them in traditional ways, the Playmate Project organizes its efforts to seek solutions in an entirely new way.

The Playmate Project is a program that embodies an image of human interrelatedness far beyond any we have ever imagined. To be a playmate is to be admitted into another's life in an extraordinary way. The playmate relationship is a human trust fund. In place of money or property, it is the human being who serves as a repository of love that forms the foundation for all other relationships.

The playmate relationship is an infrastructure of love and trust that works below the level of social roles and institutions, and can thereby serve as a basis for promoting the development of kinder human beings.

Who Is A Playmate?

Everyone is a potential playmate. To be a playmate is to be in a rather special kind of relationship, in which the myriad of differences that so often separate us are not ignored or masked, but simply allowed to be. It's not that a playmate does not recognize individuality, it is rather that to a playmate there are no differences that make a difference.

Why The Playmate Relationship?

Bruno Bettelheim wrote, "If we wish to understand our child, we need to understand his play." To be a playmate is to hold a child in your heart. You'll be sharing a gift of love. And sharing love is your greatest gift to the future:

• Because it ignores the categories with which we are taught to separate the world.
• Because it is the most profound and loving of all human relationships.
• Because through it we find the most direct way to be in touch with and touched by each other.

The power of this innovation lies in the truth that the play-mate relationship is a birthright and not an artifact of any cultural or social system. Unattached as he or she is to any cultural role, a playmate is uniquely equipped to give and receive love. In a world so conditioned by fear, the playmate relationship is primarily a bond that cancels out fear and therefore private and collective aggression.

Being a playmate is much more than reaching a certain level of competency in a physical activity, more than being a competent caregiver; it is about rediscovering a very powerful relationship with self, others and the world.

Years ago Friedrich Schiller described play as the most profound and humanizing of all human activities. In this bond lies the love and trust that may restore our imaginations and our hopes to their appropriate stature. At the heart of the Playmate Project is not any particular knowledge, technique or procedure as such, but a relationship with oneself, with others and with life itself. No matter how much we may sometimes resent and fear our human interconnectedness, we must also admit that the love and trust of our lives comes through contact with others.

We profess to value each child, allowing the child to reach his or her maximum potential, yet we promote a competitive system that thrives on failures. If it is true that we can ill afford to waste the talents and despoil the love of even a single child, then it is a moral imperative that we develop the practices that flow out of a life-enhancing vision.

My *vision* is that through play/touch, human beings will be able to transmit love and trust not only to one another but to all life regardless of culture or species. Without such a dramatic new vision, we will continue to raise children who are aggressors and victims.

The *mission* of the Playmate Project is to give and receive love through the provision of playmates for children throughout the world, thereby improving the quality of both adults' and children's lives, while bridging the gap between them.

The Project's goal's are:

• To prepare adults and adolescents to function effectively as play-mates for children.

- To create self-perpetuating playmate programs in educational and childcare facilities.
- To educate the public through in-services, workshops and courses to the importance of play in the lives of children and adults.
- To substitute play for contest in human relationships.

The Playmate Project proposes an action agenda that flows from a set of guiding principles concerning basic human needs.

Realizing The Vision

A Demonstration Project

At first our task is to select childcare facilities within which to demonstrate the Playmate Project. The project is flexible and adapts to any educational or childcare setting. A Playmate Program can be initiated within a variety of organizational settings, including a hospital, school, physician's office, clinic, community mental health office, orphanage.

Sites will be chosen based upon their willingness to participate, their willingness to consider a playmate as a permanent paid position following the demonstration year, and the number of children available.

For each site one or two adult playmates will undergo a period of training prior to assignment to a childcare institution. Following assignment, the apprentice will continue training in that institution.

Each playmate apprenticeship would be funded by an outside sponsor for a year. Following the year, the institution would then take on the responsibility of incorporating the position in their budget.

After an intensive training period, the apprentice playmates would be assigned a childcare facility in which to begin work. These facilities would have been previously consulted and agreed to have a playmate work in their institution. The apprentice would work full time. There would at first be daily on-site visits by me with each apprentice. As the year progressed, my visits would become less frequent.

These adult playmates may be recruited from the community, an assigned staff member or a new position. It is the hope of the

Playmate Project that playmate positions will be seen as imperative in childcare institutions, thus created and funded as integral
parts of these systems.

Costs And Benefits

Preventing violence and aggression before there are victims is
the most benefit- and cost-effective way to address the needs of
a troubled world. How shortsighted we are to think that an
investment in weapons is a more effective preventative to aggression than an investment in a different kind of human being. Effectively addressing the needs of children will require a tremendous commitment of courage, time and financial resources by
individuals, the private sector and government at all levels.

Without the generous support and contributions of many,
many individuals, we cannot accomplish our mission. For this
reason, the Playmate Project is directed to individuals and institutions, to the public as well as the private sectors of society.
We need the support of the childcare facilities, individuals who
have the courage to become playmates and the business community to help fund the positions. In coming together to form
a courageous blueprint for our children's future, we also strengthen our own.

The playmate is not to be thought of as a substitute for any
other cultural caretaker. Numerous providers already impinge on
children's lives. A playmate is not present to meet the needs of yet
another social system. The project is based on a one-on-one model
of relationship which requires that we get in touch with our
children.

The qualities of self-esteem, cooperation, inner discipline, physical awareness, creativity, compassion and love, developed
through the playmate relationship, are as essential and applicable
to the world of the adult and the adolescent as they are to that
of the child.

In terms of specific services the playmate is engaged in two
basic activities: (1) The experienced playmate guides adults/chil-
dren by modeling the psychomotor skills of play and (2) offers
opportunities for their practice. Although their style of engagement will typically be quite different, the playmate works in con-

junction with other professionals and families to promote well-being in an individual and their world.

There is no reason to limit participation with a playmate to high-risk populations. However, there are people whose needs may be more urgent and obvious, including teenage parents, special needs children, adolescents and adults who receive and give little, if any, touch, the elderly, aggressors and victims of aggression and abuse.

The specific costs will vary, depending on the cost of living in a community. The costs include pre-assignment training, a one year salary for the apprentice and additional training periods during the first year.

Playmate Training

Introduction

Although initially play came to us naturally, its rediscovery is by no means simple. Play requires discipline and practice. To truly understand our children, we must be willing to play with them, to "get down" on the floor and the ground. It is not enough to read, theorize, observe and analyze play; you must play to be a play-mate. As strange as it may seem, getting down to play with children is very difficult for many adolescents and adults because of personal fears about touch and the cultural designation of play as "childish."

Consequently, older children and adults are eased gradually, step-by-step into the play experience. Video and discussion are used where appropriate to present the benefits and fundamentals of play, its principles and forms and the differences between play and contests. No one, child or adult, is required to participate in an activity or to do anything they do not want to do. Sometimes people need time to watch and listen before they're ready to commit themselves to playing. To take hold, play must be entered into freely without external pressure.

Play is neither knowledge nor a skill to memorize, but rather a way of being and doing that is acquired slowly by the body and the spirit. In play, spirit and body, knowledge and action, principle and practice constitute an interdependent whole.

The training of playmates may be done at the setting under consideration. Training sessions are available individually or in groups of up to thirty participants. Introductory training can take place in workshop settings or in individual sessions. Further training will come from both Master's classes and individually directed play sessions. It is also possible for training to be provided to individuals or groups within their workplace. Eventually playmate training sites around the world are planned.

The playmate becomes a catalyst for positive change. By introducing one playmate into a school, for example, a seed is planted which begins to influence and change the interaction patterns from aggression, anger and violence to sharing, care and affection.

Those who participate in the training will:

- Develop self-esteem through play's touch and mutual empowerment.
- Be able to give and receive safe, kind touch.
- Replace the frequency and severity of their fearful, aggressive interactions with more positive relationships.

"It's Tough To Be Kind:" The Spirit Of Playmate Training

The sense of kindness inherent in play requires a mental and physical toughness that is beyond our notions of strong and weak. As adults and adolescents, it takes courage to be kind in a competitive world. To express the relationship that I am proposing in our daily lives requires endless practice. It's not easy. It takes real devotion to ourselves and other people. As we practice we are slowly transformed, something builds within us and between us. It's not by anything we memorize or figure out in our heads. We're transformed by what we do. Eventually if we're patient enough and practice enough, we have some possibility of making a contribution to ourselves and each other — a love with real strength. We all want it; we need it. So it's up to us to play.

In making play their own, playmates come to share with others an entirely new relationship unconditioned by their cultural roles. This occurs in a very personal way and may be different for each playmate. Traditional roles such as adult and teacher are not replaced but are supported by a new foundation based on mutual trust.

The play process descibed here is based on the following assumptions:

1. The universe is at play with us and is nothing to be afraid of.
2. The most important thing I have to do each day is to give and receive love. Every human being wants to give and receive love, no matter how distorted or convoluted our attempts.
3. Touch is our most direct and effective means of communicating and sharing love.
4. Play evokes love through touch.

"Smooth Moves Follow A Clear Heart:" The Practice Of Playmate Training

Practice, or "ground time," is the ground for understanding and development. Most people beyond age three or four no longer know how to play. Consequently, playmate training includes much "undoing" in order to rediscover play, to keep themselves and others safe, to give and receive safe touch and to maintain kindness in conflict situations. Playmates actually learn to reprogram their reflexes. Playmate training is divided into three phases: Introduction, Rediscovery and Interplay.

Phase 1: Introduction

Through specially designed play activities, participants are introduced to the playmate relationship. The activities have been developed from my 19 years of playing with young children and wild animals around the world. The purpose of the activities is to return us, through a step-by-step process, to what we once did naturally. These activities are based on touch because touch is our most direct way of communicating trust, kindness and love. To be a playmate requires a high level of skill in knowing how to touch.

Phase 1 may be a short period, ranging from a few hours to an intensive multiday experience. It is an introduction to the spirit and the practice of playmatehood. The nature of trust, the patterns of touch and such skills as centering and blending required of a playmate are introduced and experienced.

Phase 2: Rediscovery

During Phase 2 of training, emphasis is placed on relearning the personal art and craft of being a playmate. It is about washing away the fears of many years. Students pay primary attention to the development of personal skills such as flexibility, centeredness and balance.

Phase 3: Interplay

In Phase 3 playmates focus on their interactions with others; learning to blend without being either an attacker or a victim is stressed. The "way" of the playmate cannot be attained alone. In Phase 3 playmates learn the subtleties of touch and timing and how to blend these with surprise and change. There is constant practice in the interactive energies of following, joining, blending and contributing.

The actual practice of "playmate training" follows five guidelines:

1. Be a beginner.
2. Pay attention and be present.
3. Keep in touch.
4. Get down.
5. Allow time.

These guidelines are not intended to impart new knowledge, but to aim at a new orientation to life. What was always present, but unknown because of ignorance and fear, can now be realized.

Phases 2 and 3 are complementary processes. I separate them here only to identify the two processes — an inner and an outer one. In actual practice they are not separate but proceed together. Personal discovery leads to more creative and compassionate interactions, which in turn, lead to greater personal discovery. Through continued personal discovery and encounters with others, we make play our own. Playmate training is a lifelong endeavor.

Endnotes

Preface

Bateson, Gregory. **Mind And Nature: A Necessary Unity.** New York: Bantam, 1979, 8.

Bronfenbrenner, Urie. Quoted in **Beyond Rhetoric: A New Agenda For Children And Families.** Final Report of the National Commission on Children. Washington, D.C.: U.S. Govt. Printing Office, 1991, 40.

Campbell, Joseph. **Transformations Of Myth Through Time.** New York: Harper & Row, 1990, 16.

Daumal, Rene. **Mount Analogue.** Baltimore: Penguin, 1959, 42.

Sartre, Jean-Paul. Quoted in Wes Nisker, **Crazy Wisdom.** Berkeley: Ten Speed Press, 1990, 208.

Introduction

Bacon, Sir Francis. Quoted in Daniel Boorstin, **The Discoverers.** New York: Random House, 1983.

Bateson, Gregory. **Mind And Nature : A Necessary Unity.** New York: Bantam, 1979, 9.

Bateson, Gregory. "A Theory Of Play And Fantasy," in **Steps To An Ecology Of Mind.** New York: Ballantine, 1972, 179.

Dalai Lama. "Paradise Under Seige," *New Age Journal*, (September-October 1990) 55-60, 114.

Frank, Heidi. "His Game Playing Is Therapeutic," *Kamloops This Week*, (May 3, 1991), 9.

Lin-chi (Rinzai). Quoted in Frederick Franck, **To Be Human Against All Odds.** Berkeley: Asian Humanities Press, 1991, 63.

Mumford, Lewis. Quoted in Kenneth Heuer, ed. **The Lost Notebooks Of Loren Eiseley.** Boston: Little Brown & Co., 1987, 149.

Rilke, Rainer Maria. Quoted in James Cowan, **Mysteries Of The Dream-time.** Dorset, England: Prism, 1989, 41.

Chapter 1

Adam, Michael. **Wandering In Eden.** New York: Knopf, 1976, 53.

Boorstin, Daniel. **The Discoverers.** New York: Random House, 1983, 314.

Campbell, Joseph. **The Hero With A Thousand Faces.** Princeton, New Jersey: Princeton University Press, 1949, 58.

Chopra, Deepak. **Quantum Healing.** New York: Bantam, 1989, 17.

Eddington, Sir Arthur. Quoted in Deepak Chopra. **Quantum Healing.** New York: Bantam, 1989, 113.

Eiseley, Loren. Quoted in William H. Calvin. **The River That Flows Uphill.** San Francisco: Sierra Club,1986, 400.

Jeans, Sir James. Quoted in Deepak Chopra. **Quantum Healing.** New York: Bantam, 1989, 9.

Lilly, Antoinette. Quoted in Piero Ferrucci. **Inevitable Grace.** Los Angeles: J.P. Tarcher, 1990, 238-9.

McClintock, Barbara. Quoted in Piero Ferrucci. **Inevitable Grace.** Los Angeles: J.P. Tarcher, 1990, 228-9.

Mechthild of Magdeburg. Quoted in Whitall N. Perry. **A Treasury Of Traditional Wisdom.** San Francisco: Harper & Row, 1971, 35.

Pascal, Blaise. Quoted in Stephen Nachmanovitch. **Free Play.** Los Angeles: Jeremy P. Tarcher, 1990, 40.

Polanyi, Michael. Quoted in Robert Grudin. **The Grace Of Great Things.** New York: Ticknor & Fields, 1990, 44.

Rahner, Hugo. Quoted in Harvey Cox. **The Feast Of Fools.** New York: Harper & Row, 1969, 177.

Tagore, Rabindranath. Quoted in Piero Ferrucci. **Inevitable Grace.** Los Angeles: J.P. Tarcher, 1990, 39-40.

Wald, George. Quoted in Weber, Renee. **Dialogues With Scientists and Sages.** London: Routledge and Kegan Paul, 1986, 244.

Chapter 2

Adam, Michael. **Wandering In Eden.** New York: Knopf, 1976, 32, 52.

Aurobindo. Quoted in Piero Ferrucci. **Inevitable Grace.** Los Angeles: Jeremy P. Tarcher, 1990, 131.

Boehme, Jacob. Quoted in Whitall N. Perry. **A Treasury Of Traditional Wisdom.** New York: Harper & Row, 1971, 22.

Buber, Martin. Quoted in Piero Ferrucci. **Inevitable Grace.** Los Angeles: Jeremy P. Tarcher, 1990, 288.

Chang, Chung-yuan. **Creativity And Taoism.** New York: Harper & Row, 1963, 39.

Chopra, Deepak. **Quantum Healing.** New York: Bantam, 1989, 210, 262.

Chuang-tzu. Quoted in Whitall N. Perry. **A Treasury Of Traditional Wisdom.** New York: Harper & Row, 1971, 231.

Chuang-tzu. Quoted in Wu, Kuang-ming. **Chuang-Tzu: World Philosopher at Play.** New York: Scholars Press,1982, 43.

Doczi, Gyorgy. **The Power Of Limits.** Boston: Shambhala, 1985, 139.

Dyson, Freeman. **Disturbing The Universe.** New York: Harper & Row, 1979, 17.

Eckhart, Meister. Quoted in Mike Sayama. **Samadhi.** Albany: State University of New York Press, 1986, 3.

Eckhart, Meister. Quoted in Larry Dossey. **Recovering The Soul.** New York: Bantam, 1989, 221.

Eckhart, Meister. Quoted in Whitall N. Perry. **A Treasury Of Traditional Wisdom.** New York: Harper & Row, 1971,33.

Krishna, Sri. Quoted in Whitall N. Perry. **A Treasury Of Traditional Wisdom.** New York: Harper & Row, 1971, 33.

Makarov, Oleg. Quoted in Kevin W. Kelley. **The Home Planet.** Reading, Massachusetts: Addison Wesley, 1988.

Nisker, Wes. **Crazy Wisdom.** Berkeley: Ten Speed Press, 1990, 31.

Ochs, Carol. **Behind The Sex Of God: Toward A New Consciousness — Transcending Matriarchy And Patriarchy.** Boston: Beacon Press, 1977, 123.

Plato, Laws. vii, 796. Quoted in Johan Huizinga. **Homo Ludens.** Boston: Beacon Press, 1950, 19.

Ramdas, Swami. Quoted in Whitall N. Perry. **A Treasury Of Traditional Wisdom.** New York: Harper & Row, 1971, 36.

Ramakrishna, Sri. Quoted in Whitall N. Perry. **A Treasury Of Traditional Wisdom.** New York: Harper & Row, 1971, 33.

Rumi. Quoted in Whitall N. Perry. **A Treasury Of Traditional Wisdom.** New York: Harper & Row, 1971, 33.

Schiller, Friedrich. **Works-Aesthetical and Philosophical Essays.** Letter 15. Nathan H. Dole (ed.) Boston: The Wyman-Fogg Company, 1902.

Schweikart, Russell. Quoted in Kevin W. Kelley. **The Home Planet.** Reading, Massachusetts: Addison Wesley, 1988.

Sexson, Lynda. **Ordinarily Sacred.** New York: Crossroad, 1982, 71.

St. Gregory Nazianzen. Quoted in Alan Watts. **The Book: On The Taboo Against Knowing Who You Are.** New York: Vintage, 1966, 115.

Swimme, Brian. **The Universe Is A Green Dragon.** Sante Fe, New Mexico: Bear & Co.,1984, 120.

Van der Post, Laurens. **A Walk With A White Bushman.** New York: William Morrow & Company, Inc.,1986, 84.

Watts, Alan. "Letting Go: The Art of Playful Living," *East West Journal,* (April, 1983), 35.

Watts, Alan. **Beyond Theology.** New York: Pantheon Books, 1964.

Chapter 3

Black Elk. Quoted in Brown, Joseph E. **The Sacred Pipe, Black Elk's Account of the Seven Rites of the Oglala Sioux.** Norman, Oklahoma: University of Oklahoma Press, 1953, 74-5.

Buber, Martin. **I And Thou.** New York: Charles Scribner's Sons, 1970, 76.

Campbell, Joseph. Quoted in Conrad Hyers. **Zen And The Comic Spirit.** Philadelphia: The Westminster Press, 1973, 169-70.

Cohen, Sherry Suib. **The Magic Of Touch.** New York: Harper & Row, 1987.

Fox, Matthew. **Whee! We, Wee All The Way Home.** Santa Fe, New Mexico: Bear & Co., 1981, 214-15.

Herrigel, Eugen. **Zen In The Art Of Archery.** New York: Vintage, 1953, 33.

Leboyer, Frederick. **Birth Without Violence.** New York: Alfred A. Knopf, 1976, 90.

Maslow, Abraham. **The Farther Reaches of Human Nature.** London: Penguin, 1971, 17.

Mead, Margaret. (ed.) **Cooperation and Competition Among Primitive Peoples.** New York: McGraw Hill, 1937.

Merton, Thomas. **The Way Of Chuang Tzu.** New York: New Directions, 1965, 132.

Montagu, Ashley. **Growing Young.** Massachusetts: Bergin & Garvey, 1989, 73, 2.

Owen, W.J.B. (ed.) **The Fourteen-Book Prelude By William Wordsworth.** Ithaca: Cornell University Press, 1985, 54-5.

Perry, Whitall N. **A Treasury Of Traditional Wisdom.** San Francisco: Harper & Row, 1971, 578.

Prescott, James A. Quoted in Sherry Suib Cohen. **The Magic Of Touch.** New York: Harper & Row, 1987, 36.

Ramakrishna, Sri. Quoted in Whitall N. Perry. **A Treasury Of Traditional Wisdom.** San Francisco: Harper & Row, 1971, 573.

Saraha. Quoted in Whitall N. Perry. **A Treasury Of Traditional Wisdom.** San Francisco: Harper & Row, 1971, 578.

Sexson, Lynda. **Ordinarily Sacred.** New York: Crossroad, 1982, 72.

Sorenson, E. Richard. "Cooperation and Freedom Among the Fore of New Guinea." in Ashley Montagu (ed.) **Learning Non-Aggression.** New York: Oxford University Press, 1978.

Tagore, Rabindranath. Quoted in Jacob Needleman & David Appelbaum. **Real Philosophy.** London: Arkana, 1990, 578.

Takuan. Quoted in Whitall N. Perry. **A Treasury Of Traditional Wisdom.** San Francisco: Harper & Row, 1971, 578.

Thoman, Evelyn B. & Sue Browder. **Born Dancing.** New York: Harper & Row, 1987, 178.

Turnbull, Colin M. "The Politics of Non-Aggression." in Ashley Montagu (ed.) **Learning Non-Aggression.** New York: Oxford University Press, 1978, 169.

Watson, Lyall. **Gifts Of Unknown Things.** Rochester, Vermont: Destiny Books, 1991, 118.

Chapter 4

Attar. Quoted in Whitall N. Perry. **A Treasury Of Traditional Wisdom.** San Francisco: Harper & Row, 1971, 101.

Balint, Michael. Quoted in Berman, Morris. **Coming To Our Senses.** New York: Bantam, 1989, 27.

Becker, Ernest. **The Denial Of Death.** New York: The Free Press, 1973, 240.

Bennett, Ned. "Choosing The Public Interest," *Northern Lights,* Vol. 5, (April,1989), 12.

Berman, Morris. **The Reenchantment Of The World.** New York: Bantam, 1984, 2.

Brown, Norman O. **Life Against Death.** Middletown, Conn.: Wesleyan University Press, 1959, 38.

Carroll, Lewis. **Alice's Adventures in Wonderland.** Akron, Ohio: The Saalfield Pub. Co., 1911.

cummings, e. e. Quoted in Stephen Nachmanovitch. **Free Play.** Los Angeles: Jeremy Tarcher, 1990, 116.

Einon, Dorothy. **Creative Play: Play With A Purpose From Birth To Ten Years.** New York: Viking, 1985, 7.

Eison, George. **Children And Play In The Holocaust.** Amherst: The University of Massachusetts Press, 1988, 121.

Erikson, Erik H. **Childhood And Society.** New York: W.W. Norton, 1963, 214.

Fordham, Michael. **Children As Individuals.** New York: G.P. Putnam & Sons, 1969, 33.

Fox, Matthew. **Whee! We, Wee All The Way Home.** Santa Fe, New Mexico: Bear & Co., 1981, 10.

Fynn. **Mister God, This Is Anna.** New York: Ballantine, 1974, 38.

Hesse, Hermann. **Demian.** New York: Bantam, 1965.

Huizinga, Johan. Quoted in George Leonard. **Mastery.** New York: Plume, 1991, 116.

Kafka, Franz. **The Great Wall Of China.** Reflection, 13, 165.

Laing, R.D. **The Politics Of Experience.** New York: Ballantine, 1967, 26, 183.

Lapierre, Dominique. **The City Of Joy.** New York: Warner, 1985, 406-7.

Lawrence, D.H. Quoted in Laurens van der Post. **The Heart Of The Hunter.** London: Penguin, 1961, 13.

Miller, Alice. **For Your Own Good.** New York: Farrar, Straus, Giroux, 1984, 211.

Perry, Whitall N. **A Treasury Of Traditional Wisdom.** San Francisco: Harper & Row, 1971, 99.

Rilke, Rainer Maria. Quoted in James Cowan. **Mysteries of the Dream-Time.** Prism: Dorset, England, 1989, 41.

Russell, Bertrand. Quoted in Piero Ferrucci. **Inevitable Grace.** Los Angeles: Jeremy P. Tarcher, 1990, 146.

Sawyers, Janet K. & Cosby S. Rogers. **Helping Young Children Develop Through Play.** Washington, D.C.: National Association for the Education of Young Children, 1988, 7-12.

Schuon. **Perspectives Spirituelles** quoted in Whitall N. Perry. **A Treasury Of Traditional Wisdom.** San Francisco: Harper & Row, 1971, 238.

Sexson, Lynda. **Ordinarily Sacred.** New York: Crossroad, 1982, 9.

Shabistari. Quoted in Whitall N. Perry. **A Treasury Of Traditional Wisdom.** San Francisco: Harper & Row, 1971, 22.

Stevenson, Robert Louis. **A Child's Garden Of Verses.** New York: Crown Publishers, 1985.

Trungpa, Chogyam. **Shambhala.** Boston: Shambhala, 1984, 48.

Van der Post, Laurens. **A Walk With a White Bushman.** New York: William Morrow, 1986, 72-4.

Van der Post, Laurens. **A Story Like The Wind.** London: Penguin, 1972, 176.

Van der Post, Laurens. **Jung And The Story Of Our Time.** New York: Vintage, 1975, 72.

Williams, Margery. **The Velveteen Rabbit.** Garden City, New York: no date.

Wittes, Glorianne & Norma Radin. **The Learning Through Play Approach.** San Rafael, California: Dimensions Publishing Company, 1969.

Wordsworth, William. "Recollections of Early Childhood" Quoted in Conrad Hyers. **Zen and the Comic Spirit.** Philadelphia: The Westminster Press, 1973, 183.

Yeats, W.B. Quoted in Matthew Fox. **Whee! We, Wee All The Way Home.** Santa Fe: Bear & Co., 1981, 40.

Chapter 5

Bauman, Mark & Markos Kounalakis. "Holy War Without End," *Los Angeles Times Magazine,* (February 23, 1992), 28-31.

Becker, Ernest. **The Birth And Death Of Meaning.** New York: The Free Press, 1971, 149.

Becker, Ernest. **The Denial Of Death.** New York: The Free Press, 1973, 221.

Berman, Morris. **The Reenchantment Of The World.** New York: Bantam, 1984, 302-10.

Berman, Morris. **Coming To Our Senses.** New York: Bantam, 1989, 63.

Berry, Wendell. Quoted in "Hearth & Home." *MANAS,* (September 30, 1987), 6-7.

Best, Raphaela. Quoted in Miedzian, Myriam. **Boys Will Be Boys.** New York: Doubleday, 1991, 83.

Betcher, William. **Intimate Play.** New York: Viking, 1987, 16, 88.

Bettelheim, Bruno. "The Importance of Play," *The Atlantic,* Vol. 259 (March,1987), 35-46.

Bowlby, John. Quoted in "The Role Of Play," *MANAS,* Vol. 41, (February 10,1988), p. 5, 8.

Brady, Erik. "Bill's Smith Primed For The Big Time," *USA Today*, (January 10, 1991), 1-2B.

Brinkley, Joel. "Lethal Game of 'Chicken' Emerges for Israeli Boys," *New York Times*, (April 3, 1989), 2.

Caillois, Roger. **Man, Play and Games.** New York: Schocken, 1979, 7, 50.

Campbell, Joseph. Quoted in Conrad Hyers. **Zen And The Comic Spirit.** Philadelphia: The Westminser Press, 1973, 170.

Carazo, Rodrigo. Quoted in "A Peace-Making Nation," *MANAS*, Vol.41 (November 9,1988), 5.

Carlson, Bernie W. & Ginglend, David R. **Play Activities For The Retarded Child.** New York: Abington Press, 1961, 13.

Carroll, Lewis. **Through The Looking Glass.** London: Macmillan & Co., 1885, 68.

Carroll, Lewis. **Alice's Adventures in Wonderland.** Akron, Ohio: The Saalfield Pub. Co., 1911.

Chuang-tzu. Quoted in Thomas Merton. **The Way of Chuang Tzu.** New York: New Directions, 1965, 137.

Conn, Stephen & Marquez, Judith B. "The Social Context of Pinball: The Making Of A Setting And Its Etiquette," in Frank Manning, **The World of Play.** West Point, N.Y.: Leisure Press, 1983.

Currie, Eliott. "Wild In The Streets," *Los Angeles Times Magazine*, (December 15, 1991) 26-28;30;32;74.

De Tocqueville, Alexis. **Democracy In America.** New York: Doubleday, 1969.

Efron, Sonni & Davan Maharaj. "Vicious Circle," *Los Angeles Times*, (September 26, 1989), Part 1, 3 & 18.

Ehrenreich, Barbara. "The Warrior Culture," *Time*, (October 15, 1990), 100.

Flader, Susan. **Thinking Like A Mountain.** Lincoln: University of Nebraska Press, 1974, 1.

Franck, Frederick. **To Be Human Against All Odds.** Berkeley, California: Asian Humanities Press, 1991, 73.

Ginott, Haim G. "A Rationale For Selecting Toys in Play Therapy," *Journal of Consulting Psychology*, Vol. 24, (June 1960), 243-6.

Golant, Susan. Quoted in Mary Laine Yarber. "Some Of The Signs That Point To A Gifted Child," *Los Angeles Times*, (September 18, 1991), E3.

Gotto, John. "Our Children Are Dying In Our Schools," *NewAge Journal*, (September-October 1990), 62-4, 99-100.

Groos, Karl. Quoted in Jerome L. Singer. **The Child's World Of Make-Believe.** New York: Academic Press, 1973, 9.

Hammer, Joshua. "Vampire Agents At Play," *Newsweek*, (September 11,1989), 64.

Hans, James S. **The Play Of The World.** Amherst: University of Massachusetts Press, 1981.

Hayes, Woody. Quoted in Ashley Montagu & Floyd Matson. **The Dehumanization of Man.** New York: McGraw Hill, 1983, 195.

Homer. Quoted in Joseph Meeker. **The Comedy of Survival.** Los Angeles: Guild of Tutors Press, 1980, 72.

Huizinga, Johan **Homo Ludens.** Boston: Beacon Press,1950, 11, 89, 105.

Hyers, Conrad. **Zen And The Comic Spirit.** Philadelphia: The Westminster Press, 1973, 170.

Ikeda, Daisaku. Quoted in. Arnold Toynbee & Ikeda, Daisaku. **The Toynbee-Ikeda Dialogue.** Tokyo: Kodansha, 1976, 203.

Jolidon, Laurence. "Leathernecks Get A Lecture," *USA Today*, (September 27, 1990), 2A.

Keltikangas-Jarvinen, Liisa & Kangas, Paula. Quoted in "Aggressives May Suffer Cognition Problems Instead," *Brain/Mind Bulletin*, Vol. 14 (February, 1989), 7.

Keyes, Roger. **The Male Journey In Japanese Prints.** Berkeley: University of California Press, 1989, 44-6.

Kingham, Scott. *Sierra*, Vol.77 (March/April, 1992), p.98.

Kohn, Alfie. **No Contest.** Boston: Houghton Mifflin, 1986, 161, 163.

Koltowitz, Alex. "Day-to Day Violence Takes A Terrible Toll On Inner City Youth," *The Wall Street Journal*, (October 27, 1987) 1, 24.

Laing, R.D. **The Politics Of Experience.** New York: Ballantine, 1967, 12, 28.

Larson, Sandra K. & Field, Tiffany M. "Massage With Child and Adolescent Psychiatric Patients." in Nina Gunzenhauser (ed.) **Advances In Touch.** Skillman, New Jersey: Johnson & Johnson Consumer Products, 1990, 126, 131.

Lavoie, Richard D. "Toward Developing A Philosophy of Education: A Re-examination of Competition, Fairness and the Work Ethic," *Journal of Learning Disabilities*, Vol. 19 (January, 1986), 62-3.

Lever, Janet. "Child's Play: What Every Parent Needs To Know," *Ms*, Vol. 5 (February, 1977), 22.

Lombardi, Vince. Quoted in Myriam Miedzian. **Boys Will Be Boys.** New York: Doubleday, 1991, 192.

McMurtry, John. Quoted in Myriam Miedzian. **Boys Will Be Boys.** New York: Doubleday, 1991, 196.

Merton, Thomas. **Raids On The Unspeakable.** New York: New Directions, 1964, 47.

Miedzian, Myriam. **Boys Will Be Boys.** New York: Doubleday,1991, 181, 187, 257, 239-40.

Miller, Alice. **Banished Knowledge.** New York: Nan A. Talese, 1990, 188-9.

Miller, Annetta with Manly, Howard & Williams, Elisa. "Toys In Hamburgerland," *Newsweek*, (December 12, 1988), p.50.

Montagu, Ashley. **Touching,** New York: Harper & Row,1986, 120, 285.

Newman, Bruce. "Remorse? Not In The NFL," *Sports Illustrated*, (October 16, 1989), 112.

Novak, Michael. Quoted in Kohn, Alfie. **No Contest.** Boston: Houghton Mifflin, 1986, 163.

Overbye, Dennis. **Lonely Hearts of the Cosmos.** New York: Perennial, 1991, 277.

Ortega y Gasset, Jose. **Meditations on Hunting.** New York: Charles Scribners, 1985, 97, 122.

Papanek, John. Quoted in Debrigard, Bill. "Suiting Up At *Sports Illustrated*." *Vis A Vis*, (February, 1991), 62.

Pearce, Joseph C. **Magical Child.** New York: E.P. Dutton, 1977, 141.

Pellegrini, A.D. & Perlmutter, Jane C. "Rough-and-Tumble Play on the Elementary School Playground," *Young Children.* (January, 1988), 14-17.

Piers, Maria W. & Landau, Genevieve M. **The Gift of Play: And Why Young Children Cannot Thrive Without It.** New York: Walker, 1980, 82.

Powell, Bill & Carolyn Friday. "Deal of the Century," *Newsweek,* (December 12, 1988), 40-44.

Prescott, James W. Quoted in Simon, Sidney. **Caring Feeling Touching.** Allen, Texas: Argus, 1976, 20.

Rich, Charles F. quoted in Mary Jo Kochaklan. "Childrens' Perspectives of Games Are Different From Ours," *The Seattle Times,* (July 31, 1988).

Rockefeller, John D. **Beyond Rhetoric. The Final Report Of The National Commission On Children.** Washington, D.C.: United States National Commission On Children, 1991, viii.

Rosenblatt, Deborah, "Developmental Trends in Infant Play," in Barbara Tizard & David Harvey (eds.) **Biology of Play.** Clinics in Developmental Medicine. No. 62. London: William Heinemann Medical Books, 1977, 34.

Sahagun, Louis. "Behind A Mask," *Los Angeles Times,* (September 28, 1989), Part II, 5.

Schlein, Stuart J. (et al) "Effects Of Social Play Activities On The Play Behavior Of Children With Autism," *Journal of Leisure Research,* Vol. 22, (1990), 317-28.

"Schoolyard Bullying," *Education USA,* Vol. 32 (November 20, 1989), 95.

Sealth, Chief. Quoted in Morris Berman. **Coming To Our Senses.** New York: Bantam, 1989, 63.

Segal, Marilyn. Quoted in Schuman, Wendy. "The Importance Of Play," *Parent's Magazine,* Vol. 59 (September, 1984), 56-61.

Shantz, David W. "Conflict, Aggression and Peer Status: An Observational Study," *Child Development,* Vol. 57. (December, 1986), 1322-1332.

Simon, Sidney. **Caring Feeling Touching.** Allen, Texas.: Argus, 1976.

Singer, Jerome L. **The Child's World Of Make-Believe.** New York: Academic Press,1973, 9, 243-4.

Smith, Peter K. "Social and Fantasy Play in Young Children," in Barbara Tizard & David Harvey (eds.) **Biology of Play.** Clinics in Developmental Medicine. No. 62. London: William Heinemann Medical Books, 1977, 131.

Strick, Anne. Quoted in Kohn, Alfie. **No Contest.** Boston: Houghton Mifflin, 1986, 162.

Sutton-Smith, Brian. Quoted in Myriam Miedzian. **Boys Will Be Boys.** New York: Doubleday, 1991, 270.

Verhoeven, Paul. Quoted in Pool, Bob. "Screen Violence Would Stop If It Didn't Sell Tickets, Filmmakers Say," *Los Angeles Times*, (November 3, 1991), B1 & 6.

Washburn S.L. & Lancaster, C.S. Quoted in Terry Orlick. **Winning Through Cooperation.** Washington, D.C.: Acropolis Books, 1978, 139.

Watson, Broadus. Quoted in Ashley Montagu. **Touching.** New York: Harper & Row, 1986, 150.

Wehman, Paul. **Helping the Mentally Retarded Acquire Play Skills: A Behavioral Approach.** Springfield, Illinois.: C.C. Thomas Publishers, 1977, 124.

Wieden, Dan. Quoted in Christy Scattarella. "Still Just Doing It," *Pacific Magazine-Seattle Times.* (January 19, 1992), 4-9, 17.

Woolf, Virginia. **A Room Of One's Own.** London: Penguin, 1928, 37.

Wright, William A. **The Complete Works Of William Shakespeare.** Garden City, New York: Doubleday & Company, 1936.

Zukav, Gary. **The Seat Of The Soul.** New York: Fireside, 1989, 72.

Chapter 6

Bhagavad Gita, 2: 22-24. Quoted in Joseph Campbell. **The Hero With A Thousand Faces.** Princeton, New Jersey: Princeton University Press, 1949.

Blake, William. Quoted in George Seldes. **The Great Thoughts.** New York: Ballantine, 1985, 44.

Chang Chung-yuan. **Creativity and Taoism.** New York: Harper, 1963, 24.

Dossey, Larry. **Recovering The Soul.** New York: Bantam, 1989, 213.

Eckhart, Meister. Quoted in Chang Chung-yuan. **Creativity and Tao-ism.** New York: Harper, 1963, 52-3.

Ferrucci, Piero. **Inevitable Grace.** Los Angeles: Jeremy Tarcher, 1990, 313.

Franck, Frederick. **Everyone.** Garden City, New York: Doubleday & Co., 1978, 110-11.

Gray, J. Glenn. Quoted in "The Meaning of War," *MANAS*, Vol. 41 (October 5, 1988), p.1-2,7.

Green, Julien. **God's Fool: The LIfe And Times Of Francis Of Assisi.** San Francisco: Harper & Row, 1985, 128, 187, 194, 205, 217-19.

Huizinga, Johan. **Homo Ludens.** Boston: Beacon Press, 1950, 11-12.

Hyers, Conrad. **Zen And The Comic Spirit.** Philadelphia: The Westminster Press, 1973, 26, 30, 46-8.

"IRA-Type Bomb Defused After Boys Use It As Makeshift Soccer Ball," *Los Angeles Times,* (May 26, 1991), A19.

I-tuan. Quoted in Conrad Hyers. **Zen And The Comic Spirit.** Philadelphia: The Westminster Press, 1973, 109.

Jung, C.G. Quoted in Laurens van der Post. **Yet Being Someone Other.** London: Penguin, 1982, 351.

Mitchell, Stephen. **The Gospel According To Jesus.** New York: Harper-Collins, 1991, 179, 230.

Norwich, Julian of. Quoted in Lynda Sexson. **Ordinarily Sacred.** New York: Crossroad, 1982, 125.

Picasso, Pablo. Quoted in Paul Reps. **BE!** New York: Weatherhill, 1971, 34.

Schweickart, Russell. Quoted in Piero Ferrucci. **Inevitable Grace.** Los Angeles: Jeremy Tarcher, 1990, 276.

Sengai. Quoted in Frederick Frank. **The Zen of Seeing.** New York: Vintage, 1973, 128.

Siu, R.G.H. **Ch'i: A Neo-Taoist Approach to Life.** Cambridge, Massachusetts: The MIT Press, 1974, 25-6.

Tabriz, Divani Shamsi. Quoted in Whitall N. Perry. **A Tresury of Traditional Wisdom.** San Francisco: Harper & Row, 1971, 737.

Tagore, Rabindranath. Quoted in Jacob Needleman & David Appelbaum. **Real Philosophy.** London: Arkana, 1990, 231.

Traherne, Thomas. Quoted in Stephen Mitchell. **The Gospel According To Jesus.** New York: HarperCollins, 1991, 216.

Watson, Lyall. **Lifetide.** London: Coronet, 1980, 376.

Weil, Simone. Quoted in "A Saintly Dissenter." *MANAS,* Vol. 40. (December 30, 1987), p. 3, 7.

Chapter 7

Bachelard, Gaston. **The Poetics Of Reverie.** Boston: Beacon Press, 1969, 33, 104.

Buber, Martin. **I And Thou.** New York: Charles Scribner's, 1970, 60.

Campbell, Joseph. **The Hero With a Thousand Faces.** Princeton, New Jersey: Princeton University Press, 1949, 71-2.

Carroll, Lewis. **Through The Looking Glass.** New York: Macmillan, 1885, 133.

Chuang-tzu. Quoted in Thomas Merton. **The Way of Chuang-tzu.** New York: New Directions, 1965, 81, 133.

Clynes, Manfred. **Sentics.** Garden City, New York: Anchor Press, 1977, 180.

Fox, Matthew. **Whee! We, Wee All the Way Home.** Santa Fe, New Mexico: Bear & Co., 1981, 56.

Fromm, Erich. Quoted in Conrad Hyers. **Zen And The Comic Spirit.** Philadelphia: The Westminster Press, 1973, 181.

Fry, William F. Jr. **Sweet Madness: A Study Of Humor.** Palo Alto, CA.: Pacific Books, 1963, 134.

Gawain, Elizabeth. **The Dolphin's Gift.** Mill Valley, California: Whatever Publishing, 1981, 61.

Hoff, Benjamin. **The Tao Of Pooh.** New York: Penguin Books, 1982, 77.

Huang-po. Quoted in Stephen Mitchell. **The Gospel According To Jesus.** New York: HarperCollins, 1991, 161.

Hui-neng. Quoted in Conrad Hyers. **Zen and the Comic Spirit.** Philadelphia: The Westminster Press, 1973, 176.

Hyers, Conrad. **Zen and the Comic Spirit.** Philadelphia: The Westminster Press, 1973, 129,178.

Kasulis, T.P. **Zen Action Zen Person.** Honolulu: University of Hawaii Press, 1981, 33-4.

Ko-sahn. Quoted in N. Scott Momaday. **The Way To Rainy Mountain.** New York: Ballantine, 1969, 118.

Leonard, George. "This Isn't Richard," in Richard Strozzi Heckler (ed.) **Aikido and the New Warrior.** Berkeley, California: North Atlantic Books, 1985, 203.

McIntyre, Joan. **The Delicate Art of Whale Watching.** San Francisco: Sierra Club Books, 1982, 104.

Melville, Herman. Quoted in *Parabola,* Vol. 13. (Winter, 1988), 109.

Mencius. Quoted in Mai-mai Sze. **The Way of Chinese Painting.** New York: Vintage, 1959, 15.

Milne, A. A. **The World of Pooh.** New York: E. P. Dutton, 1985, 264.

Montagu, Ashley. **Growing Young.** Granby, Massachusetts: Bergin & Garvey Publishers, 1989, 45.

Oppenheimer, Robert. Quoted in David Miller. **Gods And Games: Towards A Theology of Play.** New York: World Publishing Company, 1970, 130.

Pearce, Joseph Chilton. **Magical Child Matures.** New York: Bantam, 1985, 79.

Robson, James. Quoted in Whitall N. Perry. **A Treasury Of Traditional Wisdom.** San Francisco: Harper & Row, 1986, 44.

Rumi. Quoted in Deepak Chopra. **Unconditional Life.** New York: Bantam, 1991, 110.

Stevenson, Robert Louis. **A Child's Garden of Verses.** New York: Children's Classics, 1985.

Van der Post, Laurens. **The Heart of the Hunter.** London: Penguin, 1961, 208.

Chapter 8

Adam, Michael. **Wandering In Eden.** New York: Alfred A. Knopf, 1976, 73.

Bachelard, Gaston. **The Poetics of Reverie.** Boston: Beacon Press, 1969, 29, 188.

Berenson, Bernard. Quoted in Anthony Storr. **Solitude: A Return To The Self.** New York: Ballantine, 1988, 17.

Brown, Norman O. **Love's Body.** New York: Vintage Books, 1968, 261.

Byrd, Admiral Richard. Quoted in Anthony Storr. **Solitude: A Return To The Self.** New York: Ballantine, 1988, 36.

Cage, John. Quoted in Fritjof Capra & David Steindl-Rast. **Belonging To The Universe.** San Francisco: Harper, 1991, 100.

Campbell, Joseph. **Myths To Live By.** New York: Bantam, 1972, 266.

Einstein, Albert. Quoted in Wes Nisker. **Crazy Wisdom.** Berkeley, California: Ten Speed Press, 1990, 114.

Ferrucci, Piero. **Inevitable Grace.** Los Angeles: Jeremy Tarcher, 1990, 208-09, 389-90.

Hesse, Hermann. Translated by James Wright. **Wandering.** New York: Farrar, Straus & Giroux, 1972, 58.

Hoff, Benjamin. **The Singing Creek Where The Willows Grow: The Rediscovered Diary Of Opal Whiteley.** New York: Warner Books, 1986, 86.

Maurois, Andre. Quoted in Robert Grudin. **The Grace of Great Things.** New York: Ticknor & Fields, 1990, 45.

Pearce, Joseph Chilton. **Magical Child.** New York: Bantam, 1985, 23.

Saint-Beuve. Quoted in William James. **Varieties of Religious Experience.** New York: Random House, 1902, 255.

Sexson, Lynda. **Ordinarily Sacred.** New York: Crossroad, 1982, 5.

Chapter 9

Abu Yazid al-Bistami. Quoted in Stephen Mitchell. **The Gospel According To Jesus.** New York: HarperCollins, 1991, 184.

Cox, Harvey. **The Feast Of Fools.** New York: Harper & Row, 1969, 179.

De Chardin, Teilhard. Quoted in Renee Weber. **Dialogues With Scientists And Sages.** London: Routledge & Kegan Paul, 1986, 127.

Ferrucci, Piero. **Inevitable Grace.** Los Angeles: Jeremy Tarcher, 1990, 251-2.

Griffiths, Fr. Bede. "Sacred Simplicity: The Style of the Sage," in Renee Weber. **Dialogues With Scientists And Sages.** London: Routledge & Kegan Paul, 1986, 127.

Guyon, Madame. Quoted in Piero Ferrucci. **Inevitable Grace.** Los Angeles: Jeremy Tarcher, 1990, 256.

Hesse, Hermann. **Demian.** New York: Bantam, 1965, 119.

Johnson, Trebbe. "The Four Sacred Mountains of the Navajos," *Parabola.* Vol.13. (Winter,1988), 40-47.

Keats, Quoted in "The Art of China and Japan." *MANAS,* Vol. 41 (March, 16, 1988), 3-4, 8.

Lao Tzu. Quoted in. R.L. Wing. **The Tao of Power.** Garden City, New York: Doubleday & Co., 1986, 49.

Nollman, Jim. **Animal Dreaming.** New York: Bantam, 1987, 57-9.

Peat, F. David. **The Philosopher's Stone.** New York: Bantam, 1991, 135.

Rasmussen, Knud. Quoted in Joseph Campbell. **Myths To Live By.** New York: Bantam, 1972, 212.

Seng-tsan. Quoted in Stephen Mitchell. **The Enlightened Heart.** New York: Harper & Row, 1989, 87.

St. Augustine of Hippo. Quoted in Claudio Naranjo. **The One Quest.** New York: Ballantine, 1972, 87.

Tagore, Rabindranath. Quoted in Jacob Needleman & David Appelbaum. **Real Philosophy.** London: Arkana, 1990, 231

Chapter 10

Bachelard, Gaston. **The Poetics of Reverie.** Boston: Beacon Press, 1969, 183.

Black Elk. Quoted in John G. Neihardt G. **Black Elk Speaks.** New York: Pocket Books, 1972, 65.

Buber, Martin. **I And Thou.** New York: Charles Scribner, 1970, 67.

Cammerloher, M.C. Quoted in Michael Adam. **Wandering In Eden.** New York: Alfred A. Knopf, 1976, 72.

Carpenter, Edmund. **Eskimo Realities.** New York: Holt, Rinehart & Winston, 1973, 132.

Doczi, Gyorgy. **The Power of Limits.** Boston: Shambhala, 1985, 25, 139.

Durckheim, Karlfried. **The Japanese Cult of Tranquility.** York Beach, Maine: Simon Weiser, 1991, 100.

Durckheim, Karlfried G. **The Way of Transformation.** London: Unwin Paperbacks, 1980, 27.

Jordan-Smith, Paul. "The Apprentice." in D.M. Dooling (ed.) **A Way of Working.** New York: Parabola Books, 1979, 37.

McIntyre, Joan. **The Delicate Art of Whale Watching.** San Francisco: Sierra Club, 1982, 96.

Montagu, Ashley. **Touching.** New York: Harper & Row, 1986, 3, 164.

Novalis. Quoted in Ashley Montagu. **Touching.** New York: Harper & Row, 1986, 3.

Ortega Y Gasset, Jose. **Man and People.** New York: Norton, 1957, 72.

Russell, Bertrand. Quoted in Ashley Montagu. **Touching.** New York: Harper & Row, 1986, 13.

Sexson, Lynda. **Ordinarily Sacred.** New York: Crossroad, 1982, 37.

Soho, Takuan. **The Unfettered Mind.** Tokyo: Kodansha, 1986, 23.

Tolstoy, Leo. Translated by Leo Wiener. **The Death Of Ivan Ilich.** Boston: Dana Estes & Co., 1904.

Ueshiba, Morihei. Quoted in Mitsugi Saotome. **Aikido And The Harmony Of Nature.** Boulogne, France: Sedirep, 1985, 168.

Van Gogh, Vincent. Quoted in Gaston Bachelard. **Poetics Of Space.** New York: Orion Press, 1964, 232.

Chapter 11

Bateson, Gregory. **Mind And Nature.** New York: Bantam, 1979, 8.

Clynes, Manfred. **Sentics.** Garden City, New York: Anchor Press, 1977, 85.

Einstein, Albert. Quoted in David Lorimer. **Whole In One.** London: Arkana, 1990, 273.

Eiseley, Loren . Quoted in David Lorimer. **Whole In One.** London: Arkana, 1990, 72.

Fools Crow. Quoted in Thomas Mails. **Fools Crow.** New York: Avon, 1979,184.

Heckler, Richard Strozzi. **In Search Of The Warrior Spirit.** Berkeley, California: North Atlantic Books, 1990, 217.

Heinberg, Richard. **Memories And Visions Of Paradise.** Los Angeles: Jeremy P. Tarcher, 1989, 96.

Heloise. Quoted in Matthew Fox. **Whee! We, Wee All The Way Home.** Santa Fe: Bear & Company, 1981, 210.

Krishnamurti, Jiddu. Quoted in Jacob Needleman & David Appelbaum. **Real Philosophy.** London: Arkana, 1990, 238, 241.

Laing, R.D. **The Politics of Experience.** New York: Ballantine, 1967, 42.

Leonard, George. **Mastery.** New York: Plume, 1991, 96.

Maslow, Abraham. **The Farther Reaches Of Human Nature.** Harmandsworth, England: Penguin, 1971, 16-17.

Merton, Thomas. **Ishi Means Man.** Greensboro, North Carolina: Unicorn Press, 1976, 13.

Mitchell, Stephen. **The Gospel According To Jesus.** New York: Harper Collins, 1991, 64,154,175,188,200.

Pascal, Blaise. Quoted in Robert Coles. **The Spiritual Life Of Children.** Boston: Houghton Mifflin, 1990, 9-10.

Pasternak, Boris. Translated from the Russian by Max Hayward and Manya Harari. **Doctor Zhivago.** New York: Pantheon, 1958.

Saotome, Mitsugi. **Aikido And The Harmony Of Nature.** Boulogne, France: Sedirep, 1985, 233.

Schweitzer, Albert. Quoted in David Lorimer. **Whole In One.** London: Arkana, 1990, 72.

Smullyan, Raymond. **The Tao Is Silent.** New York: Harper & Row, 1977, 83.

Tagore, Rabindranath. Quoted in David Lorimer. **Whole In One.** London: Arkana, 1990, 191, 226-7.

Tagore, Rabindranath. Quoted in Jacob Needleman & David Appelbaum. **Real Philosophy.** London: Arkana, 1990, 231-2.

Ueshiba, Morihei. Quoted in John Stevens. **Abundant Peace.** Boston: Shambhala, 1987, 112.

Van der Post, Laurens. **A Walk With A White Bushman.** New York: William Morrow, 1986, 31, 50.

Williams, Margery. **The Velveteen Rabbit.** Garden City, New York: Doubleday, no date.

Epilogue

Smith. Lillian. **Killers of the Dream.** Garden City, New York: Doubleday Anchor, 1961, 34.

Sultan Bin Suhmanal-Sand. Quoted in David Lorimer. **Whole In One.** London: Arkana, 1990, 256.

Wheeler, John. Quoted in David Lorimer. **Whole In One.** London: Arkana, 1990, 261.

Appendix

Bettelheim, Bruno. "The Importance of Play," *The Atlantic,* (March, 1987) 259, 35-43.

Rockefeller IV, John D. **Beyond Rhetoric: A New American Agenda For Children And Families.** Final Report of the National Commission on Children, Washington, D. C.: National Commission on Children, 1991, 4-5.

Index

Wright brothers, 138
Wu-wei, 119

Yeats, W.B., 40

Zaire, 26
Zen, 15,28,31,106,111,120, 129,143
Zen In The Art Of Archery, 31
Zukov, Gary, 80
Zulu, 74